SAVING MONEY ANY WAY YOU CAN

Saving Money
Any Way You Can

How to Become a Frugal Family

Mike Yorkey

Servant Publications
Ann Arbor, Michigan

A Note to Readers: The following names included in this book are actual people: Lou Gage, Diana Haptonstall (The Coupon Queen), Lainie MacDonald, Judy Padgett, Deb Elliss, Shaun Cano, Marianne Hering, Bob Hoffmann, Karen Ahles, Tracey McBride, Michael Ross, Karen Sagahon, Bernie and Elaine Minton, John and Dena Fuller, LeeAnn Woolley, Chuck and Sally Mosher, Fred and Suzanne Sindt, Greg Johnson, Bruce Peppin, Sandra Alrich, Chas and Amy MacDonald, Michel Schmied, Mary Hunt, Jonathan Weston, David Holmes, Rich Simons, Marc Eisenson, and Bob Welch. I have quoted them or told their stories with permission.

Vine Books is an imprint of Servant Publications especially designed to serve evangelical Christians.

Published by Servant Publications
P.O. Box 8617
Ann Arbor, Michigan 48107

Cover design by Multnomah Graphics/Printing

95 96 97 98 10 9 8 7 6 5 4 3

Printed in the United States of America
ISBN 0-89283-864-7

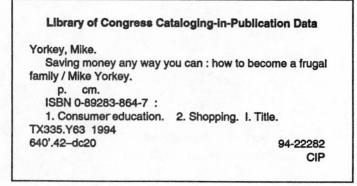

Library of Congress Cataloging-in-Publication Data

Yorkey, Mike.
   Saving money any way you can : how to become a frugal family / Mike Yorkey.
     p.   cm.
   ISBN 0-89283-864-7 :
   1. Consumer education.   2. Shopping. I. Title.
TX335.Y63 1994
640'.42–dc20
                                  94-22282
                                       CIP

Dedication

To Lou Gage
You said you knew everything
about saving money on shopping,
and you were right!

Contents

Acknowledgments

A book of this scope would not be possible without the help of many people.

To Dr. Wayne and Lou Gage, you were angels.

To Karen Sagahon, Marianne Hering, Ray Seldomridge, Barbara Crosley, Bob and Leesa Waliszewski, Tracey McBride, and Mary Hunt, thank you for your editing skills and helpful comments.

To Liz Heaney, my book editor at Servant, thanks for keeping me on track. And my thanks to Don Cooper and Beth Feia at Servant for their faith in me.

And to all those who filled out the survey and shared their money-saving advice in interviews, I know who you are. Thanks a lot!

Foreword

You will like this book.

I can't offer you a money-back guarantee, but as I thumbed through *Saving Money Any Way You Can,* four things came to mind. The first is its *practicality.* All too many personal finance books deal with the theoretical (we need those types of books, too) but they lack practical ideas. For example, I've always felt there is a lot of misunderstanding about credit cards, but as Mike points out in chapter eight, savvy couples who pay off their credit card statements every month can earn free travel or discounts on everything from cars to Apple computers. In my own business life, I use a credit card to charge all my travel, hotels, and meals so I can receive frequent-flier miles.

The second thing I enjoyed about *Saving Money Any Way You Can* is its *balance.* All too often, "frugal living" books go overboard, and I've seen families go to extremes on this stuff. Keep in mind that there is always a trade off between time and money, and you can spend so much time trying to save a few bucks that you end up being penny-wise and pound-foolish. I'm at a point in my life where I am financially able to have someone mow my lawn and take care of the garden. I view hiring a gardener as an investment in my family, because I want to spend more time on the weekends with my wife, Judy, and our five children.

On the other hand, if I'm going to buy a major appliance, I will shop that. That's what makes *Saving Money Any Way You Can* so helpful, because this book will help you save on big-ticket items. You will appreciate the balance Mike has struck here.

The third thing I appreciate is its *readability*. Mike promises that *Saving Money Any Way You Can* will be a fun read, and he has succeeded. You won't have to slog through a lot of dry prose. In addition, many "saving money" books tend to make you feel bad because of what you are *not* doing. Instead, *Saving Money* is encouraging, which is something I try to convey in my books. I prefer to encourage people to do the right thing, rather than convict them.

And last, *Saving Money Any Way You Can* is *different*. You'll find fascinating Q & As, interesting sidebars, funny anecdotes, and insightful observations on the ways we spend—and can save—our hard-earned money. That's why you need to read this book. Now get going!

Ron Blue

Introduction

"So, you're writing a book on how families can save money?"

"Uh, yes I am. It's something I've always been interested in...."

"Well, just tell your readers to spend less than they make."

Sounds so easy, doesn't it? *Spend less than you make.* But as you know all too well, the financial strain on families is incredible these days. Out of 125 Christian families who responded to my survey, 67 percent said they were struggling to stay ahead or living paycheck to paycheck. This pressure to live within our means can place tremendous stress on a marriage, causing dissension and even leading to divorce. Thus, many couples are looking for new ways to save on basic household expenses, such as food, clothing, housing, education, and health care.

If that tall order wasn't enough, most Christian families are committed to supporting their local church, which often means "tithing" a significant chunk of income—10 percent in many households. These same families may also support missionaries to foreign countries, adopt a child through various Christian agencies, or give generously to parachurch organizations.

The couples I surveyed were generous: *85 percent* said they gave at least 9 percent of their income to their local churches and charitable organizations. Compare this to the national average of 2.5 percent, according to a Christian research organization named Empty Tomb. With all this sacrificial giving, many who follow Christ live even closer to the edge than the typical family.

We also enjoy a priceless advantage: being God's children means we can go to him with our finances. He knows *exactly* where we are, and he knows our needs before we do. This brings me to the most important point of this book: *whenever you have an important buying decision, pray about it.* Just as God can direct you to a dependable used car that won't break down every other month, he can also help you find a much-needed pair of soccer shoes at a garage sale.

In one of the most comforting passages of Scripture, Jesus says, "So my counsel is this: Don't worry about things—food, drink, and clothes. For you already have life and a body—and they are far more important than what to eat and wear. Look at the birds! They don't worry about what to eat—they don't need to sow or reap or store up food—for your heavenly Father feeds them. And you are far more valuable to him than they are" (Mt 6:25-26, TLB).

Although the Lord instructs us not to worry, it's human nature to be concerned about making it to the end of the month without dipping into a limited savings account. Our consumerist society constantly contributes to that concern. Blitzed with "Sale of the Century!" ads everywhere we turn, we must be on guard against the formidable pressure to buy something.

We also face an extraordinary number of choices for *where* we can spend our money. Fifty years ago, our grandparents grew up in towns with one market, one hardware store, and one gas station. These days, ultra-modern supermarkets, expansive warehouse clubs, and bag-your-own grocery stores have sprung up in the suburbs like mushrooms.

Our grandparents shopped at a local five-and-dime store; we can choose from Wal-Mart, Kmart, Sears, and

Montgomery Ward. They had one clothing store; we have JCPenney, Marshalls, Ross Dress for Less, and Target. They had seasonal sales; we have a constant deluge of coupons, rebates, and discount books. They had a Sears catalog book; we have twenty-four-hour, mail-order companies with 800-numbers. They paid cash; we carry multiple credit cards.

With all these options, how do we keep our heads and spend wisely? How do we know what is a good deal and what is not? This book will help you answer these questions, plus give you lots of practical tips on stretching your spending dollars. My advice comes from research, interviews, and the 125 surveys I received from Christian families—people just like you and me who are trying to keep their noses above water.

Allow me to also explain one additional reason why I am writing this book. It's my belief that many moms want to stay home and raise their kids. *Saving Money Any Way You Can* is chock full of ideas to help you do that. Since families can do little to save on housing and taxes, the best chance to reduce costs involves so-called "discretionary spending." This is where stay-at-home mothers can make a big difference.

In fact, searching out good deals on groceries and clothing—which takes time—can become a part-time job. When you stop and figure out what it costs to send Mom back to the work force, most families net only a couple of hundred dollars a month after deducting the necessary child-care expenses, new work clothes, maintenance and insurance on a second car, and meals away from home (tired mothers are usually too wiped out at the end of a long day to cook meals from scratch). Meanwhile, a mom who has the time to hunt down bargains can save her family several hundred dollars a month. Some of these reasons may help justify a mother's decision to work at home.

Of course, most single moms and dads don't have the option of staying home with their kids during the day. They face the most difficult assignment of all: providing for their family on a single salary plus any child-support they can muster. The income gap can be huge. Married-couple families had a household income of $41,574 according to the 1990 U.S. Census, while female-headed families had only $17,645! No wonder most single-parent moms see their style of living cut in half after the divorce.

Saving Money Any Way You Can is written for men as well as women. None of us are off the hook when it comes to frugality. I've heard it said that when a woman goes shopping, she returns with a dress; but when a man goes shopping, he returns with a power boat. Whatever our individual spending habits, all of us can benefit from making wise buying decisions.

As editor of a national magazine for families, I understand that today's harried parents have little patience for long-winded explanations of debt service and no-load stock funds. Other authors may talk about "getting out of debt," "making your money grow," or "investing for the nineties," but *Saving Money Any Way You Can* is different. Along with learning valuable tips, you'll have *fun* reading the interesting illustrations, informative sidebars, and quick-hitting advice.

One last point: although the book title says *Saving Money Any Way You Can*, don't become an obsessive-compulsive about saving every nickel. Yes, it's good stewardship to spend money wisely and stretch your paycheck as far as you can, but don't fret over having left the twenty-five-cent JELL-O coupon back at home. The key word is *balance*. God has given us financial resources—be they limited or plentiful—and we are "to be content whatever the circumstances" (Phil 4:11). If we're not happy with a *little* money, then we certainly won't be happy with a *lot* of money.

WHO IS LOU GAGE?

Perhaps you noticed that I dedicated the book to Lou Gage. Who is *she*? Lou, now in her early fifties, grew up dirt poor in New Hampshire. In fact, her family lived without indoor plumbing until she was twelve years old. She's a mom who has chopped wood, sold antiques, and worked as a dental technician.

These days, Lou loves to buy things—for family, for friends, and for her local church, where she is the ad hoc "procurement officer." With children who are grown and married, Lou now has *time* to hunt down good deals. She also has *money* to buy things since her husband, Wayne, brings home a good salary as an emergency room physician. Don't get the wrong idea: the Gages are not wealthy. They give generously to their local church and live modestly but comfortably.

The way Lou looks at it, buying a forty-dollar sweater for five dollars means she can afford several *more* sweaters, which she often gives to friends or charitable organizations. "God gives us spiritual gifts, and mine is the gift of giving," she explains.

When you've bought as many things as Lou has, you get pretty good at sniffing out bargains. Exhibit A: several years ago, Lou purchased 743 Christmas gifts for family and friends. She started buying holiday presents during the end-of-winter sales in February and March. Each time she purchased a gift, she wrote the person's name on the ticket and stored it in her huge crawl space. (Lou also has plenty of wrapping paper. She once purchased fifteen hundred rolls for ten cents apiece at a church rummage sale!)

Another time, Lou walked into a car dealership on New Year's Eve and began dealing for a Chevy Beretta. She knew December 31 was the best time to buy because the dealer didn't want to count the car as part of his year-end inventory. Lou had to get up out of her chair to leave several times, but she drove off the lot at nine o'clock that evening in a yellow Beretta, having bargained six thousand dollars off the sticker price.

Those are just a couple of Lou Gage stories. You'll be hearing a lot more from this masterful bargain hunter in the rest of this book. Enjoy.

CHAPTER 1

We Spent
How Much?

S ometime after the college bowl blitz on New Year's Day and before the Super Bowl several years ago, I walked out to the garage where we stored an old file cabinet. Inside were stashed all the bank statements, checking account records, credit card reports, cash receipts, and sundry bills for the previous year. I pulled out one file after another and began sifting through the growing mountain of paper.

My mission was a serious one: find out where all the Yorkey money had gone that year. For months, I and my wife, Nicole, had been steadily raiding our savings account to make up for shortfalls. Sure, we paid all our bills on time and never carried a credit card balance, but that strategy had eroded our hard-won nest egg. Simply put, we were spending more than we were taking in. And if the hemorrhaging didn't stop, we were headed for financial trouble.

We had just purchased our first home, a thirty-year-old, Southern California tract-model with its original roof in disrepair. Like most young families buying their first abode, we knew money would be a little tight for a while. We tackled several home projects right away, such as adding automatic sprinklers, ripping up the shabby linoleum in the kids' bathroom, and hauling an old rock garden to the dump. We even did all the work ourselves to save money. Even so, our finances were beginning to worry me.

As I spread out the stack of bills and statements on the dining room table, I took a hard look at all these bits of paper in front of me. *Where had our money gone?* Nicole and I had never had a budget, and our periodic attempts to track our expenses were so depressing that we always quit after several months. It was time to get a handle on our finances. But where should I begin?

Friends of ours kept a logbook in a kitchen drawer. Every evening they listed that day's expenditures—even the twenty-five-cent newspaper. I found that approach too tedious. Another friend ran the family budget with the loose philosophy, "When the checkbook's empty, stop buying."

My own thoughts on spending fell somewhere in the middle. I hauled out a notebook and divided the pages into categories. First, I wanted to know exactly how much we spent on the American Dream of owning a home: mortgage, property taxes, and home insurance. To ensure keeping our priorities straight, I then totaled the amount we gave our local church and other charities.

Next I listed what Nicole spent on clothes for the four of us (yikes!) and household improvements. Other columns were reserved for groceries and bulk purchases at Pace, a warehouse membership club. I gave eating out a separate column, but I was a little fuzzy there since I usually paid cash. I tallied what we spent on utilities: electricity, natural gas, water, trash removal, telephone, and cable TV.

After that, it was on to my favorite sinkhole: cars. At that time, we owned two seven-year-old beauties—a Subaru station wagon and a small GMC pickup truck. All the repairs, gas purchases, smog tests, and insurance tabs added up to a pretty penny.

Next, I made columns for uncovered medical expenses, pharmacy visits, health insurance, and dental checkups, followed by what we spent on the kids' piano lessons and fees for soccer and baseball. Then I listed "fun money" expenditures: vacations, tennis tournaments, and day trips to a nearby ski slope. A final column was marked "miscellaneous" for all the incidentals, but, again, all I could do was make a good guess at these cash expenditures.

When the columns were tallied, I compiled a list of income and expenses, detailing what money came *in* (my editor's salary plus a small, home-based, tennis racket-stringing business) against what went *out*. That's when I confronted the awful truth: we had spent $2,534 *more* than we had taken in during 1989. As I mentioned earlier, we had been dipping into savings to cover the shortfall.

After my "profit and loss" report was finished, I made a date with Nicole. My plan was to discuss my findings over dinner at our favorite Chinese restaurant. I wanted to make the evening fun, because what couple *loves* to talk finances? I called it the "State of the Yorkeys" night.

Over a relaxed meal Nicole and I took a hard look at where our money train was headed—and where we wanted it to go. That evening helped us get our financial locomotive back on track. The following year, I'm happy to report, we came out $1,141 ahead. We've managed to stay in the black ever since, but it's been a wild ride.

The old saying "We're spending it as fast as it comes in" certainly applies to our family. It seems like we're always being hit by an unexpected bill. This two-steps-forward and one-step-back routine means Nicole and I had to cut expenses and look for ways to save money. This book includes many of the money-saving strategies we used to curb our spending.

BUDGET TIME

If you find yourselves in the same sort of financial boat, begin by tracking your expenses for several months. A spiral notebook provides an easy and cheap way to do this exercise. (If you have access to a computer and can afford the expense, software programs such as Quicken offer superb help in tracking expenses. I'll talk more about these various programs in chapter fifteen.)

Before you can get started, you need to keep all your receipts dating back at least one month. Then gather your checkbook and credit card statements and sit down with a notebook. Write a category on top of each page (groceries, clothes, medical, etc.) and assign each expense to the appropriate column. Here are the categories I used to list our monthly expenses:

- mortgage payments, including property tax and house insurance (or rent)
- groceries
- clothes
- health insurance premiums
- utilities (electricity, gas, water)
- phone
- trash removal
- cable TV
- gasoline
- car repairs and emission tests
- car insurance
- newspaper and magazine subscriptions
- haircuts and perms
- school expenses (field trips, cheerleading outfits, sports fees, school pictures)
- charitable giving (church, missionaries)
- restaurants (including McDonald's and take-out pizza)
- vacation
- kids' music lessons, Girl Scout uniforms, sports fees
- miscellaneous

If this is the first time you've tracked your monthly expenses, congratulations! After totaling your expenditures, itemize and add up your sources of income. Possible categories include:

- Dad's take-home pay
- Mom's take-home pay
- family cottage-industry income
- miscellaneous (perhaps an annual garage sale)

Now, take a cold, hard look. How much was the difference between what went out and what came in? Are you among the few who had a substantial amount of money left over? Was the difference razor thin? Or did you end up in the red?

FAMILIES ON THE EDGE

As a case in point, let's consider the spending patterns of two fictitious couples. Perhaps you can see your family's money habits reflected in one or the other.

We'll call the first couple John and Judy. John, age thirty-four, is employed as an assistant manager of a local supermarket. Judy, thirty-three, is a stay-at-home mom who does twelve hours of bookkeeping out of her home each week. They have two children: six-year-old Amber and three-year-old Tiffany. John and Judy purchased a "starter" home several years ago, and they own two well-used cars. Their monthly expenses break down as follows:

mortgage	$623
property tax	75
health	80
home insurance	40
groceries	400
clothes	125
utilities	125
phone	60
trash removal	15
cable TV	22
gasoline	100
car maintenance, repairs	100
car insurance	110
newspaper	10
haircuts	15
charitable giving	150
restaurants	100
miscellaneous	75
Total monthly expenses	$2,225

Income. John makes $14.54 an hour or $1,260 per pay period, which totals $30,343 a year. Judy earns $7.50 an hour, $90 a week, $360 a month. John uses four allowances for his payroll deductions. While his health insurance is picked up by the super-market chain, he must pay for dependents. (I had the following take-home figures checked by an accountant.)

John's take-home pay	$2,001
Judy's income	$330
Total monthly income	$2,331

Leftover to go into savings	$106

The uncertainty of whether they'll make it to the end of each month has strained this couple's emotional reserves. John and Judy know they *should* be putting aside more for a rainy day—a major car repair, an uncovered medical expense, braces for the kids—but they rarely get the chance.

We'll call the second couple Tom and Teri. Tom and Teri, both in their mid-twenties, have been married for three years and have a one-year-old named Josh. Tom has had trouble finding work in his computer field so, to make ends meet, he works in the men's clothing department at Marshalls. Teri is committed to being at home with her son. Tom and Teri live in a two-bedroom apartment and own one car, an '84 Chevy Caprice with 110,000 miles. Their monthly expenses add up this way:

rent	$550
groceries	300
clothes	50
health	80
utilities	100
phone	40
gasoline	60
car repairs	75
car insurance	50
newspaper	10
charitable giving	40
miscellaneous	50

Total monthly expenses	$1,405

Income. Tom makes $8.57 an hour, $742 twice a month, or $17,825 a year. Lately, he's been putting in overtime, which brings in an extra $100 a month. Teri has been working Fridays at the same clothing store (while Tom stays home with Josh), earning $6.25 an hour, $50 a day, or $200 a month. Tom has three allowances for his payroll deductions. His health insurance is paid for by the clothing company, but he must pay for dependents.

Tom's take-home pay (including overtime)	$1,282
Teri's part-time pay	$184
Total monthly income	$1,466

Leftover to go into savings	$61

Tom and Teri are living on the edge, and they know they must spend every dollar wisely—just like your family. Teri has been scrimping on groceries: lots of grilled cheese dinners and cold cereal breakfasts. What has been the budget buster for this second couple? Disposable diapers.

THE SQUEEZE IS ON

Teri is fairly typical of modern moms who want to stay home and raise their children. Working Fridays while her husband watches Josh is her way of fulfilling that instinctive desire. The popular culture, however, would have you believe that *both* parents are working these days. Think again. According to the U.S. Department of Labor statistics, 41.3 percent of all married mothers with preschool children are full-time homemakers. Another 20 percent work part-time, some only a few hours a week. When you add up those figures, that means 61 percent of mothers with preschool children are spending *most* of their time raising the kids!

At the same time, some moms have wonderful careers and *want* to work. Many moms, however, *must* work to augment their husband's salary or to help pay the mortgage required to live in a good school district.

If high housing costs weren't enough, Washington isn't doing families any favors. The federal tax burden on couples filing a joint return has risen from 2 percent in the early 1950s to around 25 percent today. (And that doesn't even include state, property, and sales taxes!)

Feeling squeezed? Join the club. If your financial locomotive is barely running by payday, take time to get a handle on your family's spending patterns by tracking your expenses for a few months. Not only will you know more clearly where you stand, but you'll also have a better sense of where your finances are headed. Then if you get hit with a bigger-than-usual bill—a $350 car repair, for instance—you'll know where to cut back in other areas.

Another approach is the "envelope" system. Bob Reynolds said he doesn't remember where he got the idea, but after he pays the monthly bills, he withdraws cash from the family's checking account and deposits it into various envelopes for discretionary spending. "We keep five envelopes in the pantry," said Bob. "We put four hundred dollars in one for groceries, one hundred for gas, fifty for entertainment, fifty for clothes, and one marked miscellaneous, for something like a haircut. If we run out of grocery money, then we take money from the gas and entertainment envelopes. But that means we do less driving and see fewer movies."

The Reynolds started the envelope system after getting into deep debt with credit card companies. "We're doing this to get out of the spending habit," said Bob. "Our biggest problem was that after payday, our checkbook had two thousand dollars in it, so we thought we had a ton of money. But we forgot we also faced two thousand dollars in bills. By the end of the month, we were using our Visa card to buy groceries, and that was not a good situation."

If you need to regroup and get a handle on your spending, you may want to consider using "spending envelopes." This simple tool brings home a basic lesson: if the money is literally not there, it's not there. Sure, you can borrow from Peter to pay Paul, but that means forgetting the Friday-night movie, or eating at home instead of going to Red Lobster.

If you want to take accountability one step further, consider outlining a budget, or spending plan, for the family. "Budget" is a scary word. Financial counselors say *95 percent* of American families don't have one, and that includes the Yorkeys. Budgets are a hassle, they take discipline, and they take the fun out of spending. (Did I really say that?) Still, budgets are a good idea. If you decide this more rigorous measure is called for, *The Money Workbook* by Mahlon L. Hetrick explains budgeting from a Christian perspective.

Enough said? Let's get started with the number one battlefield: the grocery store.

CHAPTER 2

Food Fight

It's a war zone out there. Supermarkets, grocery stores, and warehouse clubs are locked in Mortal Combat. Value-conscious consumers have learned that every time they stride through those automatic doors, they enter into a firefight over how many dollars retailers can extract from their wallets. They often feel like donning flak jackets before a shopping trip.

Grocery shopping used to be a fairly mundane chore reserved for Saturday mornings. But no longer. As families look for ways to cut corners, groceries come under scrutiny because of the hefty bite they chomp out of the family budget. If you're a family of four, for instance, you probably average five hundred dollars a month or six thousand dollars a year for groceries. (By "groceries," I mean all food items plus paper towels, toilet paper, diapers, aluminum foil, shoe polish, feminine hygiene products, shampoo, dog food, etc.) If your family's take-home pay amounts to two thousand dollars a month, that means you're spending 25 percent of that on groceries.

The good news is that groceries are not a fixed expense like the rent or a mortgage. Money can be saved here. To do so, I recommend the following tactics:

- buy store brands
- shop the loss leaders
- stock up on sale items
- use coupons
- frequent warehouse clubs

The overall *best* strategy is to "cherry-pick" from all five. For this chapter, I'll concentrate on supermarkets. Couponing and warehouse clubs will be discussed in the next two chapters.

SEEING THROUGH THE SELL-THROUGH

Step into a supermarket a few days before the Fourth of July, and what are you likely to see? Long banners hang from the ceiling, announcing "firecracker" savings. The employees—from stocker to lead cashier—are dressed in stone-washed jeans, red cowboy shirts, boots, and straw hats. Just inside the front door, you practically trip over a patriotic display of twenty-pound bags of barbecue briquets, boxes of canned lighter fluid, two crates of watermelon, and 7Up cases stacked in the shape of a pyramid.

Nothing is left to chance. Track lighting illuminates the fresh produce just so, while an abundance of cheery signs guide you along. The aisles are wide enough for two carts to pass each other, but not too wide: grocers want you to easily pick things off both shelves as you pass. If you shop early in the morning (many supermarkets are now conveniently open twenty-four hours a day), you can practically see your reflection in the freshly waxed, white-tile linoleum.

Supermarkets offer tremendous *variety*. You can choose from 147 kinds of cereal, 22 brands and types of peanut butter, and 25 brands of chocolate-chip cookies—several thousand different products totaling one million items. Everywhere the merchandise is stacked perfectly; nothing is out of place. A paradise of food beckons you to partake liberally of its abundance—as long as you pay the cashier on your way out.

I remember when Nicole and I were seduced by a beautiful supermarket when we moved to Southern California from a small ski resort town several years ago. The Vons Pavilion around the corner offered a gleaming white showcase of conspicuous consumption. The centerpiece was a bakery and deli with gorgeous-looking meats, Chinese platters, and European pastries. Call it designer shopping. During that first summer, I loved to get up early on Saturday mornings and walk into Vons Pavilion to purchase warm blueberry muffins and fresh orange juice. I felt like a yuppie when I walked out of the store. But it slowly dawned on us that we were paying for that feeling, so we started shopping the Price Club more frequently.

Supermarkets purposely place the produce section on one side of the building, with the milk and other dairy products *way* over on the other side. If you're dropping in for lettuce and milk, you better have your walking shoes on. The idea is to make you pass by a *lot* of mouth-watering food on your way to the high-traffic staples. The hope, of course, is that you'll drop something else into your cart.

Both ends of the aisles (called end-caps) feature specials of the week. Some are good deals, others aren't; but you have no way of knowing since you can't compare the $1.69 bag of Casa Rosario tortilla chips to other brands. They're back on aisle four.

So, where do you start? Actually, you should be well-prepared to shop *before* you ever drive into the parking lot. That means going through your refrigerator and pantry and compiling a "tight" grocery list. Next, go through the supermarket flyers inserted into the daily newspaper or mailed to your home. Inside, you'll find in-store coupons or special sales featuring "buy one, get one free" or "four cans for a dollar." Is there anything worth stocking up on? Are whole chickens reduced to 39 cents per pound? Ten pounds of Russet potatoes for 99 cents? Dannon yogurt reduced to three for 89 cents?

Take a close look at the front page of the flyer that banners the store's loss leaders—goods or merchandise sold at less than cost. Remember, these specials are designed to pull you into the store so you'll do the *rest* of your week's shopping on that same trip. Supermarket executives know how much we enjoy the convenience of one-stop shopping.

If you want to save money, however, build your shopping list around the loss leaders at your regular supermarket—as well as at the competition. "We have Safeway, Albertsons, and King Soopers in our area," said Lou Gage. "You have to play the ads, because all three supermarkets run different loss leaders. If you're a wise shopper, you'll shop the ads at all three stores, unless they're across town from each other. But if your goal is to save money, you might drop by Safeway on your way to the post office and Albertsons after soccer practice."

Rita said she regularly shops at two stores to get the lowest prices. "I check the weekly circulars for sales. After figuring out how much I want to spend, I make out a list and prioritize it," she added. "I don't buy any low-priority items until the end, when I know whether I'm over budget or not. I also shop every other week to cut down on impulse buys."

Organizing a well-planned list in advance helps to prevent impulse shopping, which the supermarkets *love*. Historically, grocery stores earn a slim profit margin—just a percent or two after paying overhead—on staples such as milk, bread, sugar, and coffee. Where they make money is on other items such as cereals, snack foods, deli items, canned chili, salad dressings, hair spray, lipstick, and deodorant.

Rhonda said she makes out a week's worth of menus, figures out the ingredients she needs, and then sticks to her list like glue. "If I can do that, then I allow myself and anyone with me *one* impulse item or treat."

Several women told me it takes upwards of two to three hours to carefully shop a supermarket each week, but that is not the norm for many busy moms. According to *EDK*

Forecast, a New York-based newsletter that tracks female consumers, "Women make buying decisions as fast as they can wheel their carts down the aisles, grabbing familiar products and pausing occasionally for a quick label scan or price comparison."

Take your time! When you're juggling coupons, reading price comparisons, and making snap judgments on which brand to buy, don't rush yourself. Remember that you're *earn - ing* money every time you make the right choice.

Know your prices; that way, you're not shopping by instinct. Type out a sample grocery list and enlist your older kids to compare prices at several different grocery chains—including a name-brand versus store-brand comparison. Also, read the supermarkets' advertising claims with a skeptical eye. A popular come-on touts "our" register tape at $57.42 and "their" tape at $72.39. The store with the lower total often jerry-rigs the test by listing its own sale items.

While it may be true that the woman of the house usually does the shopping, that is not always the case, especially in households where both parents work or a single dad has custody of the kids. When Lou Gage was growing up, her father did all the grocery shopping because he was self-employed and his wife worked full-time as a schoolteacher.

But, you ladies may want to think twice about sending your hubby alone to the supermarket. Men have a well-deserved reputation for taking a detailed grocery list and promising to "buy just a few things," then returning with eggnog, taco-flavored Doritos, Dove bars, and two six-packs of brewski.

What about shopping with kids? Cathy doesn't take her children shopping with her unless absolutely necessary. "As a rule, I leave the kids home with Robby because they add goodies to the cart. If I do take them along, I make sure they know how many items, if any at all, they will be able to pick out. I also make it a rule not to shop when I'm hungry. I always buy more when I'm famished."

Those who shop when hungry are more likely to impulse

buy! If you're a careful shopper, you should eat something *before* you shop since it may be two or three hours before you exit those automatic doors.

BATTLE OF THE BRANDS

When members of the Association of National Advertisers gathered at a convention recently, many broke out in a cold sweat at the clear-cut trend: sales of store-label goods were continuing to eat into the market share of brand names such as Folgers, Crisco, Ivory Soap, and Tide. *There goes our huge account with Procter & Gamble,* they thought.

More and more cost-conscious shoppers are snapping up "house-brand" or private-label products in recent years—with name brands taking it in the shorts. Private labels now account for nearly 20 percent of all grocery and consumer-product sales.

Feeling the heat are Kraft, Philip Morris, and the industry giant, Procter & Gamble. Rimler Buck, in a commentary appearing in *AdWeek*, said that "1993 will long be remembered as the year the brand-management community turned the pricing spotlight on itself. And it's about time. Consumers have reached the limit on the increases they can afford to shell out for essentially the same brand and package as last year."

Amen. Why should we buy Advil when Sam's Club ibuprofen is exactly the same thing? Read the label: each tablet contains ibuprofen USP 200 mg. We're starting to wise up.

Supermarket chains, in an effort to fend off stiff competition from warehouse clubs, heavily promote store brands. Many place their house labels right next to the name-brand products and hang stickers on the shelves that proclaim, "Compare to the National Brand and Save!"

That's a smart move by grocers. Store brands are anywhere from 20 to 50 percent cheaper than their name-brand cousins. What's even better—for the supermarkets—is that their profit

SAFEWAY NAME BRANDS VS. STORE BRANDS

Product	Name Brand	Price	Store Label	Price
Mayonnaise, 32 oz.	Best Foods	2.19	TownHouse	1.59
Black olives, 6 oz.	Mario	1.75	TownHouse	1.39
Ketchup, 40 oz.	Hunts	2.99	TownHouse	2.45
Mustard, 16 oz.	French's	1.65	TownHouse	.99
Tea, 100 bags	Lipton	3.45	Crown Colony	2.49
Instant coffee, 12 oz.	Folgers	4.54	Crown Colony	3.49
Dill pickles, 16 oz.	Vlasic	3.39	TownHouse	2.97
Microwave popcorn	O. Redenbacher	2.47	TownHouse	1.89
Soda, 6-pack	Coke Classic	2.70	Safeway Select	.99
Mixed nuts, 12 oz.	Planters	4.39	TownHouse	3.51
Applesauce, 50 oz.	Skyland	2.49	TownHouse	1.99
Peach halves, 16 oz.	Del Monte	1.29	TownHouse	.89
Bleach, 1 gal.	Clorox	.92	White Magic	.84
Cat litter, 10 lbs.	Cat's Pride	4.19	Trophy	1.55
Dog food, 5 lbs.	Purina Dog Chow	6.49	Trophy	3.49
Aluminum foil, 200 ft.	Reynolds Wrap	5.99	Safeway	4.99
Tissues, 175 count	Puff's Free	1.15	Safeway	.85
Paper towels, 6 rolls	Scott	4.89	Safeway	3.69
Toilet paper, 9 rolls	Northern	4.69	Safeway	2.19
Acetaminophen, 100 ct	Tylenol	8.29	Safeway	4.29
Ice cream, 1/2 gal	Breyer's	4.49	Lucerne	2.39
Tater tots, 32 oz.	Ore Ida	2.32	Bel-air	1.50
Tomato sauce, 28 oz.	Hunts	1.10	TownHouse	.99
Lasagna, 16 oz.	American Beauty	1.73	TownHouse	1.49
Spaghetti sauce, 26 oz.	Newman's Own	2.49	TownHouse	1.59
Canned green beans, 16 oz.	Del Monte	.85	TownHouse	.69
Bacon, 1 lb.	Oscar Mayer	3.29	SafewaySelect	1.79
Peanut butter, 28 oz.	Peter Pan	3.79	TownHouse	3.45
Pancake syrup, 24 oz.	Log Cabin	3.49	TownHouse	2.29
Toasted oat cereal, 15 oz.	Cheerios	3.39	TownHouse	2.09
Cranberry juice, 1 qt.	Ocean Spray	1.99	TownHouse	1.79
White rice, 5 lbs.	Uncle Ben's	4.69	TownHouse	1.99
Butter, 1 lb.	Land O' Lakes	2.49	Lucerne	1.69
Vegetable oil, 48 oz.	Crisco	2.69	TownHouse	1.79
Vanilla extract, 2 oz.	Schilling	4.99	Crown Colony	3.19
Cream cheese, 8 oz.	Philadelphia	.99	Lucerne	.79
Frozen lemonade, 12 oz.	Minute Maid	1.13	Bel-air	.87
Mouthwash, 24 oz.	Scope	4.09	Safeway	2.49

margins on store brands are often *higher* than on name brands.

Where do these private-label goods come from? Thanks to advances in technology, scientists at Perrigo Company in Allegan, Michigan, can break down the ingredients of just about any product. Head and Shoulders shampoo? Perrigo chemists can whip up batches of the dandruff shampoo with the same distinctive blue tint in no time. Result: Kroger now sells house-brand dandruff shampoo in a familiar white bottle labeled with a wavy blue line for half the price. Perrigo also produces knock-off versions of Tylenol, Mylanta, Oil of Olay, Metamucil, Crest, and Pepto-Bismol—plus nine hundred other products—to hundreds of discount retailers such as Wal-Mart, Kmart, and Rite-Aid Corporation.

As for foodstuffs, supermarkets purchase inventory from smaller manufacturers or from the brand-name makers selling off excess production. For instance, it's more cost-effective for a Tree Top processing plant to keep a second shift running at full capacity by selling its surplus apple juice and applesauce to A&P.

How much can you save by shopping store brands? I did a price comparison test at my local Safeway between name brands and the store's house brands of a number of basic items. Here are my findings:

The results were stunning. The name brands totaled $119.91, while the store brands totaled $79.40—*a savings of $40.51 or 33 percent.* (By the way, I also did three comparison shopping trips between supermarkets and warehouse clubs. The findings, which are summarized in chapter four, can be found in appendix three in the back of the book.)

THE UPS AND DOWNS OF STORE BRANDS

You won't be able to find store brands for everything on your shopping list. And some supermarkets sell store brands for products that others don't, and vice versa. When I did find a store brand, it was always cheaper—except in rare instances when manufacturers' incentives gave supermarkets "headroom" to lower the price.

But what about quality and taste? When *Consumer Reports* conducted a taste test between name brands and store labels, they judged the differences to be nil. The magazine's conclusion for many products stated: "No brand stood out. Shop by price."

I disagree. I've found considerable differences in quality and taste, especially for items such as orange juice, chocolate chips, canned meats, ice cream, and canned vegetables. Some people joke that store-brand green beans are made up of end pieces. Haagen-Daz ice cream certainly beats Lucerne Neapolitan, and I always ask Nicole to buy Hollywood mayonnaise; I can't stand the cheaper stuff.

Despite the variations in taste, I recommend buying store brands for the sake of economy. Sure, the store-label canned corn might contain a lesser grade, but you really have to be a gourmet—or just plain fussy—to turn up your nose at smaller kernels. If you're still not convinced, look at the price comparison again. Can you justify a fifty-dollar difference for the sake of your taste buds? Asked another way, wouldn't you rather spend that fifty dollars on something else? All these reasons underscore the wisdom of purchasing store brands as a rule, while making a few exceptions for personal taste.

Consumer Reports also performed a price comparison between store brands and name brands at an East Coast A&P. Their battle of the tapes showed even more lopsided results: $114.36 for name brands versus $67.76 for store brands, a whopping 42 percent difference.

Over the course of a year, savings can amount to roughly $2,600 a year by purchasing store brands every week. It makes more sense to spend less money.

DOING THE SUPERMARKET SHUFFLE

What else are supermarkets doing to stay competitive with price-wary consumers? Besides pushing store brands, many of them are fighting back with "multi-buy" discounts. For example, a local supermarket advertised a gallon of store-label 2 percent milk for $2.90 a gallon (at a time when I was paying $2.01 at the warehouse club). Under its "multi-buy" discount, however, the cost of *two* gallons of milk was two cents cheaper than at the warehouse club.

Some supermarkets devote one aisle to bulk items—35-ounce boxes of Cheerios and 66-ounce jars of Ragu spaghetti sauce—sizes and prices comparable to Sam's Club. But it's only one aisle, and the selection is limited. You might also find some generic products blandly packaged in white boxes.

A word of caution: the general concensus is that generic brands are bottom-of-the-barrel goods. Sure, some will be fine, but others will be "gross," as one woman told me. If you've taste-tested the generic brand in the past and were satisfied, then go ahead and pitch it into your cart.

Supermarkets are also starting "preferred-shopper" clubs with discounts based on the amount you spend. If you're a committed supermarket shopper or don't have a warehouse club near you, it's worth checking out.

Here are some down-and-dirty ways to save during your "supermarket sweep":

• **Ask the meat manager when reduced meats—beef, chicken, and pork—are set out for quick sale.** Most meat departments put their markdowns out at 9 A.M. on certain days of the week. Ask the same question of dairy and produce managers. If you cook a piece of meat that was marked down and it doesn't smell right, simply take the sticker back for a refund. Kroger even promises double your money back on returned meat purchases. (Some stores will want the meat back. Most supermarkets take your word, but there are dishonest people in the world.)

• **If you see some bruised fruit or wilting vegetables that are still quite edible,** approach the produce manager with a request for a markdown: "Sir, I can't help but notice these four tomatoes have bruises. If I were to buy them, what price could you offer me?" If you buy fruit at full price but get home and discover it's spoiled, take it back for a refund. If you regularly shop at that store, say so when you ask for your money back. Remember that the store wants to keep you as a steady customer.

• **Stock up on brand-name soda**—Coke, Pepsi, 7Up—when it goes on sale for 99 cents a six-pack. Such sales usually hit at least three times a year: Memorial Day, Fourth of July, and Labor Day. Soda stores well, and it can occupy a corner of your basement or garage for up to a year without losing quality.

• **Supermarkets offer huge savings the week before Thanksgiving.** Stock up on items that *don't* go on sale during Christmas: jellied cranberry sauce, marshmallows, stuffing, sweet potatoes, frozen turkey.

• **Shop the "scratch-and-dent" collection.** Ask the store manager where they keep dented cans and damaged package goods. Who cares if the tomato sauce can is pushed in a little?

• **Stay away from costly prepared foods,** such as broasted chicken, cole slaw, potato salad, frozen pizza, frozen dinners, pot pies, New York cheesecake, and goodies from the bakery department.

• **Consider purchasing an old refrigerator or chest freezer to take advantage of half-price sales on vegetables, produce, soda, and meats.** But filling a fridge or freezer can be a double-edged sword. Fresh food rots after a week or two, and freezer burn hits after three or four months. Also, some older freezers and refrigerators slurp up the electricity.

• **Most cities have a day-old bread store.** A $1.69 loaf of wheat/granola bread may run 69 cents in thrift stores. They also sell discounted Twinkies, Ding Dongs, and Ho-Hos for the kids' lunches.

• **You can shop for food at swap meets**—yes, swap meets. You can usually find two or three booths selling turkey stuffing, boxed cereal, and canned food. Be sure to check the expiration dates and inspect the package for damage.

• **If you prefer health foods, join a local co-op.** The best way to find out about health-food co-ops is to network with friends, check out newspaper advertisements, or look in the Yellow Pages under "Health and Diet Food."

• **Check to see if you have a "Share" co-op program where you live.** In some cities, you can buy several boxes of food (you don't have any say as to what groceries are put *into* the boxes) for fifteen dollars or so. One stipulation requires members to perform several hours of community or volunteer service (such as helping out in your child's classroom) to buy these groceries, which are usually available only once a month.

• **Join a wholesale food service.** If you have the storage room and freezer space, you can purchase bulk orders of frozen meats, pasta, fish, and other grocery items. Then you still buy more perishable products such as dairy and produce at the supermarket. Begin your search by checking in the Yellow Pages under "Food Plans." Colorado Prime (800-365-9498) is one of the largest wholesale food service companies.

CHAPTER 3

The Coupon Queen and Her Court

It's lunchtime, but Diana Haptonstall has work to do. She has called a meeting of the Royal Order of Couponers, and as the reigning monarch, she has important business to conduct in the kingdom of refunds. Diana began the once-a-week couponing confab as a way to network and improve money-saving skills.

Gathered around the table are several of Diana's princesses: Lainie MacDonald, Judy Padgett, Deb Elliss, and a solitary male, Shaun Cano. *(Wait a minute. How did this bachelor crash the party?)* A half-dozen other women pull up chairs.

The Coupon Queen asks the group to share any recent successes. "We'd love to hear how much you saved on your last shopping trip," she explains. "Your stories can serve as an encouragement to others."

"I bought two boxes of Kellogg's Corn Flakes for 89 cents," says one. "My husband was blown away."

"I purchased two king-size Cadbury candy bars, normally

$1.47 each, for 47 cents with my coupons. That's less than 25 cents apiece," chips in another.

"Safeway was having a special on Nestlé Toll House chocolate chips for $1.50 a package. I had coupons that lowered the price to 50 cents a bag. But then I had another Nestlé coupon that offered free milk up to 90 cents. I got a quart of milk thrown into the deal!"

For the next hour, the Queen and her court swapped success stories and traded coupons. Not only were the women—and one guy—learning how to save grocery money, but they were having fun at the same time.

CLIP THOSE SAVINGS

Coupon klatches such as Diana's are becoming more common. According to NCH Promotional Services, a research firm, more than 94 percent of grocery shoppers have dramatically changed their shopping habits over the last year. The increasing number of bargain hunters has spurred grocery retailers to find new ways of providing their customers with greater value and savings.

In this era of growing value consciousness, experts say coupons remain one of the best ways to save on grocery bills. Manufacturers are responding by issuing more coupons than ever—310 billion, enough to shower each man, woman, and child with 1,200 of the little slips of paper. But 97 percent of all coupons are never redeemed, meaning 292 million end up in landfills. To entice consumers to actually *use* their coupons, manufacturers are offering fatter discounts but quicker expiration dates, according to the D'Arcy Masius Benton & Bowles advertising agency in St. Louis. Many supermarket chains, looking to entice customers to shop their stores, double the face value of coupons worth up to 50 cents off or even those up to one dollar off most products.

For Diana, couponing began when she was fed up with monthly grocery tabs totaling more than four hundred dollars for her family of three. It was time to get serious. She walked into Wal-Mart and purchased a large coupon organizer for $1.87. She divided it into various groupings—cereals, canned vegetables, frozen foods, personal hygiene—and began stuffing it with coupons.

Today, Diana has a collection of more than five hundred cents-off coupons in her war chest. Sure, it's bulky and looks like a small safe, but she ignores the stares she receives in the checkout line. "I've noticed the funny looks on people's faces when they see my bulky coupon organizer," she said. "But then they notice how much money I save and how my cart is filled with twice as many groceries as theirs."

How much money *does* she save? Diana showed me the tale of the tape after a recent trip to the supermarket. Her register receipt measured 46 inches long, nearly 4 feet—18 inches of which tabulated red deductions for her coupons! Her original total came to $163.56, but with coupon deductions of $41.34, the final amount was $122.22, a 25 percent discount! In all, Diana purchased 122 items and used 57 coupons, many of which were doubled to a maximum one dollar off by the supermarket. She even saved two dollars for bringing in her own plastic bags! (Some supermarkets offer a five-cent credit for each bag you use.)

So, how did she do it? Couponers, replied Diana, have a four-tier strategy when they walk into a grocery store. The simplest coupon transaction is a "single play," which takes place when a consumer uses a standard cents-off coupon, such as a straight fifty cents off a box of Rice Krispies.

But you can do more, continued Diana. Experienced couponers look for double plays, triple plays, and grand slams. What's a "double play?" Let's say your local supermarket is having a buy-one, get-one-free sale on Ragu spaghetti sauce. The cost of each jar is $1.77. You pull two jars of Ragu off the shelf and take two Ragu coupons out of your file box. If you have two coupons for fifty cents off, that's a double play. Final cost: 77 cents.

But if you're shopping in a supermarket that doubles

coupons, you can go for a "triple play!" Again, you pull two jars of Ragu off the shelf for $1.77. Then, you take two Ragu coupons out of your file box. Each doubled, fifty-cent coupon is worth one dollar each, for a total of two dollars. Because you paid $1.77 for the two jars but received two dollars at the checkout stand, the supermarket just paid *you* 23 cents to purchase two jars of Ragu.

"You can even do better than that," said Diana, getting really excited. "The ultimate coupon play is a 'grand slam.' That's when you have manufacturers' coupons *and* store coupons (found in newspaper inserts) in your file box. Let's say the store is again offering the two-for-one deal on Ragu sauce. In your hot little hands, you're holding two fifty-cent manufacturer's coupons, which when doubled equals two dollars off. But the supermarket also has in-store coupons for twenty-five cents off, which double to fifty cents each for a total of one dollar. In all, you receive a three dollar refund, which means the grocer just paid you $1.23 to put two jars of Ragu into your cart." (In some states, stores will not double in-store coupons.)

Is it legal?

"You bet it is!" exclaimed Diana.

Coupons should be just another arsenal in your purse when you shop for groceries. After your first double play or grand slam, you'll be hooked.

MAKING A MOVE

Like many couples, Nicole and I never used coupons a great deal. It's a hassle to cut them out, file them in a little organizer, and then remember to take them with us to the grocery store. Besides, we buy in bulk once a month at Sam's Club, which doesn't accept coupons. Warehouse clubs are often cheaper than single-play couponing, but after hearing about Diana's double and triple plays, there's no way Sam's can beat that. Nicole and I are looking at coupons with fresh eyes.

But Nicole and I have never turned up our noses at obvious coupon deals. I enjoyed paying five dollars for my state smog test last year (half-price with my coupon), and taking Nicole out to dinner—compliments of two-for-one specials. As for the supermarket, we never purchase cereal without a coupon, but we also never knew about double plays until I heard about the Coupon Queen and her Court.

If you catch the couponing bug, invest a little money in an organizer. You can usually find one advertised in your Sunday newspaper supplements, or you can buy one for $1.87 at Wal-Mart, as Queen Diana did. Cheaper yet, you can even set up your own shoe-box file.

Where can you find coupons? Again, begin with your Sunday newspaper, where 80 percent of all coupons are distributed. If you live in a two-newspaper town, you may want to subscribe to the competing newspaper, too, if they offer a special Sunday-only rate. Check it out. The coupon savings can easily pay for the cost of the paper.

Marianne Hering said, "My local supermarket sells the Sunday newspaper for half-price on Monday, and that's a great way to fill your coupon organizer." Sometimes, convenience stores will even give you old Sunday papers for free (after they cut out the masthead on page one to receive a refund from the distributor).

You can also clip coupons from several other sources: the Wednesday food section and various inserts found in your local newspaper; women's magazines such as *Good Housekeeping* and *Ladies Home Journal*; junk mail (give it a ten-second read before you toss it); and direct-mail coupon companies, such as Carol Wright. You can also add your name to Procter & Gamble's mailing list by volunteering to fill out a product preference survey. (Write: Procter & Gamble, P.O. Box 5529, Cincinnati, OH 45201-5529.)

While you're standing in the checkout line, thumb through *Family Circle*, *Women's Day*, and *Redbook*. If you see a coupon you can use, go ahead and purchase the magazine—if it's cost-effective. Doctors' offices are also a good place to clip coupons out of magazines while you wait... and wait... and wait (always ask permission, of course).

You can also find coupons *inside* grocery stores. A new trend employs point-of-purchase coupons, dispensed from little gismos that hang right next to the product. It doesn't get any easier than that. All you have to do is rip it off and give it to the cashier. Other times, products will have coupons right on the packages themselves, or perhaps tucked inside. Again, don't be bashful about pulling it off or clipping it out when you go through the checkout line. The cashier will be happy to accept it.

Be sure to read any on-the-label offers. For instance, a jar of sandwich spread may have a coupon stating that if you buy the product, you can also pick up a free liter of Diet Coke. Pull off the coupon and present it along with the Diet Coke when you go through the checkout lane.

Some grocery stores even provide a coupon-exchange bin, and you don't need to leave any coupons to take some away. Or, if you decide not to use a particular coupon that may be due to expire soon, you could leave it on the shelf by that particular product for someone else to redeem. You can also find rebate offers from various manufacturers, usually posted on a bulletin board.

Also, have you noticed the Checkout Coupons that cashiers hand you when you pay for your groceries? This latest gimmick was developed by Catalina Marketing Network using sophisticated computer technology tied to supermarket checkout scanners. That way, the store can issue coupons tailored to each customer's buying habits. For example, if you purchase a jar of peanut butter, you might be issued a Checkout Coupon for a competing brand of peanut butter, a larger size of the same brand, or a jar of grape jelly. These Checkout Coupons have an average face value of 85 cents, which is nearly 50 percent higher than traditional mass-delivered coupons found in newspapers, which have an average face value of 60 cents.

Finally, you can swap or purchase coupons through *Refunding Makes Cents*, a monthly, one-hundred-page publication crammed with classified ads, news, columns, and advice on how to use coupons, seek out rebates, and find refund forms. (Write to *Refunding Makes Cents*, Box R-839, Farmington, UT 84025. Cost is thirteen dollars for six months, twenty-five dollars for one year.)

The want ads in this publication speak a different language. Here's a sample: "My 50 forms for your NB free coupon or $1 CQCD. LSASE." Translation: this woman is offering rebate forms for your national brand free coupons or any one-dollar, complete-qualifier cash deals, which is a refund form with all proofs attached, good for a cash refund. She also asks that you send a long, self-addressed, stamped envelope.

My favorite column is "Let's Hear Your Trashy Confession," which contains reader contributions of embarrassing moments in couponing. This story is typical: "While dumpster digging on a military base near my home, we had a surprise. My brother was at one end of the dumpster hauling out the loot when a military man opened the other end and dumped his trash. He said 'hello' and then left!"

Well, I'm not ready to "dumpster dive" to save money, but some folks are really into this coupon and rebate thing. In fact, experienced couponers don't stop at second base after they hit a double play—they're after *home-run rebates*. You have to be committed, however. It is a lot of work to fill out a rebate form, circle the item on the register tape, pack it away in an envelope, stick on a postage stamp, and wait four weeks to get a buck or two in return for your efforts.

In addition, rebate offers require that you follow the letter of the law. Some companies want a dated, original receipt. Others accept photocopies. (If you have several rebate forms, ask the cashier to ring up each item separately, subtotaling all the way. Explain that you need to send a separate receipt with each rebate form.)

Despite the hassles, rebates are getting better, with some larger offers popping up. Lainie MacDonald, one of Diana's princesses, received a rebate form for Lean Cuisine frozen turkey dinners, but she needed twenty UPC symbols (bar codes) off the box to receive a five-dollar rebate and forty UPC symbols for a ten-dollar rebate. Since the rebate offer didn't require any cash register receipts, Lainie hung up a sign in the employee lunchroom asking for old Lean Cuisine boxes. "I call it my 'Lean Cuisine farm,'" she said. "We'll see what happens."

Other rebate programs are more conventional. Lainie showed me a newspaper coupon offering *full-price* rebates on five different household items, such as Surf detergent, Downy liquid cleanser, and All washing detergent. The total rebate was fifteen dollars, the same amount as the cost of the goods.

"What these manufacturers are saying is, if you buy any of these items, you will get them for free," said Lainie. "And if you have another manufacturer's coupon, and it's a buy-one, get-one-free, it's a grand slam!"

"Why are these companies doing this?" I asked.

"They're trying to build brand loyalty," she replied. "They're looking for increased sales down the line."

To make rebates work for you, it helps to be flexible about brand choice. Many name-brand products, including Surf and Wisk, are basically one and the same. "If you don't mind using Wisk one month and Surf the next, you can save a lot of money," said Lainie.

MORE COUPON ADVICE

Coupons are also good to use if you prefer a name brand over a store brand (Nestlé Toll House chocolate chips versus A&P's, for instance). However, Diana will be the first to tell you that using a coupon to purchase a name-brand item isn't always going to be cheaper than buying a generic or store brand. "It all depends. You really have to keep your eyes open and comparison shop." If a store-brand product is still cheaper, and taste and quality are not diminished, opt for the savings.

Another caution is to collect coupons only for products you want to buy. In our household, we stay away from prepared foods, such as Healthy Choice frozen entrees, Hamburger Helper, Rice-A-Roni, and frozen apple pies. Food companies and grocery stores don't produce coupons for some of our favorite basics such as ground turkey or elbow macaroni.

Here's what other people had to say about coupons. (The appendixes contain more helpful hints from my surveys and interviews.)

- "Always remember rain checks. Once, my local supermarket ran a special coupon for Post Raisin Bran: buy one, get one free. That was a savings of $3.79. When I got there late Saturday morning, all the Raisin Bran was gone. I asked for and received a rain check with no expiration date. My plan now is to walk in with two one-dollar coupons for Raisin Bran, and then I can get two boxes of cereal for $1.79!"

- "I like the coupons for items like Soup Starter and Wyler's beef and chicken bouillon because they send you a coupon for free meat."

- "When you take an item off the shelf and put it into your cart, also take your coupon out so you don't have to find it later."

- "I've found that store-brand frozen juice isn't as good as Tropicana or Minute Maid, so I always look for coupons in the juice section. Frozen concentrate is usually the cheapest. We drink orange juice like water at home."

- "My husband didn't think my couponing would add up to much, so I decided to show him. Every time I saved three, eight, or twelve dollars in coupons, I wrote a check for the same amount and deposited it into our vacation account. After six months, these savings paid for a nice weekend in the mountains."

- "I've been couponing since high school. I find I cut my food bill by 20 to 25 percent. I get a real high from the savings."

- "Not many people know you can use coupons at Wal-Mart. In fact, Wal-Mart will accept coupons from competing

---

Does Lou Gage Use Coupons?

Of course. Why ask? When asked for her favorite coupon story, Lou told me about the time she went into a store that sells hobby and craft items. One Saturday evening before Christmas, the store was handing out ten-dollar-off coupons good for the next day only. The deal: ten dollars off a purchase of thirty dollars or more. Lou asked the salesclerk how many coupons she could have. "All you want," was the reply.

That set Lou's wheels in motion. The store was offering a special on garland, 4 feet for one dollar, or 100 feet for twenty-five dollars. Her church needed 800 feet of garland for its Christmas Eve services. When Lou had priced it at other stores, the best she could do was $297.

"My church couldn't afford that," said Lou. "So we were going to buy half that amount and make do." But a purchase of 100 feet for twenty-five dollars would leave Lou five dollars short for using the store's coupon, so she decided to help the church out by buying eight $4.99 wreaths for herself, plus eight pieces of 15-cent candy.

Lou and other members of her family had to go through the checkout counter eight separate times, each purchasing 100 feet of garland, one wreath, and one knickknack for $30.14, plus tax, but the church received the eight, 100 foot garlands for fifteen dollars each. "The total for the garlands was $120, which was a lot less than $297," said Lou.

stores, so if you have a manufacturer's coupon and a store coupon for Luv's diapers, that's a triple play!"

- "At Diana's coupon meeting, we share lists of what we want from each other. Everyone gets a copy, but if anyone finds a Tavist-D medicine coupon, it's mine. It's a new over-the-counter drug."

- "If the coupon says 'on any size,' buy the *smallest* size to save the most."

- "Don't throw those expired coupons away! Some supermarkets are so hungry for business that they accept my coupons long after the expiration date. I always inform them up front of the expiration date, however."

- "Some cashiers prefer to see the coupons before they start checking your cart; others don't care. It never hurts to ask."

- "Couponers like the challenge of seeing how much they can get taken off their shopping bill. But some women buy things they don't normally use just because they have a coupon for it. For instance, if you purchase Colgate toothpaste with a coupon but the kids won't use it, you're wasting money."

- "I keep a coupon packet, although I know some people who carry them in a shoe box. If you depend on coupons, you should cut every coupon you can find. When I go to the dentist office or have my tires changed, I clip coupons out of the magazines in the waiting room. Nobody seems to mind. 'Sure, go ahead,' is the reply I hear."

- "Never buy take-out pizza, pet foods, laundry detergent, and trash bags without a coupon. If you're not hooked into a name brand like Tide or Cheer, and you're willing to buy what's on sale, you can come out ahead. You'll also find coupons at the point of purchase."

- "Be sure to check dates on every coupon. Occasionally, they are outdated, and the checkout person won't take them where I shop."

- "We drive across town to a store that offers double coupons, and we do all our shopping for two weeks. I usually save fifteen to twenty dollars each time."

- "So many people toss mailers, but if you come up with one coupon—like having your VCR cleaned for $8.95—you've saved some money. Out of five packets of junk mail, I usually find one or two coupons, which makes it worth the two or three minutes I spent going through them."

CHAPTER 4

Get Thee to a Warehouse Club

My pulse just jumped twenty points, and sweat is beading on my upper lip. I've walked into Sam's Club, one of those cavernous, bare-bones, stack-it-to-the-ceiling, blow-it-out-in-bulk warehouse clubs. It's payday, and I'm here with Nicole and the kids to do some *serious* shopping. My motto on such occasions: *the more I buy, the more I save.*

Andrea and Patrick share push-cart duty while I blaze a trail. My search-and-purchase mission soon leads me to the electronics aisle. "Hey, Nicole, look at these new Toshiba big-screen TVs."

"They cost $1,999," Nicole points out.

"Yes, but they're just like the Mitsubishi big-screens. Wouldn't one look terrific in our living room? And what a great price! I saw Mitsubishis advertised for $2600 at SoundTrack."

Nicole and I both know we're not going to purchase any TV—48-inch screen or otherwise—on this shopping trip. But I love dreaming, and warehouse clubs are where dreams begin.

Nicole pulls out her grocery list. (The last time I solo-shopped Sam's without one I bought enough hot dogs and toilet paper to service a crowd of fifty thousand at Denver's Mile High stadium.) We start cruising the aisles, hunting for bargains. A woman demonstrating Hoover vacuum cleaners catches my eye.

"Can I show you our new Hoover upright?" she asks.

"Well, we're in a hurry...."

Wait a minute, the researcher in me thinks. *Maybe she can answer a few questions about warehouse clubs.*

"I understand that Sam's and Price Club usually mark up merchandise just a few percent. Is that true?"

"You see this unit here?" she says, pointing to an upright model for $188. "Hoover wholesales it to Sam's for $184."

"You mean they're making only four bucks on it?

"That's right."

"But, how ...?"

She shrugs her shoulders. "It's crazy, but Sam's does that sometimes."

Nicole and I continue our monthly shopping spree. We start filling our oversized cart with bulk items: thirty rolls of toilet paper, twelve rolls of paper towels, two cases of Caffeine Free Diet Pepsi, a gallon of vegetable oil, eighteen large eggs, 2 pounds of jack cheese, a 5-pound tub of Country Crock margarine, 10 pounds of sugar, 10 pounds of chocolate chips, a 51-ounce box of Kellogg's Raisin Bran, a 4-pound box of Grape-Nuts, an 82-ounce tin of Country Time Lemonade, 5 pounds of Peter Pan peanut butter, a six-pack of Kodak film....

The total tab will land between $125 and $200, *but think of all the money we saved,* I remind myself. Over the years, we have saved a bundle at Price Club, Pace, and Sam's. Whenever we have faced a major purchase (tires, stereo, VCR), I've researched and shopped around for the best price. The local warehouse club had the best deal nine times out of ten. That's a great batting average.

BEHIND THE SCENES

My fondness for warehouse clubs dates back to 1976 when the first membership warehouse opened in my hometown of San Diego. An entrepreneur, Sol Price, leased an ark-like building on Morena Boulevard and began selling merchandise and business products at rock-bottom prices. Within a year, San Diego was abuzz: the Price Club had the most incredible prices in town.

Ah, but not just *anybody* could shop there. You needed to purchase a twenty-five dollar annual membership card (plus ten dollars for family members). And to get one, you had to be a business owner with a California sales tax permit, or an employee of a bank, school, hospital, local utility, or city government—stable elements of the economy. The Price Club deemed these people as less likely to shoplift or write bad checks.

Membership cards, which included your name and photo, instilled a feeling of "ownership" among the members and also fostered repeat trips. "If I paid twenty-five dollars, then I have to get my money's worth!" was the common cry. Membership fees also discouraged frivolous shoppers.

The strategy worked. The Price Club was an instant success. Talk at cocktail parties in nearby upper-class La Jolla centered around how to score with a Price Club card. Membership, in this case, had its privileges: incredible prices on well-chosen merchandise.

As the Price Club expanded and opened new stores, other companies jumped into the warehouse game: Sam's Club, Pace, Price Savers, Costco, and BJ's. Although the industry boomed during the go-go eighties, it has slumped in recent years due to more price-competitive stores (such as Office Depot, Toys "R" Us, Best Buy, PetsMart, and The Men's Wearhouse). In addition, factory outlet malls have sprung up like mushrooms outside major cities, siphoning off cost-conscious consumers. In 1993, a shakeout led Price Club to merge with Costco, and Sam's Club to buy out Pace—and shut down many Pace stores in the process.

To help you understand why warehouse clubs offer such consistent savings on everything from groceries, tires, small appliances, TVs, refrigerators, batteries, film, etc., allow me to introduce Paul. Paul and I have known each other a long time, and he's worked in the warehouse-club industry for more than ten years in a high position. Paul agreed to answer my questions about warehouse clubs as long as I agreed not to disclose his identity.

Q. What's the average markup on merchandise?

A. The general markup is 8 to 8.5 percent. From that amount, we deduct payroll (4 percent), benefits (1.5 percent), utilities and supplies (.5 percent), taxes (1 percent), and central overhead and real estate (1 percent). All those expenses add up to 8 percent. Here's one of our bigger secrets: without membership fees, the Price Club would not be profitable.

Q. You mean you don't make any money on the merchandise itself?

A. That's right. If it weren't for the annual membership fees, we couldn't stay in business. It can be honestly said that we sell merchandise at cost, and our profit comes from membership fees, which approach 2 percent of sales. There's not much room for error in this business.

Q. How many members does a warehouse club need to turn a profit?

A. We like to see a solid customer base of fifty thousand members. The annual fees represent an up-front payment, and we try to "use" other people's money to run our business.

Membership also provides the club with a database. We

know names, addresses, phone numbers, driver's license numbers, and employers. This boosts our marketing efforts, since we have no budget allowance for newspaper, radio, or TV ads. We can analyze shopping patterns, how much each member spends every month on what items. We can target mailers to volume shoppers, encouraging them to 'sponsor' friends for membership.

Q. It used to be that warehouse clubs were good places to buy toilet paper and paper towels, but not groceries. Now you can buy just about any food item there as well. What happened?

A. We had a change in business philosophy. Grocery items increase the *frequency* of shopping. Everyone has to eat, and milk lasts only one week. Food appeals to everybody.

Q. What's your selling philosophy?

A. We operate by "The Six Rights of Merchandising." Simply put, that means we have to have the *right merchandise* at the *right time* in the *right place* in the *right quantity* in the *right condition* at the *right price.* The right merchandise includes high-demand basics and commodities, sprinkled with a mix of new and exciting products. We have to sell what the members want, which generally means name brands, but we're starting to see buyers flock to private labels.

Q. What do you mean by that?

A. We started the private-label revolution by selling our own club brand. Since then, private-label goods have grown significantly in market share. That's why you see supermarkets pushing their own store brands. Some commodities such as laundry detergent and soda pop are easily "knocked off," and smart shoppers recognize there isn't much difference in quality.

At the Price Club, we're moving more and more into private labels. We sell a certain kind of detergent that you can't buy anywhere else, and that increases customer loyalty. We have developed a line of quality food products under a label named after an original shareholder, and we use another private label for our meat products. We will be coming out with our own clothing lines, as well.

Private brands cut out the middlemen with all their brokering and advertising costs, plus it allows for differentiation from other retailers. Private labels also make it much more difficult for consumers to comparison shop when the item is not available elsewhere.

Q. Is that why it's difficult to comparison shop electronic equipment, such as TVs and CD players, because the model numbers never match up?

A. "Exactly. A lot of name-brand manufacturers create special versions for the warehouse club with different model numbers or face plates. How can a customer compare a Price Club Sony TV, which may have an extra feature on it, against a Sony over at Wal-Mart? One way to get around this barrier is to go to the library and look up the product in the current *Consumer Reports Buying Guide.* At the end of each section, you'll find a listing of equivalent model numbers."

Q. I've noticed that warehouse clubs carry high-quality merchandise and name brands but have a limited selection. What's the reasoning behind that?

A. Limited selection increases efficiency. With fewer vendors to order from and fewer items to stock, fewer mistakes are made. Errors cost money. It is also easier to maintain a limited selection. Can you imagine what life is like for the "re-order" specialist at Home Depot? "Let's see, we have one thousand and one bolts, one thousand and two...."

In fact, I think limited selection is the primary strength of wholesale clubs. Let's say you walk into a Silo or Circuit City with their walls of televisions, all playing an *Aladdin* video. Where do you begin to shop? How do you know one television is really better than another? I'd rather let the warehouse-club buyer make the decision for me than the sharkskin-suited salesman feeding off commission. That's why we offer excellent products in three price ranges: low-end, mid-range, and high-end.

Limited selection makes shopping easier and clearer for the customer because we often bring in items recommended by *Consumer Reports*, although we can't advertise that fact. But we know our customers tend to read such publications.

By focusing on limited selection, the Price Club purchasing agents gain economies of scale all along the distribution pipeline. "Another truckload of televisions for Price Club? Yep, you weigh the same as the two trucks just ahead of you. No need for a full inspection. Just roll on through." Believe me, those little savings count up. Another part of the magic is transporting full loads, because freight rates are much lower in full-truck quantities as compared to "less-than-truckload" shipments.

Q. What shopping tips can you give our readers?

A. Get to know some of the staff. They can tell you about the hot bargains or when something new is expected to arrive. They'll know which slow-movers have been marked down, or when price changes are made. For instance, Price Club usually changes prices on Saturday nights after closing.

Our stores use merchandise codes. A yellow Post-it tag on a sign means the item is in low-stock condition. 'D' means the product has been discontinued; 'I' means it is temporarily inactive and will not be reordered soon. Costco stores flag the tags with an asterisk to signify a markdown.

Take a close look at the numbers on the price tags. At the

Price Club, we identify items on initial markdowns by a price ending in seventy-seven cents. A final markdown results in a price ending in eleven cents—the point of maximum savings. Often, clothing is marked down simply because the selection is limited in color and size. If you don't mind the least-popular color, and it fits, then you can purchase a real bargain.

Q. But how come there's never any place to try on clothing at a warehouse store?

A. The extra labor of monitoring the fitting rooms and rehanging the merchandise makes it cost-prohibitive. Having fitting rooms would also increase shoplifting.

Q. What are supermarkets doing to compete?

A. Supermarkets have tried to stem the growth of warehouse clubs, but they cannot move the merchandise as efficiently as we can, nor can they generate the volume necessary to support such low prices. The "club buster" sales are actually loss leaders for the supermarkets. Their newspaper ads may feature these items, but they hope you don't buy them.

Everyone keeps a close eye on the competition. One of our biggest competitors is Target. We check their Sunday ads to make sure our prices are lower. We've noticed many of our customers bring their Target flyers with them and compare prices as they shop. If we have a particularly good deal on a Target item, we will feature it at the end of an aisle.

When customers come in and see a better deal, we win. Beating Target becomes our best advertising, because customers tell their friends, 'You should have seen what I paid for the new Super Nintendo game at Price Club today!'

Q. Sometimes I'll see some really off-the-wall goods, like Gucci handbags and Swatches. Where do warehouse clubs get those?

A. We sometimes purchase goods "unconventionally" on the gray market. For example, Levi Strauss may not want to sell to a warehouse club because that would upset The Gap, The Limited, and Miller's Outpost. But then one of those traditional retailers approach a warehouse club with an overstocked item, or someone in the distribution chain diverts those goods to us. We have to authenticate the merchandise, because there are counterfeits out there! If we sold fake Seiko watches, for instance, we would lose a tremendous amount of good will.

Sometimes, buying unconventionally involves cloak-and-dagger maneuvers. Once, a local tire store was selling Michelins for less than our wholesale prices. We sent a truck over—unmarked, of course—and bought as many tires as we could. When our truck left, their manager tailed the truck to see where it was going. Our people knew they were being followed, and made sure they lost him before delivering the tires to our distribution center. It really gets wild out there.

Q. What are your biggest-selling items?

A. Toilet paper, paper towels, low-fat milk, skinless chicken, and breadmakers. After that, whatever's hot at the moment. We recently had a shipment of Seiko watches, which carried a retail price of three hundred dollars. We blew them out in five days at thirty dollars a pop. Since we don't advertise, the only way members can find out about these special items is to drop by regularly or read our monthly mailer.

Q. How do you keep up with fluctuating prices?

A. We have spotters and competition shoppers. Let's say we have a Hoover vacuum for $79, but Target is selling it for $75. I would call our purchasing agent and ask him what can we do to lower our price. If he can't do anything, sometimes we'll pull the vacuum off the floor. In the past, we've even posted an announcement: "Dear Customer. It is against Price Club philosophy to sell at a loss. At the moment, Target is selling this item for less than our wholesale cost. We suggest you purchase the item at Target."

THE NITTY-GRITTY

Isn't that amazing? A store *telling* you to go shop the competition? While admirable, the more important question is: Are warehouse clubs actually *cheaper* on the whole for groceries and other items? The answer is yes. I made three comprehensive shopping trips over a six-month period, comparing Pace and Sam's to Cub Foods (a bag-your-own-groceries supermarket with a reputation for having the best prices in town) and Safeway (the national chain with all the modern-day shopping conveniences).

A word or two on how I conducted the tests. First, size differences were a significant hassle. I had to make some judgment calls, especially in the area of bulk buying. For instance, if Pace sold six, 16-ounce cans of tomato sauce in bulk, but Cub's sold single, 12-ounce cans, I calculated a common denominator between the two. In the case of the tomato sauce, I used three, 16-ounce cans as a reasonable amount that Nicole and I would typically buy on a shopping trip.

Second, some of the stores sold house brands and some didn't, so I wanted to be sure I was comparing apples to apples. Yes, my decisions were arbitrary, but I had to start somewhere. (It was also interesting to note the rise in grocery prices over time. Many items cost 10 to 15 percent more in just six months.)

In the first two comparison surveys, I shopped Pace as I normally would, adding a few items found on most families' grocery lists. Then I went to Cub's and Safeway that same week and compared their prices to my Pace shopping list. Some items were brand names, and some weren't. My first survey indicated that Pace offered a savings of 25 percent over

Cub Foods and 39 percent over Safeway: Pace, $107.15; Cub Foods, $135.10; Safeway, $149.55.

The second survey showed Pace saved 33 percent over Cub Foods and 48 percent over Safeway: Pace, $124.31; Cub Foods, $165.50; Safeway, $184.64. These results mirrored a similar test conducted by *Consumer Reports*. A magazine staffer shopped a Pace and an A&P in New Jersey, using a grocery list similar to mine. Pace came in at $76.71 and A&P at $128.53—a 67 percent difference! They compared name brand against name brand, however.

For my final shopping survey, Lou Gage and I conducted an extensive comparison featuring Sam's' name brands (and a few house brands) vs Cub and Safeway's name and store brands. (I've included a detailed account of my final shopping comparison in appendix two.) Sam's scored a savings of 15 percent over Cub Foods and 24 percent over Safeway: Sam's, $229.47; Cub Foods, $266.89; Safeway, $285.82.

The smaller differences in the third test occurred because I was trying hard to find store brands, even though there may have been a significant difference in quality between the supermarket house brand and Sam's name brand. Summing up, warehouse clubs have the lowest prices 90 percent of the time. Even more importantly, you can buy high-quality, name-brand products for less than the supermarket store brand in most cases.

THE BOTTOM LINE

Before you go out and purchase a warehouse-club membership, however, you have to understand its strengths and weaknesses.

The Upside
- Warehouse clubs are cheaper.
- Warehouse clubs sell name-brand cereals 40 to 70 percent cheaper than supermarkets, even with a dollar-off coupon.
- Warehouse clubs are great places to shop for small appli-

ances, lawn mowers, and electronic equipment, including TVs, VCRs, and computers.

- Tires, especially high-quality Michelins, will usually be the best deal in town and the mounting costs are very reasonable.

- Warehouse clubs' philosophy of limited selection means they can't afford to stock losers. With non-grocery items, warehouse clubs usually carry models in two or three price ranges.

- Warehouse clubs are starting to sell in smaller bulk sizes. It used to be that you had to buy a 5-pound can of tomato sauce or a 10-pound block of jack cheese to get the discount. No longer.

- Warehouse clubs have the best deals on prescription eyewear.

- It's easier to become a warehouse club member than it was ten years ago. Eligibility rules have been relaxed.

- If you're a name-brand shopper, warehouse clubs are 40 to 70 percent cheaper than supermarkets' name brands.

The Downside

- You have to spend more up front to get your savings.
- Lack of variety.
- You need lots of storage space at home.
- Many warehouse clubs are not conveniently located.
- Warehouse clubs accept only Discover credit cards (no GM rebate or airline miles).
- You have to take clothes home to try them on.
- Salespeople are hard to find, but that's getting better.
- Low-rent atmosphere: You won't find track lighting in the produce department or air-conditioning in the summer. I've had people tell me this is actually a plus, however, since the attractiveness of supermarkets causes them to stay longer and buy things they normally wouldn't.

Recommendation

If it's convenient, do your main shopping at a warehouse club, buying in bulk as much as you can. Then shop the supermarkets once a week for fresh vegetables and items you can't purchase at a warehouse club. Stock up on loss leaders, especially in the meat department, and use coupons for your favorite cereals that you can't buy at the warehouse club. And if you can make a double or triple couponing play, go for it!

CHAPTER 5

"Let's Go *Out* to Eat"

It was the summer of 1970, and I had just turned an impressionable sixteen years of age. My huge appetite had trouble keeping up with a body that was growing by leaps and bounds. I ate seconds and thirds so often that my mother wondered if she should peel up some kitchen linoleum and serve it to me. Pry, my younger brother by just one year, matched me bite for bite.

That summer one of my mother's cousins, Bob Hoffmann, rented a room from us. We called him "Uncle Bopper" because of his crazy sense of humor. One evening, as he watched Pry and me wolf down our fourth pork chop and third baked potato, he announced a brilliant idea. "You know that all-you-can-eat smorgasbord in Pacific Beach? I think Mike, Pry, and some of their friends could eat out that smorgie. Then I could sue for breach of contract and false advertising."

Uncle Bopper wasn't serious about the lawsuit part, but he liked the idea of sending a hungry, SWAT-eating team into an unsuspecting smorgasbord. So we enlisted some heavy eaters in the neighborhood and even made up team T-shirts. On a Saturday night, our troupe of twelve walked into Sir George's smorgasbord. We hadn't eaten in *hours*. As we giggled and punched each other in the shoulders, Uncle Bopper asked to speak to the manager.

"You see these kids?" he said. "They are poised to consume all the food you have. We can settle this right now, or I can turn these voracious eaters loose." Then Uncle Bopper whipped out a parchment containing a lot of Latin words and subjunctive clauses. The legal-looking but bogus document set forth the reasons behind the threatened "lawsuit."

The manager was a recent Greek immigrant who didn't quite comprehend what was going on. Managerial training had never prepared him for this sort of challenge. "What does this mean?" he asked, pointing to the parchment.

"It says if these kids eat everything you have, then you will have to pay damages for false advertising and breach of contract, since this is an *all-you-can-eat* establishment."

The baffled manager shrugged his shoulders. He muttered something in Greek and then replied, "Be my guest."

My friends and I attacked the buffet line, filling our plates with salads and breads. Then we returned and devastated the fried chicken and roast beef entrees. It was a mismatch—like the Notre Dame football team against a high school squad. The kitchen scrambled to keep up, but when we returned for seconds on roast beef, the slices were decidedly rare and cool to the touch.

After watching us gorge for an hour and a half, the manager asked to speak with Uncle Bopper. "Please, sir, can you tell your boys to stop? I've only been manager for one month." We were stuffed anyway, so Uncle Bopper called off the dogs.

That evening at Sir George's was probably the last time a restaurant lost money on me. These days, I still count eating out as one of life's joys, although restaurant food is not a very good deal when compared to home cooking. But it's nice to be served, eat a delicious meal, and have somebody else do the cleanup.

When eating out, it's important to pay attention to *value*. Sure, you and your family could eat at Joe's Greasy Spoon for ten bucks, but oily food, smoke-filled air, and dirty forks won't make for a pleasurable dining experience. At the other end of the pendulum, you and your family could dress in your Sunday best for an evening at L'Hermitage, where you could indulge in a degustatory delight of *gigot d'agneau aux flageolets* or *escalope de veau aux morilles.* Then the bill would arrive, giving you an instant case of heartburn. *I could have made a car pay - ment for what I'm paying tonight,* you might groan to yourself.

Sensible restaurant eating falls somewhere in the middle. But before I get into some money-saving strategies, let's take an overview of the industry.

FROM ROADSIDE DINERS TO FINE DINING

The least expensive eateries are **coffee shops, diners, and cafes,** where the clientele often look like they've stepped out of a ZZ Top video and the waitresses wear beehive hairdos. The menu—mostly short-order fare—can range from inedible to tasty, but the price is right: $1.99 for eggs, sausage, and toast; $3.75 for a hamburger and fries; $5.50 for chicken fried steak and mashed potatoes. And it's fun to people-watch in diners.

The emphasis is different at **fast-food restaurants,** where high volume and quick turnaround are gospel. An assembly-line process produces tacos, burgers, hot dogs, sandwiches, and fries in a hurry. Families with kids frequently eat in fast food restaurants—especially when they're on the road. A Big Mac tastes the same in Portland, Maine, and Portland, Oregon. Cost per person: $2.50 to $5.00. (Besides coupon fliers sent through the mail, fast-food restaurants such as Wendy's and Burger King sometimes print coupons on their carry-out bags and paper place mats. I recently saw a coupon good for a 49-cent liter of Pepsi on a Wendy's bag.)

The next step up includes **moderate-priced restaurants,** such as Denny's, Village Inn, International House of Pancakes,

Shoney's, and Big Boy. The service is good and you don't have to dress up. The waitresses cater to families with high chairs for infants and crayons for the kids. The menu focuses on salads, burgers, sandwiches, and "skillet" meals. I also include ethnic restaurants in this category: Italian, Mexican, Chinese, Thai, Japanese, and German. Many are family owned and serve delicious meals at moderate prices. Cost per person: $4.00 to $9.00.

Families with teens and insatiable appetites tend to frequent another category in this moderate-priced tier: **smorgasbords, cafeterias, or "country buffets"**—one-price, all-you-can-eat restaurants. Chains such as Perry Boy's, Furr's, and Morrison's lead the pack. The downside is an uninviting atmosphere: bright lighting, a high noise level, and toddlers in the adjoining booth tossing food your way. But when you've got a couple of teenage boys with raging hormones, they're going to eat a lot of food.

The next level encompasses **sit-down restaurants,** where a hostess or maitre d' escorts you to your table. Steak and chicken seem to rule places such as Stuart Anderson's, Smugglers, Galley Hatch, Steak and Ale, Red Lobster, and Marie Callenders. High-end Chinese, Italian, and Mexican restaurants can also be found in this category, such as Olive Garden and Acapulco's. These lunch and dinner establishments with a bar serve beer and wine. Entrees, which usually include a dinner salad, run $7.00 to $16.00.

What's the Best Fast-Food Restaurant?

Everyone has an opinion, but I'll weigh in with mine: Taco Bell is my favorite fast-food restaurant because the food is cheap and seemingly healthier. The kids can eat three tacos for $2.07 and still get a little green stuff and cheese in the process. Yes, I know the tacos are the size of a Liechtenstein postage stamp, but we're consistently pleased with our runs "south of the border."

The ultimate experience is **fine dining,** the bastion of "foodies" and lovers of haute cuisine. Fine linen tablecloths and napkins grace your table, lemon wedges flavor your water, and a lighted candle and a fresh rose bud add the final touches. The lighting is muted, and live piano music fills in the background.

Well-trained waiters (and perhaps an occasional waitress) attend to your every need. Portions will be small. The chef puts as much emphasis on how the food *looks* as on how it tastes; presentation is everything. Everything on the menu is a la carte, so you can expect to pay a separate price for appetizer, salad, entree, dessert, and coffee. In fact, you can expect to pay through the nose. Cost is $20.00 to $50.00 per meal.

No matter where you eat, it's going to cost more than you think. Let's say you and your spouse order two inexpensive manicotti dishes for $7.95 each. By the time you leave the restaurant, your wallet will be $25.00 lighter. How's that? Well, it's not out of the ordinary to order a beverage with your meal. This will add in many cases at least $5.00 more, which pushes the total to $20.90. Sales tax (6 to 8 percent in most states) takes the bill to $22.15, and when you add a 15 percent tip, the grand total comes to $25.47. And you didn't even order an appetizer, another round of beverages, or dessert, which would have pushed the tab closer to $35. And that's at the low-end of fine dining.

I wish we could transport the Swiss system of eating out to this country. Restaurant patrons in Switzerland pay no tax or tip. The 15 percent *service compris* is included in the price of the meal. If the menu says *poulet et pommes frites* (chicken and french fries) are ten dollars, then you pay ten dollars.

Granted, restaurants are a labor-intensive industry struggling to make a profit just like any other business. But when our family of four eats at Chili's (a low- to medium-priced chain), it costs a cool $25.00 for hamburgers, fries, and lemonade. That's a lot of money for a no-frills meal, and we usually feel rushed to "turn over" the table in an hour.

HOW TO KEEP THE LID ON

Enough bellyaching. Restaurant meals are a pleasure, and the cook always appreciates a break from kitchen duty. Eating out, however, can blow a hole in the family budget unless you keep the following ideas in mind:

• **Make it an "occasion" to eat out.** Perhaps you've seen this scenario in your house: Dad arrives home from work, just as Mom pulls into the driveway with the kids after soccer practice. It's six o'clock, and everyone is tired and hungry. Dinner hasn't been started yet. The next thing you know, the family is sitting down at a nearby Italian joint. The kids' spaghetti is doughy, and you're not impressed with the chicken cacciatore. But the thirty-four-dollar tab catches your attention.

Eating out should be reserved for an *occasion*. It doesn't have to be a special one, but impromptu meals out should be discouraged. If you eat out on a Thursday night, what's your family going to do on Saturday night when everyone feels like going out? Restaurant meals should be planned and anticipated.

If the above scenario happens in your household, you might want to consider these alternatives:

1. Cook something fast, like grilled cheese sandwiches and ramen soup. Better yet, eat up your leftovers. Dad and the kids can pitch in and help Mom.
2. Order take-out pizza. If the idea is to get something hot into your tummies, Little Caesar pizza will feed a family of four for $8.50. I always keep take-out pizza coupons around in case of need. Little Caesar and Pizza Hut are just a couple of blocks away from my home, so I pick it up myself and save a two-dollar tip.
3. Go to McDonald's. Not very original, but kids' meals are just ninety-nine cents after 4 P.M. on select days.
4. Take a pre-cooked meal—not a frozen entree like Healthy Choice—out of the freezer and pop it into the microwave. I'll be talking more about this option later in the chapter.

If you and the family decide to go to a sit-down restaurant, here are some ways to trim the bill.

• **Take advantage of "early bird" specials.** Many families overlook this idea, but if you can get the family out of the house by 5:30, you can save 25 percent on your meals. Most kids are hungry early anyway.

• **Use newspaper coupons.** You can usually find worthwhile coupons in the Wednesday and Friday editions of your local newspaper. Often, the coupons are good for weeknights only, evenings when restaurants need to stimulate business. Another idea is to ask a restaurant chain if it's running a coupon special. At Denny's or Shoney's, the hostess will hand you a coupon on the spot, or the restaurant may honor the discount even though you don't have the coupon in hand. This policy is at the manager's discretion, however. Many restaurants even honor the competition's coupons.

I heard one story about a couple who asked some friends to join them at a certain Italian restaurant, but they didn't tell their friends they had two-for-one coupons. They let the other couple order first, then they ordered entrees for equal or less value. When the check arrived, this fellow grabbed it and announced to the unsuspecting couple their share of the bill. Then he walked over to the cashier and paid the full amount. With his hidden twenty-five-dollar discount, he and his wife nearly ate for free. I do not recommend this kind of subterfuge!

• **Look for weeknight specials.** Does your favorite Italian restaurant have a two-for-one "pasta night" every Monday? Some restaurants let kids eat free on certain weeknights.

• **Don't worry what the help thinks of your discount dining.** Restaurant owners and managers do not resent customers who use coupons, although the waitresses and busboys may be wary because they fear a smaller tip. When I use a two-for-one coupon, I always tip 15 percent of what the total *would* have been. It's OK being cheap on yourself by ordering the least expensive item on the menu. It's not OK to stiff the servers.

Karen Ahles, a friend of mine who recently sold an Italian restaurant, told me, "If you're trying to save money on restaurants, pay attention to the nights when special deals are offered, like Mondays or Wednesdays. The specials are an incentive for customers. As for coupons, we always encouraged them because we figure families would *not* have come into the restaurant without one."

• **Order complete meals.** Look for entrees on the menu that come with appetizer, soup, or salad. In restaurants where salad is a la carte, pass on the more expensive salad bar and order a smaller dinner salad instead—unless you're really hungry. When scanning the menu, remember that chicken is always cheaper than fish, fish is always cheaper than beef, and beef is always cheaper than lobster and shrimp.

• **Do "date nights" during lunchtime.** When times are tight, one of the first "spending cuts" Nicole and I make is eating out. This strategy has never enhanced our romance, however. To save money (and our marriage, Nicole jokes), we usually hold our "date nights" during lunchtime. She comes to my workplace and we eat out at a nearby restaurant. Noontime meals are always less expensive than evening dining, plus no babysitting costs.

• **Drink water.** Not only is water healthier than soft drinks, but ordering Cokes and 7Ups can soak up gobs of money. (That's why Lou Gage often takes a can of soda in her purse. "That's highway robbery, paying two dollars for a little 7Up and a lot of ice," she says.)

We often drink ice water in restaurants, including fast-food places. At Taco Bell recently, the four of us ate for $8.43. Ordering four of the cheapest soft drinks would have added $3.16 or 37 percent to the bill. The "drink water" trend is growing: McDonald's now provides a large water cooler at the end of the counter. If you do order soda, ask for it without ice; then you'll get 12 full ounces, not 6 ounces of ice and 6 ounces of beverage.

• **Watch the add-ons.** Waiters and waitresses will try to get you to order appetizers, soup, specials of the day, and dessert. If you indulge, you can double the cost of your meal—and ingest enough calories to keep you on the treadmill for a week.

• **Go out for breakfast.** If you order the no-meat, egg breakfasts, you can eat well for under four dollars, sometimes for a mere $1.99!

• **Purchase a "dining club" membership.** Nearly every city has a dining club that offers two-for-one entrees. I recently won a year-long membership, which turned out to be a great bargain. Around sixty restaurants—in different price ranges and food styles—participated in the program. The annual membership cost is usually twenty-five to thirty-five dollars. If you want to know if you have a dining club in your hometown, call Premiere Dining (800-346-3241).

• **Double check the check.** All too often, errors are made— for you or against you. If you think you've been overcharged, ask humbly if a mistake has been made. When mistakes have been made in my favor, I've always felt I should point them out. More often than not, the staff will thank me for my honesty and wave it off! (Plus I feel better.)

• **Be leery of group checks.** Have you ever eaten with a bunch of friends—maybe six or even twelve at the table—and then wondered what to order because you're not sure how the bill will be split? *Hmmm, should I get something inexpensive? Or do I order the poached salmon since everyone else is getting prime rib?* It can be a little frustrating to eat spaghetti carbonara for $6.95 while your tablemate raves over the $16.95 lobster, and then hear someone announce that your "share" of the bill is $16.00.

Group dining can be a delicate situation, especially if the check is placed in the hands of someone at the far end of the table. We all know waitresses do not like separate checks. Most of the time, you're going to have to shrug off any inequality or go ahead and order a more-expensive entree like everyone else. It isn't easy taking charge in a group atmosphere.

Although it's out of character for me, I do remember the time I acted assertively. I was eating with a group of fifteen, and I ordered a vegetarian entree for eight dollars. But several guys at the end of the table went hog-wild, having the waitress bring out plate after plate of appetizers, lobster *con guacamole* and *schwartzwald torte*. The wine flowed freely, too. When the check arrived, they informed me my share was twenty-four dollars. I replied, "Hey, I ordered the vegetable lasagna, drank water, and didn't eat any appetizers. Here's twelve bucks, which should more than cover my share of the tax and tip." It was hard for them to argue with the truth.

• **If you're dying to go out, make it dessert.** We've gone to the Chart House for its famous mud pie and Chili's for its brownie fudge sundae. It's a cheaper way to itch the urge to go out.

• **Let your parents or your company take you out to eat.** If somebody else is paying…. Be kind, however.

COOKING AT HOME, WITHOUT PAYING FOR PROCESSING

Anytime you cook at home, you're saving money. And I mean *cooking*—not popping a frozen dinner into the microwave. We are fast becoming a nation that rarely cooks from scratch. It seems like everything we buy at the supermarket has already been chopped, diced, carved, crushed, peeled, pureed, sundered, sawed, sniped, split, rend, cut up, torn, dis-limbed, dismembered, deboned, or deskinned by someone else—all of which costs money.

Consider cooked shrimp, for example. If the supermarket's meat department shells and deveins the little crustaceans, you pay $9.99 a pound. If you buy cooked shrimp with the shell and veins, you pay $6.99 a pound, a 42 percent savings. I remember the time our family was invited over to a friend's house for dessert. They set out several half gallons of ice cream, chocolate syrup, and a box of Oreo Cookie Bits, which Nabisco sells for those too lazy to crush cookies themselves! Anytime we buy convenience foods such as prepared salad, cole slaw, Rice-A-Roni, frozen country chicken, Stouffer's spinach, we're paying treble rates.

Did you know you can make your own convenience foods and save money? If you like Stovetop stuffing or JELL-O pudding, take a look at *Make Your Own Groceries* by Daphne Hartwig, which tells you how to duplicate these popular foods in your own kitchen. *Confessions of a Happily Organized Housewife,* by Denise Schofield, describes how you can make your own taco seasoning, spaghetti seasoning, and cake mixes.

Tracey McBride, who publishes *The Frugal Times,* has cooking down to a science. She will cook more beef in the winter and stock up her freezer because she knows beef prices are usually cheaper during that time. "The popularity of the cut of meat also affects the price," said Tracey. "One meat that is more expensive in the summer is steak because it is in demand for grills. That drives the price up. Roasts are more expensive in late fall and winter, however, because families consume heavier meals when the weather turns colder. I recommend buying less expensive cuts, such as ground beef, round steak, rump roast, stew beef (but not precut), pot roasts, beef shank, brisket, short loin, and the heel of the round roast. If you are into lamb, lamb shanks, short loin, and shoulder cuts cost forty or more cents less per pound. If you have a big family, it adds up.

"Tender cuts of meat should be barbecued or broiled, while tougher cuts should cook longer in a crock pot for tenderness. Cook meat at no higher than 325 degrees in the oven because it will dehydrate and shrink. If you're splurging on meat, examples of more expensive cuts are blade and arm steaks, flank steak, sirloin tip, and bottom round. Any broiling steaks, such as porterhouse, will almost always be expensive unless they are on special sale, in which case, stock up!"

Tracey is a believer in home freezers because of the savings that can be gained on meat. "Just a couple of weeks ago, my local supermarket was selling top sirloin for $1.98 a pound, as compared to $4.99 a pound regularly. When those sales come along, I try to buy fifty pounds. I can make fajitas one night, stir fry the next, then put it on the barbecue or broil it."

But how long does frozen meat last? "My butcher told me if I rewrapped the meat in freezer paper and tape, it could last six months to a year. He said not to put all the steak in at once, since that could raise the temperature of the freezer for a short time and could cause spoilage. Instead, he told me to put the freezer on its lowest temperature the day before, and then put the meat in. Freezers are a great idea because they save you wear and tear on the car, plus shopping and cooking time. And I always remember that it's 'first in, first out' when I take something out of the freezer."

"It's important to know your meat prices," added Tracey, "so you can take advantage of supermarket 'stock-up' specials. If you spot top sirloin on sale for $1.98 a pound, you know it's a good buy because it's nearly the same price as lean hamburger.

Can you save on meat by cutting it up yourself? For chicken, the answer is yes. For beef, it's not worth it. A Safeway butcher walked through the meat department with me. "See this rib-eye roast," he pointed. "It costs $4.69 a pound. If you saw the roast into slices, it becomes rib-eye steak. We sell that for $4.99. Is it worth the extra thirty cents a pound to cut roasts into steak yourself?" asked the butcher. "I don't think so." Indeed, I would have needed a sharp hacksaw to cut through those bones.

"Chicken is a different matter," continued the butcher, pointing to another section of the display case. "We have whole fryers at 79 cents a pound, but if we cut them up, we sell them for $1.29 a pound." I calculated the savings at 63 percent.

"You wouldn't believe the number of people who don't know how to cut up a whole chicken," he said, shaking his head. "They pick up the chicken here and ask us to cut it up for them."

"But doesn't that cost money?" I asked.

"No, we don't charge for that since customers just expect us to do it for free. But all you need is a good knife or kitchen shears, and you can cut up chickens yourself."

The butcher picked up the skinless, boneless chicken breasts for $3.99 a pound. "You can buy regular chicken breasts for $2.19 a pound and debone it and take the skin off yourself," he said. Again, the savings would be 45 percent—even a little less since you're paying for some breastbone.

Sometimes, the butcher said, whole fryers are not the cheapest chicken to buy. That afternoon, for instance, cut-up legs were 59 cents a pound—20 cents a pound less than the whole fryers.

When Tracey shops for meat, she calculates its protein value against the cost per pound. For instance, one pound of rib roast contains approximately thirty grams of protein and usually costs $4.49 a pound. Tracey takes along a calculator and a calorie/gram counter book (which can be found in magazine and book racks at your local supermarket). Most calorie-counter books also list the grams of fat, an important health consideration these days.

When she's at the meat case, Tracey divides the thirty grams of protein in a rib roast by the price per pound ($4.49), which comes out to 14.29 cents per gram of protein. She then compares that to round steak, which has approximately eighty grams of protein per pound, and sells for $2.19 a pound. This means her cost-per-gram of protein for the latter is lower at 3.29 cents. "Round steak is a better value for protein, so I'll serve that more often to my family," said Tracey.

Over in the produce department, Tracey is amazed at the number of city people who aren't aware of when produce is in season. These days, supermarkets are importing more and more produce from South America, New Zealand, and Israel. An uninformed (or unconcerned) shopper may see New Zealand strawberries in January and Israeli avocados in July and plop them into the cart. But these fruits and vegetables are two or three times more than in-season produce from U.S. farms and orchards.

Since homegrown fruits and vegetables cost so much less during the summer, consider blanching and freezing your favorite fruits and vegetables for the winter. Canned and frozen vegetables go on special at the end of the summer because wholesalers want to liquidate their surplus inventory. "You should have a pantry to stock up on these items, even if it's under your bed," said Tracey.

Tracey looks for ways to do less food preparation and cleanup. For instance, she prepares most of her fresh vegetables and salad makings after she comes home from the market. She stores her washed and torn lettuce in a salad spinner, which keeps it fresh for four to six days. Most of her fresh vegetables, such as carrots, broccoli, and cauliflower, are washed, chopped, and stored in airtight containers. Again, they'll stay fresh for nearly a week.

"When I go to start dinner, all I have to do is toss the salad, put the vegetables in the steamer or my wok, and I'm in business. I think a lot of people don't have fresh vegetables because they think they are a lot of trouble, but they're not if you work ahead."

ONCE-A-MONTH COOKING

The April 1992 cover of *Focus on the Family* magazine featured Mary Beth Lagerborg standing in her kitchen and chopping onions and carrots. For years, Mary Beth and coauthor

What's for Lunch?

Michael Ross, the editor of *Breakaway* magazine (*Focus on the Family*'s teen publication for boys), dropped by my office one day. "Gee, it's sure hard to save any money," said Michael, who's a single guy.

"Having trouble, huh?

"Well, you know...."

Well, I *did* know. Each workday at noon, Michael and a bunch of his friends would go out to eat at Red Robin's, Chili's, TGIF's—nice restaurants.

"You go out to lunch every day, right?" I asked.

"Yes, I guess so."

"Do you know how much that's costing you?"

Mike shrugged his shoulders. I did the math for him. "With tax and tip, it's probably costing you six to seven dollars a shot." He nodded. "Multiply that out, and it's thirty dollars a week or one hundred twenty a month, minimum."

"You're kidding!"

Most people don't realize the true cost of eating lunch in a restaurant—even at Subway Sandwiches—every day. On the rare occasions I've gone out with the office gang (maybe someone's good-bye party), I've felt a little funny. After all, since Nicole and I have to limit the times we can eat out, why should I enjoy lunch in a restaurant when she can't?

So I brown-bag each day, either making my own peanut-butter-and-jelly sandwiches, or taking a Tupperware container full of leftovers that I can pop into the office microwave. When I see colleagues leaving work to go out for lunch, I remember how determined I am to save more than one hundred dollars a month.

Mimi Wilson had worked on a manuscript that taught families how to cook just once a month. Dozens of publishers passed until *Focus on the Family* took on the project, and *Once-a-Month Cooking* became a runaway best-seller!

Mary Beth's and Mimi's concept boils down to this: Do most of your monthly grocery shopping one day, cook all the next day, and store the ready-made meals in the freezer. It's an interesting formula, and one that has struck a chord with many busy moms. When I told Nicole about this "once-a-month" concept, she immediately turned up her nose. "Why would I want to do that?" she asked. Nicole *likes* to cook.

But I've read the testimonials of those who say once-a-month cooking works for them. If you can make it work for you, go for it. Although I couldn't get Nicole interested, she still practices some of the concepts in a modified way. Around our kitchen, we call it "thrice-a-week" cooking. Nicole always cooks enough to make two meals, which saves on food costs and preparation time. Fortunately, she has a family that *loves* leftovers.

Tracey recommends browning lots of hamburger meat at one time (maybe 10 to 15 pounds) and then packaging it in 1-pound freezer bags. You can also sautee onions prior to browning the meat, drain, and put them off to the side. Next brown the hamburger and add the sauteed onions at the end. This will improve taste later on. Then when you need a quick meal, pull a bag out of the freezer, heat it up in the microwave, and voila! You can make tacos, chili, spaghetti sauce, sloppy joes, or hamburger casserole in a matter of minutes.

Tracey will also buy a couple of chickens and use them as the basis for three meals. On Monday, she'll serve a roast chicken dinner with baked potatoes. After dinner, she'll dice up the chicken breasts for chicken tacos the following night, and then later in the week, she'll serve homemade chicken noodle soup made from the leftovers.

I can recommend two other resources. Rhonda Barfield, author of *Eat Well for $50 a Week* ($11.95, write Lilac

Publishing, P.O. Box 665, St. Charles, MO 63302), believes you can do just that. Does it work? I asked Diana Haptonstall, the Coupon Queen, to read Rhonda's book and try out her system. "*Eat Well for $50 a Week* had some great tips," reported Diana. "I believe some people can spend fifty dollars a week and get by, but not all. Mine was about sixty dollars a week, but I had to purchase diapers. I also think you have to take into consideration which states offer double coupons." As I thumbed through Rhonda's book, I was impressed by her meal plans and detailed shopping lists to make those meals.

One last resource is *Dinner's in the Freezer* by Jill Bond, which is similar to the "once-a-month" cooking concept, except Jill explains how to cook for the next six months! Her book also has a savory Christian flavor running throughout.

CHAPTER 6

Never
Pay Retail

I'm standing in the ladies' dresses section of Joslins, an upscale department store. It's a few minutes before eight o'clock on a Saturday evening, and a crowd of thirty shoppers is anticipating the next "dress riot," a ten-minute clearance sale on specially marked clothes.

"Why do you call these 'dress riots'?" I casually asked one of the salespeople.

"Oh, we don't like to use that term, but that's really what they are," she replied. "You should have seen the dress riot this afternoon. Two women grabbed a $229 navy-and-white Pendleton ensemble at the same time, and then began fighting over it. It was marked down to $19.99. You should have seen them rolling on the floor, trying to pull the dress from each other's grasp. Finally, our store manager took a bullhorn and announced, 'Ladies, if you don't stop right now, I'll have to call security.'"

"Things really get that crazy?" I asked.

"They sure do."

Just then, four clerks wheeled out four racks of dresses, each containing fifty to seventy-five pieces. Bedlam broke out as the horde of women—and a few brave men—stormed the barricades to grab the heavily discounted dresses, all priced at just $4.97.

A friend of mine, Karen Sagahon, reached for a white Leslie Fay dress with black polka dots, but a man brusquely swooped it off the rack—along with twenty other dresses. Karen shrugged her shoulders. "I guess I'm not a fighter," said the diminutive young woman, who weighs slightly over one hundred pounds.

The dress riot was over in five minutes. Poof! One hundred fifty dresses had vanished, except for an odd-colored straggler or two. The feeding frenzy left the clothes racks resembling goldfish carcasses stripped by a school of piranha.

Lou Gage, my shopping confidante, managed to hold her own. She claimed a half-dozen dresses, although she wasn't shopping for herself. Lou enjoys buying dresses and passing them on to friends. One ended up in my wife's closet: an azure-blue Liz Claiborne with white buttons, originally $148. We were glad to pay Lou five bucks in reimbursement.

The dress riot was the highlight of Joslins' "Moonlight Madness Sale," a sixteen-hour, shop-til-you-drop bargain bonanza. Lou stayed until half past eleven, finding good buys in women's accessories and shoes. The next morning, she laid out all the clothes and merchandise on her living room floor, added up the receipts, and compared them to the original retail amounts. On this particular shopping excursion, Lou spent just over five hundred dollars, but the regular retail amount would have been $3,085, an 83-percent savings. "I've never done worse than 82 percent, and my best is 90 percent," she said. "It's gotten to be a challenge: *How much can I get off?*"

THE SHOPPING GAME

Granted, most of you aren't going to buy five hundred dollars worth of clothes at a clip, with the idea of giving many of them away. And you may not have dress riots in your town.

But Lou's experiences are a reminder that those who seriously shop department store sales can purchase high-quality clothing at a fraction of the original price.

But department stores aren't the only shopping game in town, no siree. Let's take an overview of the retail family:

• Perched at the high end are **department stores,** such as Nieman-Marcus, Hudson's, Saks Fifth Avenue, Carter Hawley Hale, and May Company. They sell merchandise at a full markup but pride themselves on customer service and shopping assistance. Best of all, they have liberal return policies.

• **Power retailers,** such as Sears, JCPenney, and Montgomery Ward, have the financial muscle to buy in huge quantities and push vendors for discounts, which can be passed along to consumers. A small markup keeps prices low.

• Next we have the **moderate-priced stores,** such as Mervyns and Miller's Outpost. They buy lower-priced clothes but still sell at a full markup. Customer services are good.

• **Discounters** include Target, Kmart, and Wal-Mart, which sell medium-quality clothes at a lower markup and offer fewer shopper services.

• Stores such as Ross Dress for Less, Marshalls, and TJ Maxx are called **off-pricers.** They buy from a variety of manufacturers and vendors—or closeouts from department stores—and work off a smaller markup. The selection may be limited and the styles a few months behind. Few special services are offered.

• **Closeout stores** include Pic 'n' Save (also known as McFrugals) and off-site department store outlets, such as, Nordstrom Rack and Macy's Bargain Basement Store. They dispose of unsold inventory and returns at rock-bottom prices.

• **Warehouse retailers** such as Sam's and Costco buy in huge quantities from manufacturers willing to cut them a good deal. Selection is limited, but with minimal markups, prices are excellent. As I mentioned in the chapter on warehouse clubs, you won't find a fitting room.

• **Factory outlets** have sprung up outside many major cities. Manufacturers such as Nike or Eddie Bauer sell surplus production, returns, and discontinued merchandise in these stores. For information or to order a list of outlets near you, call (800) 336-8853.

Big discounts can be had at all these stores, *if* you know how to play the shopping game. Lou offers this advice:

"Nearly every retail store has a selling system which boils down to this: move the end-of-the-season merchandise when the next season of clothes arrives. Because stores have to make room for their hot-selling profit-makers, *no one should ever pay retail for clothes.* Someone is always having a sale or just about to have one. Be patient.

"People tell me they can't afford a new dress for their daughter's eighth-grade graduation, but I say you just have to work at it. You start by getting familiar with the way clothing stores sell things. If you can invest a few hours, then you can find *what* you want at a *price* you can afford. You do this by buying clothes *off-season* or during the stores' *big sales* three or four times a year.

"An example of buying off-season would be walking into Mervyns a couple of weeks after Labor Day. The summer merchandise has got to go since the fall and holiday stuff is arriving. That means you should buy your children's shorts or shortsleeve shirts after Labor Day—not in the spring, when they're sold at full retail. The same goes for other seasonal items, such as winter coats, gloves, and beach sandals. Although it may seem funny buying a ski jacket in April, you'll be glad you did the following November."

MAKING THE MOST OF SALES

"Many people don't shop at department stores because the clothes are expensive," continued Lou. "That's understandable when you're paying retail. But if you wait for their once-a-quarter sales, you can purchase high-quality merchandise at 50 percent off or more. Remember, quality clothes last longer—and look better."

As for buying on sale, you do that by:

- **Shopping the department stores' "doorbuster" sales three or four times a year.**
- **Keeping an eye out for sales at the off-price stores, such as Ross Dress for Less and Marshalls. Many of them are not advertised.**
- **Checking out the clearance racks.**
- **Looking for closeouts at the clearance stores.**
- **Knowing prices so that when a deal comes along, you can pounce on it.**

"Mike told me he was skeptical of department store sales until he accompanied me to a 'Moonlight Madness Sale.' Now I'm convinced these huge department store chains sell clothes for dimes and nickels on the dollar to rid themselves of excess inventory headaches. I saw great prices on leather handbags, shower curtains, towels, small area rugs, kids' shoes, linens, bedspreads, and pillows—items hard to buy on discount. The markdowns averaged 50 percent, and some items—like the $119 quilted comforters for $29—were incredible bargains."

Before attending a big department store sale, you should be adequately prepared.

- **Check your expenditures for the month.** Do you have enough set aside to do some clothes shopping?
- **Know what you want to buy.** Does your husband need

some new dress shirts? Does your teenage son's Levis have holes? Make a list.

- **Go the night before when the markdowns are being made.** Typically, all the advertised markdowns are made between 6 P.M. and closing. If you find something you like, you can usually buy it at the next day's discounted price. All you have to do is ask.

- **On the morning of the sale, the first thing you should do is ask for the ten-minute special sheet and the ad for the "doorbusters."** You can usually find these at the store's information counter. If the salespeople say they don't make these sale sheets available to the public, ask to *look* at them. They generally will not refuse such a request. Be sure to take notes of the ten-minute specials' "batting order."

- **Scan the ten-minute special sheet and figure out which ones you can skip.** You can use that time to run things out to the car, get a bite to eat, or visit the restroom.

- **Don't carry a purse; use a fanny pack.** You need freedom and flexibility as you hurry from one ten-minute special to the next.

- **Arrive five minutes before the store opens.** Early birds really do get the best worms, especially at the doorbusters which run from eight to eleven in the morning. In blow-out sales, the size selection is often skimpy.

- **Follow the ten-minute specials.** These are the extra markdowns made on clearance merchandise that has already been marked down several times. You have to be fast on your feet.

- **Shop for classic styles.** Elaine Minton, a friend of mine, says she buys jackets, slacks, skirts, shoes, belts, and purses to match basic color schemes of beige, white, or navy. "I don't buy fad items," said Elaine. "I buy in one classic, tasteful color scheme so replacements are easy to find. I can always add an inexpensive accessory to update the style or the color."

- **Leave the kids at home.** They'll get bored, and you'll get on each other's nerves. Plus, you need to concentrate on the task at hand.
- **Taking your husband along can be a two-edged sword.** On the one hand, he can help stand in line at the cash register while you go on to the next special. Then again, he can be a pain. (I'm speaking from personal experience.)
- **Keep your cool.** Like a shrewd Las Vegas poker player, have a spending limit in mind and stick to it.

RATING THE RETAIL OUTLETS

To give you a better overview of the clothes shopping landscape, I've given each retail outlet a "bargain rating" on a scale of one to five shopping carts (five being the best). The bargain ratings take into consideration the following variables: the final sales price; quality in comparison to other stores; frequency of sales; selection and size of the inventory.

Some stores are lumped together into one category, some are rated on their own. Keep in mind that we are talking about *clearance merchandise* and *loss leaders*. We'll begin with department stores, which are rated as a group since they are regional.

Sometimes major retailers will send merchandise that doesn't sell to other parts of the county or state where the economy is not as strong and the people are poorer, with the assumption that those shoppers will be less picky. If you live in a rural area, for instance, you might find your local Kmart sells dresses and shoes for less than the big-city Kmart.

Department stores

(Carter Hawley Hale, Dayton-Hudson, May Co., Nordstroms, etc.)

Name of sale: varies.

Frequency: three or four times a year.

Best buys: clothes, luggage, silverware, jewelry (not fine jewelry), and household items.

Downside: it's crowded; the hours are long; the doorbusters start early in the morning.

Comment: If you play your cards right, department stores can be a great dollar-for-dollar deal.

Bargain rating: five shopping carts (for a ten-minute special or a doorbuster).

Power retailers

I have given separate ratings to the "big three" in this category: Sears, JCPenney, and Montgomery Ward.

Sears

Name of sale: The Great Take-Off, 50 Percent Off Red Tag, or Baby Days.

Frequency: three or four times a year.

Best buys: children's and infants' clothes, baby furniture, paint, and Craftsman tools.

Downside: fashion styles are not on the cutting edge.

Comment: Sears has been around forever, and they usually won't hassle you with returns. While not flashy, the chain is dependable.

Bargain rating: two shopping carts.

JCPenney

Name of sale: Red Tag Sale.

Frequency: three or four times a year.

Best buys: ladies' and kids' clothing, accessories, and shoes.

Downside: sales lack variety and certain sizes because you're dealing with end-of-season merchandise.

Comment: JCPenney will take an extra 30 to 50 percent off its clearance price.

Bargain rating: two shopping carts.

Montgomery Ward

Name of sale: Clearance Plus.

Frequency: three or four times a year (depending on the volume of seasonal merchandise on hand).

Best buys: apparel.

Downside: limited selection, variety, and size.

Comment: Montgomery Ward doesn't usually take more than 40 percent off the clearance price, and they never feature housewares and other hard goods.

Bargain rating: two shopping carts.

Moderate-Priced stores

I have chosen Mervyns and chains that sell teen clothing to represent this category.

Mervyns

Name of sale: Super Weekend Sale or the 50 Percent Off Clearance Sale.

Frequency: twice a year (end of January and late fall).

Best buys: school clothes, nightgowns, lingerie, towels, sheets, comforters, pillows, napkins, and cookie jars.

Downside: limited selection.

Comment: Meryvns frequently holds sidewalk sales, but you're better off waiting for the Super Weekend Sale.

Bargain rating: three-plus shopping carts.

Miller's Outpost, The Gap, etc. (chains that sell teen clothes).

Name of sale: varies.

Frequency: not very often.

Best buys: Levis and Dockers.

Downside: the infrequent sales never take more than 25 percent off.

Comment: occasionally, these stores have clearance racks where you can find slightly damaged items. If your teens are looking for hot fashions, this is the place to go.

Bargain rating: One shopping cart.

The discounters

National chains such as Kmart, Target, and Wal-Mart are perhaps the best known stores in this category.

Kmart

Name of sale: Blue-Light Specials or After Christmas Clearance.

Frequency: after each season (back-to-school, Christmas, end of summer).

Best buys: family clothes, accessories, shoes, and infants' clothes.

Downside: you have to be willing to buy out-of-season, and variety and selection are limited. And yes, those flashing blue lights are pretty silly.

Comment: You never know when Kmart is going to run a blue light special. You may arrive ten minutes after the last one, and they won't run another one just for you.

Bargain rating: three shopping carts.

Target

Name of sale: Red-Tag specials.

Frequency: quarterly.

Best buys: shoes and toys.

Downside: a reluctance to mark down clothing more than 40 to 50 percent.

Comment: "Tar-zhay," as my wife calls the store, has improved its shopping ambience in recent years, but the chain is reluctant to sell clothes at low, low prices. Its weekly advertised specials, however, are still good deals.

Bargain rating: three shopping carts.

Wal-Mart

Name of sale: Seasonal Clearance.

Frequency: seasonally and after each holiday period.

Best buys: children's clothing, shoes, Christmas toys, and non-perishable food items after holiday periods.

Downside: Wal-Mart doesn't clearance household items, hardware, automotive, appliances, and electronics.

Comment: The nation's biggest retailer isn't number one for nothing. You need to drop by often because it offers many "Manager's Unadvertised Specials."

Bargain rating: four shopping carts.

The off-pricers

Chains such as Marshalls, TJ Maxx, and Ross Dress for Less have carved a niche in the market by always selling at a discount.

Marshalls

Name of sale: Down-and-Out.

Frequency: two or three times a year (usually February, August, and October).

Best buys: ladies' apparel, shoes, children's clothing, men's sweaters, and some housewares.

Downside: At beginning of the Down-and-Out sales, merchandise is plentiful but discount is low. At end of sales, discount is high but pickings are slim. Selection is depleted daily.

Comment: The Down-and-Out sales last until the clearance merchandise is gone, and that might be one week or three weeks. During that time, the staff is constantly marking down merchandise.

Bargain rating: four shopping carts.

TJ Maxx

Name of sale: Red-Tag or End-of-Season Clearance.

Frequency: seasonally.

Best buys: all apparel.

Downside: TJs is reluctant to take deep cuts like Marshalls. Lou theorizes that each outlet ships the stuff they can't sell to other TJ Maxx stores, where the market is better for that particular line of clothes.

Comment: TJ Maxx does not advertise its sales. Its clearance philosophy is to take the regular merchandise and mark it down only 20 to 30 percent. That's why you should wait a couple of days until the second or third markdown.

Bargain rating: two shopping carts.

Ross Dress for Less

Name of sale: Red-Tag specials or End-of-Season Clearance.

Frequency: seasonal.

Best buys: name-brand separates for men and women, shoes, accessories, and fragrances.

Downside: limited selection and sizes.

Comment: Ross does not advertise its clearances. Occasionally, it will take an additional 20 to 30 percent off at the cash register without your asking for it—at the manager's whim.

Bargain rating: three-plus shopping carts.

Clearance or close-out stores

I chose Pic 'n' Save to represent this category, which includes stores such as McFrugals and Harry and David's.

Pic 'n' Save

Name of sale: none.

Frequency: whenever.

Best buys: brassware, candles, baskets, toys.

Downside: selection is poor, and you have to be careful about the quality of the merchandise. The Buster Brown clothes may be seconds.

Comment: Pic 'n' Save buys endlots and closeouts from other retailers. But on some items, quality doesn't make any difference (i.e., candles and baskets).

Bargain rating: two shopping carts (depending on quality).

Department store "rack" outlets

Name of sale: none.

Frequency: all the time.

Best buys: designer-label merchandise, shoes, and accessories.

Downside: they never have the same thing twice.

Comment: The "rack" stores are stocked with unsold goods and returns from the parent stores. Because of their liberal return policies, you might find twice-worn pumps for $20 instead of $115.

Bargain rating: three-plus shopping carts.

Warehouse outlets
(Sam's, Price Club, Costco, and BJ's)

Name of sale: none.

Best buys: leather jackets and sneakers.

Downside: no place to try on slacks or pants, and selection is limited.

Comment: Incredible bargains here, but some people are turned off by the shopping "experience." If you don't mind seeing other women trying on blouses over their own clothes while you scan the racks, good deals can be had. Shoppers never have any problems returning clothes they purchased and tried on at home. Just be sure to keep your receipt and not cut the tags.

Bargain rating: four shopping carts.

Factory outlets
(Laura Ashley, Geoffrey Beene, Toy Liquidators, The Book Warehouse, Carter's, Nike, etc.).

Name of sale: none.

Best buys: anything!

Downside: Most outlet malls are located an hour or two from metropolitan areas—or in another state. If you're traveling, ask the local tourist information office if an outlet mall is in the area.

Comment: Outlet malls are good places to shop while you're on vacation. Discounts can vary. Watch out, however, for the tendency to loosen the purse strings too much while on holiday.

Bargain rating: three shopping carts.

Shopping at Home

If you have cable TV, then you've probably come across QVC and the Home Shopping Network. Seventeen percent of Americans say they have purchased something from a shopping channel. QVC sold over a billion dollars worth of goods in 1993, and this phenomenon shows no signs of disappearing.

The shopping channels sell home furnishings, jewelry, electronics, clothes—just about anything. The prices are generally good. Markups range from just 30 percent for camcorders and VCRs to 50 percent on jewelry. You might be able to buy clothes by fashion designer Diane Von Furstenberg for half what a department store would charge. But many of the fashions sold on TV appeal to larger women who prefer to shop anonymously and not in a crowded mall.

But buying clothing through QVC and Home Shopping Network is fraught with potholes. You can't touch or feel the merchandise, which means quality is an unknown. More importantly, you can't tell how the clothing will fit. And although the Von Furstenberg dress may seem like a good deal, don't forget the shipping and handling charges. Yes, the return policies are liberal, but you usually pay the freight for the return.

I personally find the shopping channels to be a lot of techno-hype. You're not going to find any "door-

SHOPPING STRATEGIES

Of course, you don't have to buy clothes at national chains to get a good discount. Local clothing stores have to keep up with the majors, and many compete very well. Use a similar strategy by keeping an eye out for sales and rifling through the clearance racks at your own local stores.

John Fuller, a colleague of mine, found a new navy-blue suit for $1.99 at a Fashion Bar "damaged" rack. "I just walked into

---

busters" or "red-tag" specials. The same warning applies to those who purchase by mail-order catalog. Unless you're a difficult size to fit, stay local. You'll usually save money.

I asked Lou Gage if she had ever purchased something from the shopping channels. (In case you're wondering, Nicole and I never have.) "Do I have to confess?" asked Lou. "It's like being sucked into a vacuum cleaner. It happened one afternoon when there was nothing on TV, no Haagen-Daz in the freezer, and I was bored. So I turned to the shopping channel. I saw three gold-filled chains for sale, and they looked very pretty. They said the chains were gold but, when I received them, they were plated with microns of gold."

Once Lou made a purchase, she was a prisoner of the shopping network marketing department. She started receiving a monthly mail-order catalog with "super-savers" for those who ordered within ten days. She was also given her very own "super code number" so she could call toll-free and simply punch in that number and the item code to order the product. The purchase would be automatically billed to her MasterCard, which means she would never have to talk to a human voice.

Sound tempting? "It's so hokey, and I can't believe people fall for it," said Lou. When you channel surf, steer clear of the waves of merchandise being hawked on QVC or the Home Shopping Network. Take a pass.

that one," said John. "From what I could see, there was a little thread that had been pulled out of one of the sleeves."

His wife, Dena, bought a winter coat for $1.99 with a button missing. She later found the button tucked away in a pocket. "I also bought three sweaters for two dollars," she said. "They all had little holes in them, but I took them home and sewed them up. I give God the glory on those bargains."

It helps to be patient. LeeAnn Woolley said she once saw a sweater she liked for thirty-nine dollars, but decided to wait a month as a test to see if she *really* liked it. When she returned, the sweater had been reduced to twenty-four dollars! "If you can wait, clothes often go on sale," she said. "But sometimes I decide I no longer want the item."

Here are a few other subtle ways to tip the scales in your favor.

• **Look for the salesperson's name on his or her identification tag and use it.** If you're in a Kmart, you might say, "Jenni (or Greg), are you running any blue-lights today? I have several errands to do, but I'll stay if there's going to be a blue-light." Lou Gage has found that salespeople become very friendly when you address them by their first name.

• **Decipher the price tags** so you can figure out when the item was put out on the sales floor. If you approach the salesperson in a friendly way, he or she will often tell you how to read the coded tags. At Joslins, the upper left-hand corner of the ticket might say: 9339. That means the item was put on the floor in 1993, in the third week of the ninth month, or September.

At Kmart, look at the upper left-hand corner, where you should find a number between 1 and 52. If the number 22 is there, that means the merchandise came in the twenty-second week of the year. With that in mind, look for clothes that have been on the rack for six months or more. You can take the article of clothing to a department manager and say, "This looks like last season's merchandise. Perhaps it missed the clearance rack. Is there any way I can get it marked down?" You will usually receive an affirmative response—the manager *wants* to sell it!—so be prepared to buy if you get your discount.

• **Deal directly with store or department managers because they are the only ones authorized to reduce prices.** Lou said she has often received a discount on slightly damaged or imperfect clothes by showing the item to a manager and pointing out the flaw. When I told my wife, Nicole, she used Lou's tip the next time she went shopping.

Nicole was going through the racks at JCPenney in search of a pair of tennis warm-ups for our daughter, Andrea. The store had only one pair they liked—a colorful top with white pants. Just one problem, however: a small, black smudge on the back of one pants' leg. Even though Nicole judged the imperfection to be insignificant, she approached a manager and pointed it out. "Would it be possible to get a further reduction on this outfit?" she politely asked. The manager immediately reduced the price from twenty-nine dollars to twenty-two dollars!

My Favorite Thing: Christmas Shopping

What is it like to shop on the Friday after Thanksgiving, the busiest shopping day of the year? Normally I avoid malls after Thanksgiving like the Dallas Cowboys' Emmitt Smith avoids tacklers, but I wanted to find out what the big attraction was. So I followed Lou Gage on her shopping rounds, meeting her at 7 A.M. sharp at Wal-Mart, her first stop. Only sixteen cars dotted the lot when I arrived. *continued on page 102*

Despite the early hour, Lou came ready to shop. She had spent an hour going through the thicket of newspaper ads the night before. She had made out a store-by-store shopping plan, and for the next two-and-a-half hours, we shopped the loss leaders in a half-dozen stores. I didn't see anything I wanted to buy, but some of the bargains were terrific. It was obvious that the retailers were trying to get holiday shoppers out of the house early with their loss leaders good only between eight and eleven.

Christmas shopping is a cat-and-mouse game anyway. If you've been a smart shopper, you've been buying gifts all year long when you found them on sale. If you haven't planned ahead, you should wait until the last week of Christmas, when price reductions of 20 and 25 percent start appearing.

About this time, the store managers are starting to panic, wondering if they will be stuck with one hundred fifty Betsy Wetsy dolls. Some stores may hold out until the last couple of days before Christmas—but don't worry—they'll start cutting prices. They have to. When I was growing up, my parents did most of their toy shopping on Christmas Eve because they knew the local toy store put everything on half-price that night.

Another money-saving tip is to wait until *after* Christmas to shop for gifts. All the stores launch huge sales December 26 with great deals. Although many families are tapped out, the stores are trying to sell whatever they can in preparation for the annual inventory beginning January 15. Anything in stock is subject to an inventory tax, which can cost large stores tens of thousands of dollars. They figure it's cheaper to put it on sale than to count it.

CHAPTER 7

Trash or Treasure?

We've been talking about buying *new* clothes, but what about *used* clothing? This statement may belabor the obvious, but used clothing will *always* be cheaper than new duds—unless you're caught up in a dress riot bonanza.

Where can you find good used clothing? Some of the more common sources are garage sales, estate sales, thrift shops, consignment stores, and hand-me-downs from friends and relatives. As usual, each one carries its own set of risks and benefits. Let's take a closer look at each of these options.

GARAGE SALES

I grew up in a home that majored in garage sales. Every Saturday morning, my mother took my brother and me to a half-dozen sales, and we always had a great time sifting through other people's gems and junk. Whenever we visit my folks these days, three generations of Yorkeys join forces to continue the Saturday morning tradition. It's inexpensive family fun, and Andrea and Patrick love it. More importantly, my children are learning some valuable lessons: the value of a buck; how to bargain; and humility. We shouldn't be too proud to wear or utilize someone else's used stuff if it's in good shape.

Garage sales make sense, especially for families with young children who leapfrog from one size to the next every fortnight. They can also be a great place to pick up used sports equipment, an unexpected budget-breaker for families. Better yet, you don't pay any sales tax. Several strategies prove helpful in shopping garage sales. You've probably learned some of your own through the school of experience.

• **If you have a special need, ask God to open the door.** Because garage-saling is like shopping for the proverbial needle in the haystack, we usually need a miracle to find those cute OshKosh overalls for the baby or used roller blades for the kids. Praying with your children can build everyone's faith, especially when you find the items on your prayer list.

Once, when Lou Gage was asked by her church to "procure" toy furniture and bookcases for the Sunday school classrooms, she brought the request before the Lord. The next Saturday, she was making the rounds at several garage sales. "I'm looking for a toy stove and refrigerator and twelve bookcases," she told the woman behind the card table. "Would you have any of those items available?"

"Oh, I think I have what you're looking for in the basement," replied the woman. "I didn't put them out because I didn't think anyone would want them." Lou proceeded to purchase one dozen bookcases for two dollars each and the toy furniture for several more dollars. The church was thrilled. "That was a wonderful answer to prayer," said Lou.

If you're on the lookout for a particular item, such as a baby stroller, be sure to ask the people holding a garage sale if they have one for sale. They may not have bothered to put it out.

• **Be prepared.** On Friday night or early Saturday morning, look through the newspaper's garage sale listings and circle the ones that seem more promising. Then locate those streets on a city map before you leave home so you don't waste time driving around or asking for directions. If you do happen to get lost in search of that great garage sale with used hockey equipment, call a cab company for directions. They can set you right every time.

Also, bring plenty of cash, especially fives and ones, as well as a roll of quarters. Some garage sales, especially the bigger ones involving two or three families, often run out of change.

• **Start early.** As you make a list of promising garage sales, do you see any that start at eight o'clock? If so, you want to hit those first so you can arrive on time (or even a little early if you're sneaky) for the nine o'clock sales.

A significant part of the shopping strategy is *when* you arrive at a garage sale. Sometimes when a sale lists the start as nine o'clock, they really mean eight. People do this knowing that if they advertise an earlier opening, dealers will show up on their doorstep at seven! Other families say nine o'clock and mean it. Let's say you arrive early for a garage sale, but the family is still getting set up. If you spot a couple of items that look promising, you could say something like, "If I help you get ready, can I have first dibs?"

Being an early-bird shopper can work for and against you. If you arrive early, you have first crack at the bargains. If the prices are right, you're a winner. However, if the prices are high, the sellers may not be in a mood to bargain since they're expecting more customers. On the other hand, if you arrive late in the morning or in the early afternoon, you can pick up some incredible bargains on unsold items. The last thing the family wants is to cart their junk back into the house.

• **Go to garage sales in "yuppie" neighborhoods.** You can sweep up special deals where young urban professionals live. These families tend to sell nice children's clothing, the latest toys, and classic books simply because their kids have outgrown them. And they often have lots of things to sell.

Every city features great, good, and mediocre areas for garage sales. The most affluent neighborhoods are not always the best sections to shop because wealthy people tend to be older. Their kids are grown and gone, so you won't find many Tonka toys or children's clothes. But you might find a nice dining room table or china hutch.

• **Be a good bargainer.** Unless items cost only a quarter, most sellers expect to be chiseled down. If you're buying a lot of small items that add up to five dollars, offer four. A buck saved is a buck earned.

Sometimes people don't do a good job displaying clothing. They may set out several cardboard boxes filled with children's shirts and pants, but after several people have rummaged through them, everything is a mess. Don't be deterred. Look at each item carefully and imagine what the shirt or pants will look like after being washed and ironed. Are there any holes? Any buttons missing? Permanent stains?

If the clothes are in good shape, you should pay a quarter or fifty cents for T-shirts, fifty to seventy-five cents for dress shirts, one dollar for sweatshirts and ties, one to three dollars for sweaters and OshKosh overalls, and a couple of bucks for skirts and out-of-fashion dresses. Department store dresses worn only a couple of times usually sell for five to ten dollars.

Look for brand names: Healthtex, Benetton, Maui & Sons, Levis, Guess?, Cavarrichi, and Esprit. Nike and Reebok sneakers are excellent buys for infants and toddlers because the shoes aren't worn out. Actually, until your child is six years old, you can do a lot of your shopping at garage sales since the clothes haven't faded and usually don't have holes. They're just outgrown.

Little girls' dresses are another good buy. Polly Flander dresses, which retail in stores for thirty to one hundred dollars, can be found at garage sales for between one and five dollars. You shouldn't pay more than a quarter or fifty cents for children's books and tapes.

• **Make sure the item isn't torn or broken.** Shopping garage sales requires serious consideration of the saying, *caveat emptor,* "Let the buyer beware." You can't trust anybody these days! Always check out electric appliances—irons, blenders, televisions, cassette players—by plugging them in to see if they work. Remember, it won't be worth paying someone to repair an appliance or a piece of electronic equipment.

You're on surer ground with furniture, among the most sought-after merchandise. It's such a big seller because most people can't afford retail. Sellers have the upper hand here. Buyers will have to make a snap judgment on whether the price is fair and fits their available funds.

Be on the lookout for "moving sales." Families relocating to another city or state are typically more willing to bargain on chests of drawers and dressers.You know people are serious about getting rid of stuff if the garage sale is held during the winter or in the nippy fall or chilly spring months. Often, garage sales in cold weather are a sign that the family is either desperate or about to move out of town. Not only can you bargain accordingly, but you won't be competing against as many shoppers.

ESTATE SALES

Estate sales are a whole different breed from garage sales. By definition, estate sales occur after a death in the family. The surviving family members—or a third party—often sell off the effects. Thus, estate sales are more organized. Since they're often held in private homes, those holding the estate sale limit the number of buyers who can enter. They naturally want to prevent light-fingered customers from shoplifting Grandma's silver and jewelry.

Unless you arrive before the advertised time (which will *not* be moved ahead), be prepared to stand in line. Lou Gage said she used to stand in snowy Colorado weather for two hours to enter some estate sales. The antique dealers were the only other people braving the frigid temperatures.

Prices are generally non-negotiable in the morning. If you want to negotiate, ask "Are your prices firm?"

The person behind the table may reply, "We are firm until 1 P.M."

"Are you going to go to half price then?" If he or she says yes, come back at 12:30, make your selections, and carry them around until one o'clock.

THRIFT STORES

Thrift shops can be found in most towns, but it's hard to generalize nationally as to which one is better. In your town, a St. Vincent de Paul may be better than Goodwill, or a Disabled American Veterans store may beat them all.

In most states, Goodwill stores do a fine job of reconditioning the clothes—repairing holes, doing a thorough cleaning, ironing—before putting them out on the sales floor. If you're wondering whether your favorite thrift store reconditions clothes, smelling them will give you a good indication as to whether or not they've been reconditioned.

Thrift stores offer great deals. OshKosh overalls, which wear like iron, may cost twenty-five dollars new at Target, but only five dollars used at Goodwill. Like garage sales, you want to be on the lookout for quality name brands.

When college students and young couples are starting out, thrift stores provide inexpensive places to shop for forks, spoons, plates, towels, and all the little items needed to furnish an apartment. A new towel, for instance, may cost ten dollars at Sears, but only two bucks at the Goodwill store.

The best time to shop thrift stores is April, May, and June, after people have done their spring cleaning. Another good time is at the end of summer. Families who hold garage sales during the summer often box up the stuff that didn't sell and donate it to the Goodwill.

If you need a bed, try shopping for one at Goodwill. For those a tad queasy about sleeping on a used bed, Goodwill wraps new "ticking" material around it so the fabric is essentially unused.

"The Goodwill beds are clean," said Lou. "You might be getting a Simmons mattress for fifty-nine dollars when it originally cost almost ten times that. If you're unmarried and moving into your first apartment, that's better than sleeping on the floor. Not only does Goodwill recondition the whole bed, they spray the insides with insecticide to ensure the absence of critters."

You can also purchase bed frames at Goodwill. "When my daughter Nadine moved out, she needed a bed frame," said Lou. "They're very expensive in stores—about seventy dollars. Hers was only twelve dollars at Goodwill."

The best thing about thrift shops? They're wonderful places to buy costumes for yourself or the kids, or for the church's annual Christmas pageant.

CONSIGNMENT STORES

Like a Mercedes Benz dealer who sells "pre-owned" cars, consignment stores view themselves as a cut above thrift shops and second-hand stores. Many consignment stores are middlemen who sell name-brand clothes and dresses in superb shape. A good-sized city may have a dozen consignment stores, which you can find listed in the Yellow Pages under "Clothing—Used."

Consignment stores sell a broad spectrum of high-end merchandise. You can buy everything from an expensive ladies' teddy to a full-length mink stole. You're going to pay considerably more than garage sale prices, but you're also going to pay considerably less than retail. Consignment stores like Rags Fifth Avenue and Second Hand Rose sell single-owner dresses, ladies' wool suits, cocktail dresses, expensive furs, fashionable blazers, jewelry, leather belts, hats, alligator purses, and Bally shoes—all at tremendous discounts.

How much of a discount? You can figure 60 to 80 percent off retail. In a retail store, a woman's Pendleton wool suit—perhaps worn only a few times—might run almost two hundred dollars for the jacket and one hundred for the pants. At a consignment store, you can buy both pieces for sixty to ninety dollars, and the Pendleton suit will look like it has never been worn. If you're shopping for an Easter hat, it will run from two to ten dollars, a considerable discount from ten to fifty new.

Consignment stores offer a wide selection, with varying sizes, colors, designs, and styles. If you have a teenager going to the senior prom, these shops carry the latest fashions at prices you can afford. Consignment stores are always fun for browsers. Keep in mind, however, that some cater to children's clothes or to adults.

In comparison to their distant thrift-shop cousins, consignment stores offer a pleasant atmosphere—usually well lit, air conditioned, and nice smelling. One stipulation is that all clothes coming into the store must be either dry cleaned or laundered before they can be set on the rack. Most consignment shops keep half of the sale price and pass the other half on to the previous owner.

If you're in the market for second-hand sports equipment, consider stores such as Play It Again Sports and Recycled Sports, although the prices aren't cheap. I've purchased used baseball gloves and ice skates for my kids at Play It Again Sports, which has four hundred fifty franchises in the U.S. and Canada. Popular items at these stores include ice skates, mountain bikes, and NordicTracks—all hard to find at garage sales.

If you don't want to pay the higher prices at these recycled sporting goods stores, then keep an eye out for seasonal "swaps" for items such as bikes, skis, soccer shoes, and ice hockey equipment. Bike and ski swaps are often advertised in the newspaper. To find when such swaps are held for other sports equipment, you could network with parents who have children in a particular sport, or you can call someone like the soccer league commissioner or ice hockey coach. And be sure to check the bulletin boards where games are played.

We make it a point to go to the local ski swap every first Saturday in November. I think it's the only way to buy ski equipment. We usually find serviceable skis for the kids at thirty-five dollars and new boots for only twenty. We've saved enough money to pay for a couple of days skiing each winter!

While we're on the subject of sports equipment, mail-order is a great way to purchase tennis rackets and golf clubs—if you know what you want. Specialty stores are fighting the mail-order companies by being service oriented, so don't take advantage of the local retailer. It's not fair to try out a racket at a tennis shop and then order it from the mail-order company. Instead, borrow a friend's racket if you're going the mail-order

Scooping Up What's Left

I don't necessarily recommend this, but some people buy up *everything* at the garage sale.

When Lou Gage was into garage sales, she would drop by around two o'clock and cheerfully announce, "I see I've come just in time. What would you say if I backed up my car and took it all away—the good, the bad, and the ugly?"

Three times out of ten, they would reply, "Make me an offer I can't refuse." Usually twenty-five or fifty dollars bought the whole show. Lou then turned around and sold the worthwhile items to used furniture stores, consignment places, and at her own garage sales. If you're the entrepreneurial type, go for it. But that's a lot of work to make a buck.

route, or talk to the customer representatives at the mail-order company.

Also, sporting goods manufacturers are changing their lines all the time, which means last season's models quickly end up on a sale rack. Buying at the end of the season offers another way to save. Last May, I purchased new ski bindings for Nicole at a significant discount. What makes the story even better is that I got an extra twenty dollars off because I asked the salesman if he would sell me the display model. They were glad to get rid of it!

You can also ask salespeople if they sell slightly damaged or scratched equipment at a significant markdown. A new racquetball racket with a cosmetic chip on the frame works just fine. Besides, the racket will look a lot more beat up after you've played a few times.

Get to know the owner or manager of your local sporting goods store. Ask him or her to tip you off when certain merchandise goes on clearance. With early notice, you might even be able to drop by the evening before the sale and get first choice. Also, discount stores such as Kmart and Target may sell sporting equipment cheaper, but the quality isn't likely to be the same unless you buy brand names, such as Prince, Spalding, and Wilson. I recommend sticking to the specialty shops and buying on sale.

Sneakers and tennis shoes are another matter. If your children can resist the peer pressure to wear $125 Air Jordans or $150 Reebok Pumps, you're going to save a chunk of change. What happens if your youngster just *has* to have the latest Shaquille O'Neil sneaker? Tell him that fifty dollars (or whatever amount) is your limit, and if he wants Shaq's Reeboks that badly, then he will have to cough up the difference. You can also check out the mail-order companies in the back of basketball or tennis magazines. Occasionally, you can find closeouts or end lots of Nikes and Reeboks at Marshalls, TJ Maxx, and Ross Dress for Less.

Keep in mind that some stores sell "blemished" shoes that

really aren't all that damaged. Somebody may have worn them for a morning and returned them, or perhaps the sole wasn't glued perfectly. Deep discounts can be gained here. If you live near a factory outlet mall, you can find great prices on blemished Nikes or LA Gear seconds.

FRIENDS AND RELATIVES

If you're like Nicole and me, perhaps you wouldn't feel quite right sleeping on a stranger's used bed. That's where friends and family come in. My comfort level always rose when I bought a bed from my aunt and uncle, or purchased a chest of drawers from a friend for a few bucks.

Perhaps you feel the same way about used clothes. But hand-me-downs from friends and family can be a great way to pare your clothing budget. We've received boxes of clothes from relatives at times when we badly needed them. Then when our kids outgrew them, we passed them on to other relatives. Our friends Chuck and Sally Mosher have a daughter three years older than our Andrea, and once a year we receive a box of ski outfits and sweaters. That really helps.

Don't forget to look within your family for hand-me-downs. Make your needs known, and watch the Lord provide. It's important to get the word out among your friends and relatives that you would gladly receive donations of clothing, boots, books, and toys—and that you'll send them back when you're done with them.

A final option entails buying used clothing from a private party. Elaine Minton said when her boys were under three, a woman advertised used children's clothing in her local shopper's guide. Because this woman worked, she bought enough clothes to last for the week until she could do laundry on the weekends. She bought quality items, and her son quickly grew out of his clothing long before it was outworn.

"She sold me items for a dollar or two that cost her fifteen dollars or more when they were new," said Elaine. "I bought everything she had and asked her to call me whenever her son outgrew things. I could have never invested in the expensive brands she purchased if I was buying those clothes new. My boys were two of the best-dressed kids in school."

CHAPTER 8

Something for Nothing?

For fifteen years, I rarely took my Bank of America Visa card out of my wallet.

Sure, it came in handy the few times I ordered new slippers through L.L. Bean's 800-number or guaranteed a Days Inn reservation in another city, but most of the time I paid cash. Our credit card total rarely topped one hundred dollars, and many months Nicole and I charged nothing at all.

Besides, I never bought into the idea of "credit" cards. What do you mean not pay off the monthly statement in full? With the 1.5 percent interest they sock you with every thirty days, I'd just owe more money the following month. Believe it or not, Nicole didn't even know we had the option of *not* paying the entire balance each month!

That was our attitude until the spring of 1992, when we had some friends, Fred and Suzanne Sindt, over for dinner.

Suzanne, like Nicole, is a native of Switzerland. She and Fred had taken us under their wings when we moved to Colorado Springs. The Sindts, who had lived in the area nearly thirty years, had answers to our Big Questions: Where should we go to church? Which neighborhood should we live in? Where does everyone play tennis?

So when Suzanne started describing the benefits of the Citibank Visa card, I quietly listened. I had never heard anyone *rave* about a credit card.

"It's a great deal," she continued breathlessly. "For every dollar you charge, you get a mile with American Airlines' frequent-flyer program. Sometimes, American will run specials. I went to Switzerland last year—twenty thousand miles for one hundred dollars. Now I charge *everything* I can. Even when I fill up my car with gas, I'm twenty miles closer to Zurich."

Whoever heard of a *good* credit card? On the contrary, horror stories abound: the family who rang up tens of thousands of dollars in credit card debt and lost their home; the over-their-heads couple still collecting new cards so they could keep one step ahead of the collection agencies; the marriage busted up by the overspending of one spouse.

Despite the dangers, many of us have become hooked on credit like a junkie on smack, an addictive habit confessed by the growing ranks of Debtors Anonymous. Seventy percent of American families have at least one credit card, up from 35 percent ten years ago, and the number of bankcards now in circulation totals nearly three hundred million—more than the entire U.S. population. And only 21 percent of those cardholders pay off their monthly statement in full every thirty days. According to several estimates, the average "revolving" or unpaid credit card debt per household ranges from eleven hundred to twenty-five hundred dollars!

If you are among the 79 percent who do *not* pay off your monthly statement in full each and every month, please read no further. Your first priority is to get out from under the potentially staggering debt that threatens your financial future. You may have to work overtime, find a second job, or have your spouse work part-time. No matter what the choice, you need to wipe that credit card slate clean as soon as possible.

If you are one of those fortunate or disciplined enough to avoid the credit card trap, please read on.

What Credit Really Costs

How much is the cost of credit if I make the minimum monthly payment of 3 percent? I used Marc Eisenson's "The Banker's Secret Credit Card Software" to calculate three examples.

Item	Interest rate	Minimum payment
A $1,050 GE side-by-side refrigerator	18%	$31.50
Time needed to pay off 47 months	**Total interest** $416.57	**Total cost** 1,466.57

Item	Interest rate	Minimum payment
A $580 Zenith color TV	14.2%	$17.40
Time needed to pay off 43 months	**Total interest** $161.95	**Total cost** $741.95

Item	Interest rate	Minimum payment
A $2,100 dining room table (with six chairs)	15.8%	$63
Time needed to pay off 45 months	**Total interest** $683.04	**Total cost** $2,783.04

Notice that these three credit card purchases take almost four years to pay in full with minimum monthly payments. The money saved by avoiding that compounded interest—either paying at the point of purchase or through the following month's credit card statement—would be enough to buy something nice for your home.

CHECKING IT OUT

After Suzanne finished describing the benefits of her Citibank Visa, I stared ahead, lost in thought.

"You don't believe me, do you?" she asked.

"Well, it does sound too good to be true," I replied. *There has to be a catch,* my skeptical mind assumed.

"It's a marketing ploy," continued Suzanne. "Citibank does this to get you to use its card."

And how. When AT&T launched its Universal card in 1990 by offering discounts on long-distance calls, they kick-started a whole wave of rebate credit cards. The General Motors card, launched two years later, sent the credit card industry into overdrive, reflected by a 25-percent jump in credit purchases the following year.

It used to be that credit cards were a tool for living above your means. Why else would cardholders run up several thousand dollars of unsecured debt? Then, as consumers reached their credit limits, they typically cut back on spending. Banks and credit card issuers responded by developing a strategy called "co-branding," in which cardholders received some sort of premium for whipping out their plastic. A big push by MasterCard increased its market share for the first time in fourteen years in 1992 after issuing seven million General Motors cards and 70 percent of AT&T's Universal cards.

Credit card companies have always been looking for ways to boost their customer base. It's an incredibly profitable business. First off, they rake in a 2 to 3 percent "transaction fee" from the merchant on every purchase. Then, if the consumer doesn't pay the statement off each month, usurious interest rates kick in. The industry average is 18 percent, which means a borrower would pay $360 a year on a $2,000 balance. That's $30 a month into thin air!

What expenses do the credit card companies incur? They must process the charges and mail out statements each month, write off a few deadbeats who never pay (typically 5 percent of their customer base), and swallow charges on stolen cards.

I don't have much sympathy with these losses, however. Many issuers hand out credit cards like party favors. For the six months leading up to this book, I decided to count the number of credit card solicitations I received. It was thirty-five! And requiring merchants to see proof of identification could put a big dent in losses due to stolen cards. Even taking inevitable losses into account, Visa, MasterCard, Discover, and American Express pocket a lot of change.

What to Do if You Have Credit Card Debt

As you know all too well, the interest clock ticks relentlessly. The first item of business: stop charging right now! The twenty-five-day grace period ended the day you didn't pay your monthly statement in full. Consequently, every credit card purchase from that date starts accruing interest *the same day* it's posted. Several authors suggest melting your credit cards in the oven as you start your credit card diet. Cutting them up with a pair of scissors may be neater, but the melted mess would provide a graphic reminder of the mess you've gotten yourself into.

Next, formulate a battle plan. What are your highest-interest-bearing cards? Pay those off first. Then think about how you can earn more money to get out of this hole. If you need help, find a Christian financial counselor. As a stopgap measure, write the Bankcard Holders of America (524 Branch Drive, Salem, VA 24153; phone 703-389-5445.) and ask for their "Debt Zapper" report. This ten-dollar report will help you calculate the most efficient way to pay down your debt.

OK, I thought. *Let's check this Citibank Visa thing out.* I called for an application, and Suzanne was right. I *could* receive mileage credits for all my charges, which could be used for future travel. Twenty thousand miles qualified me for a free trip anywhere in the forty-eight states, and forty thousand miles would net a trip to Switzerland from fall to spring (or sixty thousand if I wanted to go during the preferred summer season).

Hey, this isn't bad, I thought. *I make a couple of business trips a year, and that mileage, coupled with my monthly purchases, could net our family a free flight or two.*

But could I charge enough to make it worthwhile? That may sound like a dumb question, but I wasn't going to go on an Eddie Bauer spending spree just to pad my frequent flier account. Those would be expensive airline miles.

Looking over our spending patterns, I saw that we could easily charge one thousand dollars a month.

- *Groceries: $400 a month.* Nearly all the supermarket chains in our area take credit cards (Albertsons is the lone holdout). Sam's Club is cash or check only for those without Discover cards.

- *Gas: $119 a month.* We drive two cars for a total of twenty-five thousand miles a year. At twenty miles per gallon of $1.15 gas, annual cost is $1,437.50.

- *Restaurant meals: $75 a month.* The whole family eats out twice a month, plus I take Nicole on lunch dates.

- *Clothing: $150 a month.* As a family of four, we spend around $1,800 a year.

- *Home improvement: $50 a month.* This can range from shampooing the carpets to having pictures framed to purchasing new grass seed.

- *Car maintenance and repairs: $100 a month.* Until we got rid of the '82 Subaru, we were averaging $2,500 a year for repairs. With our new minivan, we spend $1,200 a year maintaining both it and my '82 GMC pickup.

- *Miscellaneous: $100 a month.* This includes Christmas and birthday gifts, doctors visits, dental bills, pharmacy drugs, even charitable donations to parachurch ministries.

All these items which I had been paying by check or cash would come to a grand total of $994 monthly on our charge card. Before Nicole and I made the plunge, we agreed to this guideline: *we will pay off the balance each month; otherwise, we lose.* Sticking to this resolve has required discipline because using credit makes it easier to spend. Christian financial adviser Ron Blue has found that families spend 34 percent more when credit cards are used. We couldn't afford to be snared in that credit card trap.

In the two years since Nicole and I decided to buy intentionally on credit, we've looked for ways to charge at no cost. When at a restaurant with a group of friends, I'll offer to charge the entire bill and let the others reimburse me on the spot. When I travel to conferences or on assignment, I charge all my expenses—including flight, hotel, and rental car—and receive a reimbursement check. Once, when Nicole's brother and his family vacationed in Colorado for two weeks, I had him charge two thousand dollars for his hotel and rental car on my card. He then reimbursed me with traveler's checks.

We have already earned one Christmas trip to Switzerland, which costs around one thousand dollars round-trip from Denver to Zurich. This "free" flight will cost us one hundred dollars (two years of annual fees for the Citibank Visa card).

GOING FOR THE PERKS

Some credit card companies have hooked up with other merchants to add miles to your account. For instance, AT&T and MCI will give you five frequent-flier miles for every dollar of long-distance charges. My long-distance bill averages seventy-five dollars a month, which means I earn five thousand miles a year just by using my phone. In addition, nearly all car rental agencies and major hotel chains (Hilton, Hyatt, Sheraton, and Holiday Inn) will give you bonus airline miles.

Before jumping in with both feet, it's important to think through which card will benefit you and your family most. Appendix five lists various credit card options to help you sort through what's available, but I chose not to include each card's interest rates. Why? Because interest rates are *irrelevant* to this discussion! You'll be paying off your balance each month, right? Otherwise, you shouldn't even think about pursuing this option.

Before getting an airline credit card, ask yourself: Can I get there from here? Does the airline fly to where I want to go? In other words, if you live in Seattle but your parents live in Charleston, Virginia, Alaska Air might not be a wise choice for you.

As a case in point, Nicole and I chose American because it flies to Switzerland, but we probably should have chosen United, which also flies to Zurich. Why? Because from Colorado Springs, American flies to only one city: Dallas. We have to drive to Denver International (about ninety minutes away) and take an American flight to Chicago before we can catch a nonstop to Zurich. United, on the other hand, has a major hub in Denver, with convenient shuttles from Colorado Springs.

Nearly every airline offers frequent-flier credit cards, but the mileage requirements and the annual fees are subject to change. In fact, many of the major airlines have raised or will raise the minimum frequent-flier miles to 25,000 by the end of 1995. The reason? To save money. In 1990, airlines gave away nearly seven million free flights, and that figure jumped to nine million in 1992. With air travel costs rising dramatically, the squeeze is on.

I've learned that when something goes wrong with a flight,

it pays to write the airlines about it. When Fred and Suzanne Sindt's long flight from Zurich to Chicago was delayed because of engine trouble, they missed their connecting flight to Denver. The first thing Suzanne did when she got off the plane at O'Hare was ask for a complaint form. The result: a check for two hundred dollars.

I thought of Suzanne's story on a recent trip to Toronto for a book interview with my colleague, Greg Johnson. Coming home, we left on American for the hour-long hop to Chicago. About ten minutes outside of Chicago, the pilot informed us that the de-icer on the DC-10s wings was malfunctioning. After considering the options, they decided to turn the plane around and return to Toronto.

Back in Canada, it took three hours before we could board a United flight to Chicago and resume our journey home. Meanwhile, instead of landing in Denver at mid-morning and enjoying the rest of Saturday with my family, Greg and I trudged into Denver late that afternoon. Not a happy camper, I asked for a complaint form and an address. My letter and American's response appear on the following pages. I don't think I was harsh on American at all, which I noted in a thank-you note to Miss Ferguson. (It's never a bad idea to send letters of thanks. People are human.)

When I asked Lou Gage what she thought about airline credit cards, I secretly wished that she hadn't heard about them—that I knew something she didn't. Fat chance! Lou received a Continental Airlines One Pass credit card back in 1986 when the program first began. Each year, she and her husband, Wayne, take at least two free trips, and when she last looked, she had 140,000 miles in her account!

Do you have to be a Daddy Warbucks before these airline mileage cards result in actual free tickets? If you listen to Gerri Detweiler, executive director of the consumer credit group BankCard Holders of America, the answer is yes. "You've got to be a big spender to earn the maximum benefit or rebate, and you've got to use the rebate for a particular brand or

December 13, 1993

Miss J.L. Ferguson
MD 2400
Consumer Relations
American Airlines
P.O. Box 619612
Dallas/Fort Worth Airport, TX 75261-9610

Dear Miss Ferguson:

I am enclosing the following complaint form. I was booked on AA
flight 615 from Toronto to Chicago on Saturday, October 30. The
DC-10 took off and was a few minutes out of Chicago when the
pilot announced that the de-icer was not working, and that the
plane would have to return to Toronto. Back in Canada, I was put
on another flight, but the delay cost me five hours.

As a "make good," could I request some extra mileage to my AA
frequent flier account? My number is WWU0948. I really do like
American Airlines and use it for all my business travel when I
can.

Thank you for your attention to this matter.

Sincerely,

Mike Yorkey
Editor
<u>Focus on the Family</u> magazine
1017 N. War Eagle Dr.
Colorado Springs, CO 80919

enc: copy of boarding pass

product or you lose." One financial advisor counseled against
rebate cards, noting that since the average family charges
$2,200 a year on credit cards, it would take nearly ten years to
gain a free trip.

All those are true statements. But Nicole and I *intentionally*
increased our credit card spending from $1,200 a year to over

AmericanAirlines

December 20, 1993

Mr. Mike Yorkey
Editor
Focus On the Family Magazine
1017 North War Eagle Drive
Colorado Springs, CO 80919

Dear Mr. Yorkey:

Please accept my sincere apology for the difficulties you encountered when attempting to travel with us to Chicago on October 30. Without question, we did not provide the level of service you expect and deserve.

In a business such as ours, delays and cancellations cannot always be avoided. When these situations occur, however, we should make every attempt to minimize the inconvenience. I truly wish we had done a better job of overcoming the challenges we faced that day, and I am sorry for disappointing you. A copy of your comments has been forwarded to the appropriate management personnel with an eye toward improvement. The details you provided will help us to better serve our customers in the future.

Still, I am sorry these lessons have come at your expense. Per your request, we have taken the liberty of posting 5,000 bonus miles to your AAdvantage account as a gesture of goodwill. This should be reflected on your next statement, if not, on the one after that. We do appreciate your patience.

Mr. Yorkey, I hope you are persuaded to think a little less harshly of us. We value you as a customer and are eager to restore your confidence. Please give us another opportunity to serve you. In turn we will do our best to make your trip pleasant and trouble free.

Whether you are traveling this holiday season or staying at home, we wish you all the best as we head into the new year. Happy Holidays!

Yours truly,

Ms. D. A. Shaffer
Staff Assistant
Executive Office

$10,000 a year. If you have a household income of $30,000 or more, you should be able to charge close to $1,000 a month.

Do you do any company travel? Do you own a small business? Are you the "purchasing agent" for your women's club? You can be reimbursed. You might work in a profession that lends itself to credit spending. My father, for instance, is a general contractor. Every time he goes to Home Depot to buy building materials for a job, he hands over his Citibank Visa card. He's reimbursed, of course, but last year he netted 30,000 miles for airline travel.

QUESTIONS AND ANSWERS

Q. What's the best card?

A. Tough call. Based on pure rebate, it would have to be the GM or Ford cards, but then you have to buy or lease a new car to take advantage of it. With the GM card, for instance, you would have to spend $70,000 over three-and-a-half years to get a $3,500 rebate. If you spent the same amount with a Continental One Pass, you would be entitled to at least three round-trip tickets, with 10,000 miles leftover. Would those three plane tickets be worth $3,500 to you?

Steve Thurman, my pastor, ordered a GM card a year ago. "I am very careful with how I use it," he said. "Every time I charge something, I write a check for the same amount and put it in an envelope. That way I know exactly where I am."

Another way to track your credit card spending is to write down each charge in your checkbook and keep a running tally in the column marked for deposits. Or, you can do what Nicole and I do: We put the receipts into a large envelope and periodically add them up. Our Citibank monthly cycle ends on the twenty-second of the month, so if we've reached our limit by the fifteenth, we cool our spending jets for a week or so.

I asked Steve if he's able to charge enough to make the GM card work for him. He replied that with his travel reimbursements for church conferences and family spending, he typically charges $20,000 a year, which qualifies him for a $1,000 discount on a GM car.

"Does that mean you want a GM car?" I asked.

"You mean I have to get a GM car?" exclaimed Steve. "I really want a Porsche!"

Q. Do banks ever drop their annual fees?

A. Several years ago, I called up Bank of America and said I was thinking of canceling my card because of its eighteen-dollar annual fee. Immediately, the teleservice operator put me through to somebody who sweet-talked me into keeping the card. He said I had been a valued customer for over ten years, and that the card had so many benefits.... Never did I think to ask him to waive the annual fee.

Since then, I've read in business magazines that cardholders—if they complain loudly enough—can get a thirty-dollar annual fee erased. Just explain that you're planning to get a no-annual fee card, but offer to keep your business with the current company—if they'll match the offer. Remember, however, that only a supervisor or a manager can authorize this decision.

Q. What should I do if I charge too much one month?

A. Assuming that you can't dip into savings, you should cut up the cards until you pay off the balance. Then, when you've caught up, contact the credit card company and tell them you had to slice up the cards, but are now ready to resume the account. They will happily issue a new card at no charge to you.

Q. Doesn't the cost of credit drive up the cost of our goods and services?

A. Yes, it does, but we lost that battle a long time ago. Try to walk into a Safeway, Target, or Chili's these days and offer to pay cash for a 3-percent discount. The answer will be no. I do realize cash discounts can still be had at certain gas stations and small mom-and-pop stores, but you won't find many large merchants who will offer them.

Another thought: large retailers, such as Wal-Mart, pay the credit card companies considerably less than 2 or 3 percent of the transaction. They may pay as little as one-half of 1 percent because of their huge amount of credit card volume.

Q. What are some credit card do's and don'ts?

A. If you do pay off your credit card balance each month, get a card that can do *something* for you. There really aren't many do's, just a lot of don'ts. Here are a few:

- Don't get more than one credit card. You have to track your spending before the statement comes in, so having more than one card complicates things. Nicole and I each carry a Citibank Visa card and, believe me, that is more than enough.

- Don't use any in-store credit cards, such as Sears, May Co., or Nordstrom's. Besides, most of these stores accept regular plastic anyway.

- Don't purchase anything for which you don't have the money in the bank. Ask yourself: Can I write a check for this amount today?

- Do be cautious about "ninety-days-same-as-cash" or "six-month, no-interest" deals. Why? Because the retailer is charging you interest all that time in case the amount is not paid in full on the ninetieth day or at the end of six months. Believe me, there will be a hefty interest charge on day ninety-one or one day past six months if you are delinquent.

To avoid interest charges, make monthly payments to your savings account so the money will be there at the end of six months. If you are determined to pay on time, you can purchase big-ticket items without paying interest. Another thing you can do is turn the salesperson's "no-payments-until-April" hype around. If you've got the money, ask: "OK, what sort of discount could you give me if I pay cash today?"

• Take advantage of the credit card companies. Dena Fuller said she doesn't do this often, but when a department store offers a one-time, 20 percent discount on purchases for opening a charge account, she plans a shopping trip during a big sale and uses her card that single time. Then she pays off the statement and never uses the card again.

Once Dena received a solicitation for the GE Rewards card along with a ten-dollar coupon, plus a promise to pay her ten dollars if she canceled before one year. "I'm going to cancel it," Dena told me. "I can handle that. But I have to write myself a reminder on the calendar to do so before the year is up; otherwise I don't get the ten dollars."

• If you're not interested in the airline mileage or car company cards but feel you need a card for emergencies, request a no-annual-fee card.

Q. My daughter is going away to college next fall. Should she have a credit card?

A. After country singer Wynonna Judd went on a shopping spree at New York's Saks Fifth Avenue, her mother, Namoi, quipped: "Never loan your credit card to someone you've given birth to."

As for *your* daughter, this juncture would provide a good opportunity to take her out to lunch and explain credit cards from top to bottom. She will have to learn how to use credit cards sooner or later, and, for now, that may mean not having one. Or, you might get her a card, but with the understanding that it's for emergencies only. Emphasize that the first month the balance is not paid in full, you will immediately reclaim the card.

The worst thing you can do for your daughter is to have *her* monthly statements arriving in *your* mailbox. If you do, you will teach your child this lesson: My spending doesn't affect *me*.

Q. What's the big deal about American Express? That seems like a lot of money for a credit card you have to pay off each month.

A. I put that same question to Lou Gage. She said many people carry an American Express simply for the status it brings. "When you flash an American Express card, it says you're a wealthy person, or you wouldn't be spending $55 or $75 or $300 a year to own one. It's strictly a status thing." Then she whispered an aside: "A lot of those people are *not* paying off their statements every month." I receive American Express solicitation letters all the time, and their cover letters drip with snob appeal.

Here's an example of how some American Express cardholders have fallen for hype. Shortly after I graduated from college, I took my first job selling ski lift tickets at Mammoth Mountain in California. I worked in a ticket booth with a young woman, and we would usually sell a thousand tickets in a morning shift. We handled hundreds of customers every hour.

One time, a skier nonchalantly tossed his American Express platinum card at us and asked for four tickets. "I bet you don't see too many of those," he said with a swagger.

"That's only the tenth one this morning, sir," quipped my colleague.

Remember, credit cards are only a modern-day tool to pay for goods and services. No more, no less. Don't get caught up in the image game that credit card companies try to create.

Q. Every now and then, my credit card company will offer me a "bank holiday," saying I can skip my monthly payment. What should I do?

A. Again, read through the fine print. All too often, the interest doesn't skip a month if your card has an outstanding balance. Many cardholders who have an outstanding balance aren't aware that interest starts the *day* the transaction reaches the credit card company—not the day the bill is due.

Q. What are some other ways credit card companies try to get you?

A. Annual fees are rising—45 percent in the last year. Often, that fee is just another line in your statement, so the companies are hoping you don't notice. The other gimmick is to charge you ten to twenty dollars for going over your credit limit. If you absolutely *have* to go over your existing limit, call the company and ask for a higher one.

My favorite "gotcha" is the cash-advance fees. They make it sound so easy to pop your credit card into an ATM machine, but then they charge 1 to 2 percent for the privilege! Get a bank ATM card.

Q. What's the best piece of advice you can give me about credit cards?

A. It's far easier to go *into* debt than it is to get *out* of debt.

CHAPTER 9

"Gonna Save Up My Money, and Buy a Little GTO"

Having grown up in the shadow of Pasadena's Colorado Boulevard during the sixties and early seventies, Bruce Peppin was practically raised on the "car songs" of Jan & Dean and the Beach Boys. When he turned twenty, he was ready to buy his first set of wheels. And as a new Christian, Bruce wanted to make a wise purchase. But his swirling hormones also made him yearn for a cherry-red two-door that would impress the babes and take off in a blaze of burning rubber.

In quest of just the right car, Bruce was scanning the classifieds one weekend. One ad set his heart pounding: "68 Pontiac GTO, white, Hurst 4-speed stick shift, leather, mag wheels, top shape, $800." And when he laid eyes on this beauty, he fell in love. With its jacked-up rear end and foot-wide Tiger Paws, the gleaming GTO screamed muscle to any onlooker. Under the hood, a 455 V-8 engine growled to the slightest touch of the accelerator.

Bruce quickly agreed on a price with Billy, the GTO's owner. The following day, Billy picked up his buyer for a ride to the bank, where the transaction would be completed. Meanwhile, our novice car buyer aimed a few perfunctory prayers heavenward, asking the Lord for one red light after another if this car was a lemon.

From the shotgun seat, Bruce noticed the gas gauge was a little below half full. They quickly hopped on the freeway for the ten-mile jaunt to Pasadena. The throaty engine roared as Billy slammed the accelerator to the floor and merged quickly into the passing lane. He kept up a steady stream of chatter. "Your first car, huh? Oh, you're going to love this beauty! Believe me, the girls will go crazy. They'll be putty in your hands...."

That wasn't exactly at the top of Bruce's priority list. He glanced again at the gas gauge, which now showed one-quarter tank. A noticeable shift. *Hmmm,* he thought. *I have a real gas hog here. God, am I making the right decision?*

They sped down the freeway off-ramp onto Pasadena's Lake Avenue. Up ahead, a pedestrian stepped into the intersection. They were traveling a little too fast, but Billy had time to jam on the brakes. Unfortunately, a car following a little too closely skidded into the GTO, denting the rear fender.

Bruce and Billy jumped out to inspect the damage. The fender was bent in a couple of places, but the damage was manageable. "It'll be OK," Billy said. "A body shop can pop that out in no time. Whaddya say we keep that appointment at the bank?"

"But ..." started Bruce.

"Hey, what do you have to worry about?" asked Billy, spreading his palms upward. "This is nothing. You're gonna *love* this car." My friend was too timid to speak up. They drove a few more blocks and then turned into a gas station. The gauge was resting squarely on empty. Billy jumped out and put in a dollar of premium. *What a cheapskate,* thought Bruce. *Man, this car sure slurps up the gas.*

Billy popped the hood. From his seat, Bruce could see him pulling out the dipstick. Then he quickly stuck it back into the engine block and hotfooted it over to the attached ministore. Bruce stepped out and checked the dipstick himself. It was as dry as a desert bone.

Billy returned with a couple of quarts of oil. "She's a little low," he explained, as he poured in the oil. Back on the road, Bruce slumped into his seat. *This is not looking good,* he thought. *But the Lord will protect me. I'm sure it's nothing.*

Back on Lake Avenue, they hadn't traveled more than a mile when the GTO started lurching. They had just enough power to get off the road before the engine quit. Billy jumped out and popped the hood. The radiator hose was twice its normal size, and steam rose everywhere.

Finally, the Lord had Bruce's attention.

"I'm not going to be able to buy this car," he announced.

"Whaddya mean? It's probably just a minor repair."

"Maybe, but I'm not going to buy your car."

Billy slammed the hood and cussed a blue streak. They stared at each other for thirty minutes before the tow truck arrived.

"Afterward, I was so thankful," said Bruce. "I felt like the Lord was saying, 'Bruce, you weren't catching on too quickly, so I needed to teach you a lesson.' I depended on God, and I felt like he closed the door that day for my own good. A couple of weeks later, I came across a guy selling a '65 Mustang, a burgundy GT with a black vinyl roof, tach, tuck, and roll, all for eight hundred dollars. That car served me really well for five years. In fact, I ended up selling it for fourteen hundred dollars because Mustangs had become a collector's item. That was an incredible lesson not to jump the gun, but be willing to wait for God's timing."

THE ROAD TO RUIN

I wish *I* had learned that lesson in *my* twenties. The Lord could have saved me a lot of car-buying grief—and several thousand dollars. I also grew up in Southern California during those same years, but my Achilles heel wasn't muscle cars—it was *status*. At the same time Bruce was tooling around in his burgundy Mustang, BMWs were taking this country by storm. Germany's *Bayrische Motoren Werke* had created a sensation with its boxy coupes and sleek, expensive sedans. I was living at home with my parents and paying fifty dollars a month for room and board, so I had stashed a few bucks away. I decided I could afford the "ultimate driving machine."

A San Diego BMW dealership had the perfect car waiting for me: a white, three-year-old 2002 with sunroof, CB radio, and dual Weber carburetors. The salesman told me that Beemer could do thirty-five miles per hour in first, fifty-five in second, and seventy-five in third. I didn't have the courage to ask about fourth gear.

The slick salesman pumped me up, claiming that BMWs were in such high demand that they were *appreciating* in price. When I asked why, he explained that the new models were costing more and more, due to the dollar's shrinking value against the German mark. This pushed up prices for used cars. If I played my cards right, I would be buying an *investment*. At that point, I might have well said, "Here, put the hook in my mouth."

Cost? The asking price was $7,300, but the salesman said he could "sharpen his pencil" and "let it go" for only $6,700. Such a deal! I didn't even bother to dicker. With a few thousand down, the car payments worked out to a mere one hundred fifty dollars a month. With an annual salary of twelve thousand dollars, I could handle that with ease.

But then I met—and fell in love with—Nicole. When we became engaged, I knew the Beemer had to go. It had been an expensive toy. In eight months, I had spent twelve hundred dollars on repairs, but the engine was still overheating. Insurance for a twenty-four-year-old single male wasn't cheap either. It was time to unload my "investment."

Finding someone to take the BMW off my hands wasn't as

easy as the salesman had promised. After two weeks, my only offer came from a couple of Iranian students, who worked me over pretty good. I sold the car for fourteen hundred *less* than I paid for it. The cost of my one-year, ten-thousand-mile fling with status: a cool three thousand dollars, including insurance, sales tax, high registration fees, and gasoline.

Ouch.

A bit wiser, I turned around and bought a '69 Dodge Polara for three hundred fifty dollars. This nineteen-foot boat was just the money-saving ticket for our early years of marriage.

WHEELING AND DEALING

Perhaps you have a similar story to tell about the impertinent days of your youth. Now you're a little older and a little wiser. You've heard financial counselors say in a deep tone of voice that cars are the "second biggest purchase you'll ever make." But the truth is that autos are the biggest purchase you'll ever make of a *depreciating asset.*

Unlike homes, which usually increase in value, automobiles (especially new ones) are monetary sinkholes. But most of us rely on this convenient mode of door-to-door transportation. We drive to work, we carpool the kids to school, and we go grocery shopping. Unless we live in a small town or a large city with plenty of mass transit, cars are almost essential to everyday living.

So, how can you save money on this "essential" of modern-day life?

• buy new or used cars as cheaply as you can
• keep a car well-maintained
• shop for the best insurance deal
• look for ways to drive less miles

Let's expand on the last suggestion. The American Automobile Association calculated the driving costs for two 1993 cars: a Ford Escort LX and a Ford Taurus GL. Fuel costs were based on an average price of $1.22 per gallon of regular unleaded fuel; insurance figures were based on personal use of vehicles driven less than ten miles to work, with no young drivers. Each car was driven fifteen thousand miles per year. They calculated operating costs and ownership costs separately.

	Ford Escort	Ford Taurus
Gasoline and oil	4.8 cents	6.0 cents
Maintenance	2.2 cents	2.4 cents
Tires	0.7 cents	0.9 cents
Operating cost per mile	7.7 cents	9.3 cents
Annual operating cost	$1,155	$1,395
Comprehensive insurance ($250 deductible)	$133	$107

	Ford Escort	Ford Taurus
Collision insurance ($500 deductible)	$266	$232
Bodily injury and property damage ($100,000, $300,000, and $50,000)	$385	$385
License and registration fees	$147	$183
Depreciation	$2,412	$2,883
Annual ownership cost	$3,343	$3,790

Annual operating cost	$1,155	$1,395
Annual ownership cost	$3,343	$3,790
Total annual operating cost	$4,498	$5,185
Total cost per mile: cents	30 cents	3 4 . 5

(Finance charges, which were not included, can add five hundred to one thousand a year to the cost of driving. We'll talk more about the high cost of financing later.)

If you want to calculate how much it costs you to drive without going through months of bills and receipts, you could use these AAA calculations as a rough guide. If your car is more like a '93 Escort (a late-model economy car with good gas mileage), then your cost-per-mile would be approximately thirty cents. If your car is more similar to a '93 Taurus sedan, your cost-per-mile would be 15 percent higher or roughly thirty-five cents per mile. In other words, a one-hundred-mile round-trip to a baseball game would cost you around thirty to thirty-five dollars, while fifty miles of running errands would be fifteen to seventeen dollars. You can see how this could begin to add up.

We know that driving an older car can cut transportation costs. But how much? Suppose you drive an '87 Escort or an '88 Taurus. Obviously, depreciation costs would be lower because older cars are worth much less. If you figure a generous annual depreciation of five hundred dollars for the Escort and one thousand dollars for the Taurus, and drop your collision insurance as no longer necessary, your cost per mile would come to 14.4 cents and 19.2 cents, respectively. That's a savings of up to 50 percent over the '93 models. If you own two older cars, your savings could add up to approximately five thousand a year!

"Wait a minute," you might argue. "It doesn't cost *that* much to operate a car." Yes, it does. Even driving two '88 model cars probably costs you approximately seventeen cents a mile. Putting fifteen thousand miles on them over twelve months would cost you $5,100 or $425 a month. And that's if you make it through the year without a major repair!

Cutting mileage puts money in your pocket. Sure, it's a hassle to carpool to work, but can you arrange to share a ride even two days a week? Carpooling the kids to little league with another mom would save money, as would doing all your daily errands in one trip.

A VISIT TO THE SHOWROOM

You should base your decision to drive a new or used car on what you can afford and how much you want to spend. But if you're thinking of buying a new car in the near future, I could offer a few tips. I confess that I bought a new family car in 1993. I divulge this information hesitantly because those of you driving '79 Dodge Darts might think I can no longer identify with you. But I can. I've owned my share of "mature" cars over the years. In fact, I still drive to work each day in my 1982 GMC S-15 pickup with 105,000 miles. Dents and all, I have no desire to upgrade.

We purchased a new minivan because our family car, a Subaru GL station wagon with 170,000 miles, was dying. I saw the handwriting on the wall as we chugged up Colorado's mountain passes in second gear and spent over two thousand dollars in repairs in one year. With the Suby obviously on its last legs, Nicole and I brought the matter before the Lord. We wanted to buy a minivan as a practical family car, but we asked God to help us answer the question: new or used? In the end, we purchased a new Mercury Villager—which tapped out years of savings. Why did we make this decision?

• **First, good used cars still cost a lot.** We shopped the dealer lots and found that two-year-old Dodge Caravans with

20,000 miles—clean but with their share of nicks—were selling for $16,000 to $18,000. We couldn't find anything for sale through a private party; most families either hang on to their minivans or trade them in for new models. These versatile vehicles always seem to be in high demand. In the end, I was able to purchase a new Villager GS for just one thousand dollars more than a year-old Caravan.

• **Second, our research pointed us toward the Mercury Villager**, rated number one by *Consumer Reports* in the minivan category. I also kept a file on what other consumer and automobile magazines said about minivans. They all agreed the Villager was an excellent car.

• **Third, we considered this as a purchase for the long haul.** Consumer advisors say a new car pays for itself if you keep it at least seven years. We're prepared to do that.

In the last few years, three developments have leveled the playing field when it comes to buying from a dealer: "no-dicker" stickers; value pricing; and *Consumer Reports'* Auto Price Service.

"No-dicker" stickers. More and more dealers are switching to "one-price" shopping. Perhaps you've seen ads in which a local dealership makes a big deal about slapping their best price on the window and not deviating from it.

No-dicker dealers, which number more than fifteen hundred across the country, are following a trend started by General Motors in 1990 with the introduction of the Saturn and its one-price, take-it-or-leave-it price structure. Many auto dealers continue to resist the idea, however, believing profits will be trimmed. They tend to make more money when they control the negotiating. Those who have tried this new approach report that business is better because customers prefer to avoid the hassle of negotiating.

How do you find "no-dicker" dealers? You'll be able to tell the minute you walk onto the lot. Next to the sticker price will be a dealer sticker advertising "Our Low As We Can Go" price.

You can confirm the "no-dicker" policy when a salesperson approaches you.

Recommendation: a "no-dicker" sticker may not get you the very best deal, but it can still get you a very good price. Those who prefer to haggle with salespeople over a few hundred dollars difference should buy from a traditional dealer. But for those who know negotiating is *not* their forte, no-dicker deals could be a wise route to go.

Value pricing. GM and Ford are wising up. The automakers are cranking out special editions of their cars with a fixed set of options (air conditioning, power windows, anti-lock brakes, cruise control, and stereo system), putting one low price on the rear window, and relying on volume to make a profit. Value pricing is also a move by Detroit to streamline its byzantine price structure and patchwork array of rebates and discount gimmicks.

A few import automakers are starting to adopt "value-pricing" as well, but Detroit's latest move will certainly put pressure on imports to cut prices. These days, American-made models typically enjoy a two-thousand-dollar price advantage over similarly equipped imports.

In the past, new cars came in three models: a stripped-down, "base" version; a regular version (usually called a GS, GL, or an SE); and a luxury version (often called an LS, LX, or LE). Customers almost always passed on the base version. Who wants a minivan without back seats or side windows? Sometimes, a good salesperson could talk people into buying upgrades they didn't need—pricey items such as leather interior, computerized dash instruments, sunroof, and "surround-sound" stereo systems. (Remember, a car purchase is often ruled by emotion.)

Detroit now begins with a GS or an LS version, adds options that 90 percent of consumers want (usually air conditioning, power windows, power locks, and stereo), and offers a discount for the entire package. Here are some sample prices for comparably equipped models ("MSRP" stands for manufacturer's suggested retail price):

Chevrolet	1993 MSRP	1994 MSRP	Savings
Caprice Classic	$20,042	$18,995	$1,047
Caprice Classic LS	$22,542	$20,995	$1,547
Lumina minivan	$19,975	$17,495	$2,480
Oldsmobile			
Cutlass Supreme	$20,086	$17,995	$2,091
Eighty-eight Royale	$24,572	$22,995	$1,577

These prices are actually cheaper than the stripped-down versions. For instance, Ford sold a lot of '93 Thunderbird LXs when it began "value-pricing" the car for $16,392. Compare this figure to the '92 MSRP, which was $17,602 for the base model and $19,497 for the loaded model.

Recommendation: if you want to buy American, look for dealers who offer value-pricing. New car buyers come out ahead because the dealers are making less profit on each car in hopes of increasing their sales volume.

Consumer Reports' **Auto Price Service.** I had read auto pricing books such as *Edmund's New Cars* and had never been able to figure out how much the dealer invoice was. But then, I have trouble reading an IRS tax booklet. Then I heard about the *Consumer Reports'* New Car Price Service (303-745-1700) when I was shopping for a new car. I ordered computer printouts for the Villager and the Dodge Caravan and found them easy to read.

Each computerized report (which costs eleven dollars for one car model, twenty dollars for two, and twenty-seven dollars for three) lists the dealer invoice in one column, with a second column that tallies the manufacturer's suggested retail price. A cover letter explains the codes and offers a few negotiating tips.

I found one sentence especially telling: "Unless the car is in very short supply... you should pay closer to dealer-cost than to bottom-sticker." That's true. From the auto dealers I've talked to, most deals are struck around 2 percent, or four to five hundred dollars over invoice.

You *can* buy new cars for less. Occasionally, you will see dealerships advertising "All '94 Buick Centurys at Invoice!" or "Factory Blow-Out Below Invoice!" Are the dealers making any money? Yes, because an invoice does not reflect true dealer cost. Each dealership receives a 3 percent "holdback" from the manufacturer, which the dealer receives sometime during the year.

Example: Let's say you purchase a loaded Chrysler New Yorker at invoice for about twenty thousand dollars. You were a tough negotiator. You know the deal is on the up-and-up because your *Consumer Reports'* New Car Price Service print-out matches the dealer's invoice. If that's the case, the dealer still made a 3 percent profit of six hundred dollars on the deal.

TIPS FOR MAKING A WISE CAR PURCHASE

Before buying a new car, take the matter before the Lord. Ask him for guidance. After all, you'll probably pay more for this car than your parents did for their first house.

Pay in cash. Interest charges, even though they're more advantageous these days, still add up. If you have to get a bank loan, plan to pay it off in twelve to eighteen months. Otherwise, stick to a cheaper used car. (Leasing is another option which I'll talk about shortly.)

Do your research. Study the newspaper ads. Go to the library and look through back issues of *Consumer Reports, Consumer Digest, Car and Driver,* and *Road and Track.* Read the *Complete Car Cost Guide* and the *Consumer Guide* auto books. Talk to friends about their new cars, especially their likes and dislikes. Where did they purchase the car? Was it a good deal? Were they treated fairly? Continue to network. Can you find any Christian-owned dealerships or salespeople in the area?

Generally speaking, try to purchase a GS or GL version with a packaged set of options. An LX model is usually three thousand dollars more for extras you really don't need, such as leather interiors and on-board trip computers. When you've narrowed your choice down to a couple of models, call the *Consumer Reports'* New Auto Pricing Service and use their computerized report to figure out the cost of the dealer invoice.

When you finally walk onto the lot, employ the following strategies:

- Play your cards close to the vest and try not to get too excited. Salespeople can take advantage of people who lose their heads.

- Test-drive the cars. You can learn a lot about the handling, engine power, traffic visibility, and interior noise levels.

- When the salesperson asks what you want to pay, start at $150 above dealer invoice. Be patient: this dance may take several hours.

- Don't tip your hand on what color you want; otherwise, you might be told that color is in "short supply" and costs more. (That happened to me when I purchased my burgundy Subaru.) Green is the hot color these days; will purple be far behind?

- Be ready to walk. That's the *last* thing a salesperson wants you to do. You will probably have to get up out of your chair a few times to get the best price.

- Recognize who is "controlling" the negotiations. Remember, salespeople are experts at this game.

- Bring your spouse with you. He or she can act as a "holdout," someone who's not quite convinced that this is the deal to make. You may have to employ a few acting skills.

- Remain firm. You're the buyer, and there aren't *that* many people buying new cars these days.
- Finally, seek out a Christian dealer or salesperson. I bought our Villager through a Christian dealership, and not only was it a pleasurable experience, I got an excellent price.

Automobile brokers are middlemen who shop the car for you, then present you with the best price they find. For example, the Automobile Club of America provides a broker service for its members. These brokers are knowledgeable and can keep you from being taken advantage of in the showroom. But informed buyers can usually do better shopping themselves.

After *Kiplinger's Personal Finance* magazine endorsed auto-buying services, reader Don Page countered that advice in a letter to the editor: "The truth is, the chief value of buying services is that they save time for buyers who are too busy to do their own shopping. Particularly among services that charge hundreds of dollars before coming through with a vehicle, the final price is likely to be higher than the deal a person can find on his or her own." I agree.

WHAT ABOUT USED CARS?

The used-car market has revved up in recent years. While a new car costs $18,000 on the average, the average price of a used car is less than half that amount: $8,700.

Depending on where you live, you should be able to find a good supply of clean, used cars for sale. The upswing in car leasing provides dealers with a steady stream of used cars with between twenty-five thousand and fifty thousand miles. Besides selling the best trade-ins, dealers also have "program" cars for sale. These are used cars with low mileage that were driven for promotional purposes (such as the Tournament of Roses parade or the Pikes Peak Hill Climb), or were used by auto executives and their families.

Generally speaking, you're going to find the best used cars at dealerships because they sell the *creme de la creme*. Dealers can't take the chance of selling shoddy products. Then again, used cars typically cost more from a dealer—and it's impossible for buyers to find out what the dealership paid for them. Some dealers are taking a cue from the new-car market and trying no-dicker stickers, improved warranties, and even liberal return policies, such as having seven days or five hundred miles to return the car for a full refund, no questions asked.

You can also find used cars at smaller "mom and pop" lots and from car-rental agencies, such as Hertz and Avis. These cars have been well maintained, but you never know who drove them. Here are some tips on the best way to shop for a used car:

- Go to your bank or library and ask for the Blue Book and the National Association of Auto Dealers' used-car price book.

- Be patient. The best price comes from private party transactions, but those are fraught with peril, too.

- Have a good mechanic standing by to give the car the once-over. He can save your hide.

- Be a good negotiator. You do this by noticing who is in "control" of the bargaining process. Many salespeople will start you off by asking a lot of yes and no questions in order to soften you up for the sale. Remember: you're the buyer, the one with money in your pocket. You can walk out at any time.

REPAIRS

A friend who used to work as a dealer mechanic once told me a revealing story. One morning, he pulled a service ticket for a Chevy Corsica, in for a standard three-thousand-mile oil change. Unfortunately, he misread the handwriting and spent three hours taking this off and putting that on. The final bill came to several hundred dollars.

When he finished, his supervisor noticed the mistake and walked the ticket into the service manager. "I guess we're going to have to write off this work," he said.

"Are you kidding?" replied the service manager. "Here, give me the ticket. I'll sell it to her."

The service manager called the unsuspecting woman and explained that during the service, the mechanic discovered several things wrong with the engine. "We went ahead and did the work, Mrs. Robinson, which we know is a little unusual, but since you're a valued customer, we didn't want you to break down somewhere on the New Jersey Turnpike...."

Mrs. Robinson bought it.

Other auto dealers have told me that's an aberration. Even so, how can you avoid such a horror story? Most important, employ an honest mechanic. The odds are in favor of being able to trust a Christian. Again, network to find a reputable mechanic. For example, ask your Sunday school friends if they know of a church member who does this kind of work. Another source might be a Christian yellow pages or business directory in your area.

Whenever I try out new mechanics, I always announce that someone else recommended them as performing good, honest work. I want the mechanic to know me as an individual rather than just another anonymous service ticket.

Sandra Aldrich, a single mom, dropped by my office one morning. Her '86 Pontiac Parisienne with 120,000 miles needed major repairs. The service manager at a local dealership relayed the grim news: the car needed a new or rebuilt engine. Estimated cost: $3,500.

"What should I do?" asked Sandra.

"It sounds like you need a second opinion. Why don't you call my mechanic, Jack, and see what he says?" Jack was a Christian fellow who had worked on my aging Subaru and pickup.

After Sandra outlined her dilemma to Jack, he called the dealership and asked some questions "as a friend of Sandra's." Their explanations sounded fishy to him, so Sandra retrieved the car and drove it to Jack's. He did some poking around and discovered the "engine repair" sensor was blinking because it was broken. The engine was fine! He charged her thirty dollars to replace it and saved her over three grand.

An honest mechanic is worth his weight in gold!

A BEHIND-THE-SCENES LOOK

The following interviews were conducted with two dealers in separate parts of the country. Read their answers carefully, because what they have to say will help you understand more about the car-selling business. They agreed to be frank as long as I protected their identities. Dealer A is the owner of a Ford dealership in the Southeast.

Q. Can you give me any tips on how I should negotiate for a car?

A. Everyone has this impression that car salesmen are a bunch of wolves waiting to tear you apart. That will never happen to informed buyers who take their time. Only people who rush into a salesroom, get dazzled by the pretty colors and the smell of new upholstery, end up paying more than they should. Car salesmen work on commission, and if customers aren't sure what kind of car they want, salesmen will make money on them. They do this by totally enthralling customers and then getting them to make a snap decision.

Q. So what should I do before I walk into a showroom?

A. Get educated about the type of car you want, right down to the particular model. Let's say you're looking at the Taurus and Hondas. Go the library and read what the consumer magazines have to say. Drop by the dealership and pick up the color brochures. Take them home and compare the two products.

Let's say you decide to buy a Taurus. If you see a man getting into his Taurus in the church parking lot, ask him what he thinks. Does he like the car? Has he had any trouble? What's the gas mileage?

You should shop for cars just the same as you would shop for a home. You wouldn't buy a house just because a real estate agent recommends it. Instead, informed customers check out the neighborhood schools, talk to neighbors, ask questions about the builder. They talk through the pros and cons with their spouse, and then pray about it.

You can also go into a service department and talk to somebody waiting to pick up his or her car. I'm serious about that. You don't have to make it obvious, but start a conversation like this: 'I'm thinking of buying a car here. Can you tell me how you were treated as a customer?'

I think it's important to find a Christian dealer. You can only know that by reputation. That's not something I advertise because believers don't want to degrade their spirituality by advertising. The best way to find one is to talk to other Christians. Word gets around.

Q. I've done my homework and I'm ready to buy a car. Now what?

A. First, figure out how much money you have to spend. You would be surprised how many buyers aren't sure how much money they've got to work with. You also have to know what your trade-in is worth. If you don't, you'll get the short end of the stick.

Q. How can I find out what my trade-in is worth? Are Blue Books reliable?

A. Most banks carry Blue Books, as do libraries, but a lot of dealers don't follow the Blue Book because it gives nationwide prices that may not be applicable in certain parts of the country.

I use the "black book," which is compiled from auto auctions held in several large cities and counties in the Southeast. There's a different black book for other regions of the U.S., and they are generally more accepted.

Unfortunately, many people think their car is worth a whole lot more than it is. If they want to get as much money as they can out of their used car, they should sell it before they buy a new car.

Q. I'm ready to buy. I've got the *Consumer Reports'* Auto Buying Service listing the invoice and manufacturer's suggested retail price. What should I do next?

A. In a negotiating session the salesman will ask you what you want to pay. I would start at one hundred fifty dollars over invoice. That won't work for cars in short supply like Mustangs or Explorers. If you make that offer on an Escort, however, you'll probably get it if you hang tough.

Let's say you offer one hundred fifty over invoice for a standard, run-of-the-mill Taurus. The salesman will try to get you to pay more, but informed buyers usually win because they know the Taurus is in good supply at any Ford dealership. They can leave the salesroom and probably find one for that price at another dealer. Nationally, most deals end up at four to five hundred dollars over invoice. It really depends on the type of car you're trying to buy.

Q. What about the old stories of car salesmen throwing keys on the roof to keep the buyer negotiating?

A. Those days are over. The sales environment is totally different now. This is a competitive business, and no dealer wants to sell a car to a person they'll never see again.

Let me tell you why dealers are so concerned about customer satisfaction. At Ford, we call customer satisfaction the QCP, or Quality Care Professionals. GM and some others use the term CSI, or Customer Service Index.

When customers buy a car from us, they immediately receive a survey from the factory asking them about their buying experience with the dealer. These surveys are taken very seriously in Detroit, which uses the results to rate the dealers. Ford makes a big deal about it, and the QCP has become a point of pride among the dealers. If you have bad scores, you're a bum in the industry.

The QCP is one of three measures I track at my dealership: market share and profit are the other two. I pay my general manager a commission based on how we did in all three categories. I can't maintain a high market share if we don't have a high QCP, and without high penetration, there won't be a profit. All three work together.

I will not take advantage and misrepresent the facts to customers. It's just not worth it. In fact, if customers don't like—or can't afford—a car, I want it back. If they're going around town complaining about my dealership, I would rather they return the car and let us refund the money. We'll even return the trade-in, if it's still available, or refund the appraisal price. If it's a new car, we have a thirty-day money-back guarantee. For used cars, we have a three-day money-back guarantee. Selling cars isn't like it used to be.

Q. You've got to be kidding.

A. No, I'm not. Our challenge is to meet customer expectations no matter what they are. The dealer who can accomplish that will succeed. Let me tell you something. All the cars being built today are basically the same. Japan had the reputation of making the best-built cars, but that's no longer the case. The playing field is totally level, and the defining difference these days is the way the dealer treats the customer.

Q. A recent magazine article reported that American cars have a two-thousand-dollar price advantage over similar Japanese cars. Is this true?

A. Yes, that's true. We are also on a par with the Japanese on quality. Our initial quality is as good as anybody's. What we don't know is if we are on a par when the car is eight years old and has 150,000 miles. Will a Ford be as good as a Toyota with 150,000 miles? We won't know that until we get there. What we do know is that we are as good for 60,000 or 70,000 miles.

Q. How much profit are you looking for?

A. A dealer can't stay in business if he sells every car at invoice. With just the holdback, that's an overall profit of six hundred dollars a car. I can't pay all my expenses on the holdback—unless I sell two thousand cars a month.

Like any business, we have to make a profit to keep the doors open and to pay our employees. We are the only industry in the world where people think you should give them the merchandise at invoice. We're supposed to be Santa Claus and the Good Humor Man all wrapped up in one bundle. Look, I *have* to make a profit. I have to pay that guy who sold you a car, and we want to pay our service technicians a fair wage so they can put food on the table.

I'll tell you another thing that might surprise you. Generally speaking, dealers are a lot more honest than the customers who bring us a trade-in. I don't know why, but it must be something about the automobile business that makes it possible for people to feel it's OK *not* to tell the dealer their car leaks oil like a sieve, or that they put heavy-weight oil in the car to cut down on exhaust, or that the transmission slips every time the car hits fifty miles per hour. Somehow, people think dealers are fair game for that sort of stuff. I tell you, we are a lot more honest.

But I would look out for dealers who put 'addendum stickers' on their new cars. That's where you'll find add-on prices for paint sealants, fabric protectors, undercoating, pinstripes, or even a blatant charge for "market adjustment." A lot of these add-ons cost fifteen dollars to dealers, but then they might bump the sticker price by four hundred dollars. If you see a lot of that stuff going on, that's a pretty good indication of what type of dealer you're working with.

Q. What about leasing?

A. I love it because I get a two-year-old car with low miles, which I turn around and lease or sell to the customer who's in the market for a good used car. Everyone makes out with the two-year leasing plans: the customer gets a new car, the factory gets to make more cars, and we have prime used cars to sell.

Factories are giving a lot of incentives to lease a car for two years, and it's great for customers. They will have few problems with the car because if anything goes wrong, they're covered by warranty. And when they turn it in after two years, we do the big thirty-thousand-mile maintenance.

Ford is experimenting in Las Vegas and several other parts of the country with a *twelve-year lease* in which the customer gets a new car every two years. Ford is saying, "if you like this Taurus and will sign a contract for twelve years, we will guarantee you a certain lease payment for twelve years."

Q. Is it cheaper to lease a car or buy outright?

A. "You're always going to be better off buying a new car and driving it for a 100,000 or a 150,000 miles. That will always be cheaper. If you're the type of person who has to trade in a car every few years, then you should lease. Leasing is coming on strong. Nationally, 25 percent of all new cars are leased, and I expect to see that figure increase in coming years."

Q. What can you tell me about servicing a car at a dealership? It's always more expensive, and you hear a lot of stories.

A. Dealer service departments are more expensive because we purchase top-of-the-line computerized monitoring equipment and the latest body-repair equipment. Last year, we spent a hundred fifty thousand dollars on new equipment for our service department. We bought a forty thousand dollar paint booth for the body shop, plus recovery systems for freon and antifreeze to help the environment. We also paid for upgrade training of the technicians.

Servicing a car isn't what it used to be, and there will come a day when the mechanic around the corner won't be able to fix your car because he won't have a computer to diagnose the problem. All he'll be able to do is change the brakes, oil, and lube.

To Lease or Not to Lease

While researching this topic, I noticed many newspaper and magazine articles with headlines like "Auto Leasing Gains Favor" and "Leasing a Vehicle Makes Good Sense for Some." Leasing is suddenly a popular way to finance a car. It used to be that leases were for folks who didn't have enough money for a down payment and high monthly payments. Many people then took it in the shorts at the end of the lease when they had to make up for the shortfall in the residual value of the car.

Like new-car buying, the leasing game has changed in the nineties. The Detroit automakers are subsidizing lease arrangements so that dealers can actually offer lower monthly payments than a standard loan. If you don't plan on keeping a car for more than two or three years, it really is cheaper to lease than to finance.

A couple of years ago, I heard a top honcho at Ford tell fifteen dealers that in the not-so-distant future, our service departments wouldn't be doing much repair work. In other words, the cars won't break down like they used to. He said if we didn't start selling maintenance work like oil changes and changing brake pads, we weren't going to have anything to do. Five years ago I would have laughed at him, but not today. We're getting to the point where all we do is plug the car into the computer and that tells us everything we need to know.

What happens if you have a periodic problem, like a car that stalls at a stoplight? We can attach a computer to the engine and it will record what's wrong. Then our service techs look at the computer printout and get to work fixing the problem. It's amazing what is coming. I'm not knocking the little guy down on the corner, but he won't be able to keep up. It's economics as much as anything. That's why dealers are working hard to satisfy customers. We have the ability to know what is coming and to stay up-to-date. We are the ones in touch with the factory.

If you want to know how good or honest a service department is, drop by the dealership and catch a customer coming out of the service department. They can tell you a lot of things about the car and how they were treated. You can also stop people in the mall parking lot when you notice a dealer identification on their car. Ask them 'How was the service?' or "Would you trade with that dealer again?"

Q. What about extended service warranties? Are they worth it?

A. I would be very skeptical of extended service agreements. Most cars come with a standard manufacturer's warranty, which covers the car in its early years of service. Ford has a three-year/36,000-mile warranty, for instance. About the only thing it doesn't cover is a rental car if your car has to be in the shop for more than one day, or overnight expenses if you're out of town.

What dealers will try to sell you is a warranty from 36,000 to 100,000 miles. These warranties usually cost seven hundred dollars and have a fifty-dollar deductible. They cover engine, drive train, air conditioner, things like that, but not wear-and-tear items like brakes. A lot of people never use them, so what you're buying is an insurance policy. If you do end up using it, it pays for itself three or four times over.

The problem is that a lot of companies sell those warranties, and some go out of business or don't pay when they should. If you really want the peace of mind, buy only a manufacturer's extended warranty. Then you can go to any dealership and have your car fixed, and the dealer will bill the factory.

Dealer B is the general manager of a Ford/Mercury dealership on the East Coast.

Q. When is a good time to buy a car? Some people say you can work a deal at the end of the month because the dealerships have to make a quota. Is this true?

A. Sometimes that's true. We have a big nut to crack, and we'll take a deal that has less profit at the end of the month. I don't see too many customers trying to buy at month's end, however. I guess they don't know about it.

Q. How much money are we talking about?

A. Really, the savings is a couple of hundred dollars at the most, maybe fifty or one hundred. We sell cars awfully close to the invoice these days.

Q. What do you mean by that?

A. We don't make much money per vehicle. We have to sell a lot of volume to survive. We have some cars with only three hundred dollars profit, like a Ford Festiva. The Escort has a four hundred dollar profit, and the Crown Victoria has nine hundred.

Q. Should people try to buy a car at the end of the year because the auto dealers want to keep down inventory tax?

A. We used to have to pay inventory tax at the end of the year, but we got that repealed in our state, so it doesn't make sense to buy year-end here. For the states that still have an inventory tax, it does make a difference. Those dealers must pay three to five hundred dollars a car. An honest dealer should tell you whether your state has an inventory tax. December is our slowest month because we're competing against Santa Claus. But the week between Christmas and New Year's, we make it up.

Q. Have you ever sold cars at a loss?

A. Yes, we have, and it hurts. Sometimes we get a one-of-a-kind car on the lot, and it just sits there. We're paying interest. We have to move it out of there.

Shifting Profits

As an example of how dealers are selling new cars for less, car dealerships are reporting that 15 percent of their total profit comes from new car sales. Fifteen years ago, that figure was *75 percent!* Where has the slack been picked up? Answer: the service department. Service and parts now account for 55 percent of the average dealer's profit, as compared to just 2 percent fifteen years ago.

Source: National Automobile Dealers Association

Q. Are consumers better educated today? And what do you think of the Auto Pricing Service from *Consumer Reports*?

A. I can't think of any other business operated this way. You can go into a bookstore and find out our cost, but if I tried to find out what an appliance dealer paid for his washing machine, I couldn't do it. As for the auto pricing services out there, actually I would prefer it if every customer used one. That way, people would see that we have to make a profit, too. In fact, it would make our job easier because some folks think we have a ten-thousand-dollar markup when it usually totals one thousand.

Q. What is your profit margin?

A. We have no set rules on profit. Our philosophy is to sell to everyone who walks through the door with a price we can live with. Ford is making cars every day, and we have to sell them. Some models, however, are in short supply. For us, it's the Explorer and the new Mustang. They're the hot cars now. But we don't gouge our customers, although some merchants will. If they're old customers, we'll be very fair.

CHAPTER **10**

Fancy Stuff without a Fancy Price

When Chas and Amy MacDonald sold their home in Southern California and moved to Denver a couple of years ago, they built a dream home in a new subdivision. Amy had her heart set on furnishing their new house exquisitely, so she went shopping for a dining room set and master bedroom furniture—by phone.

Touch-tone furniture shopping? Why not? As you will see, buying furniture by mail-order is the equivalent of dialing for dollars. The MacDonalds had heard about several furniture discounters based in North Carolina, which produces 60 percent of American furniture. These mail-order companies sell name-brand furniture at deep discounts—20 to 50 percent less. When you're spending thousands, that can add up.

Amy called Edgar B (800-255-6589), one of the largest discounters, and asked for the 128-page color catalog (cost is twenty-five dollars). Although Edgar B, owned by furniture magnate Edgar Broyhill, didn't sell high-end Drexel-Heritage or Baker, the discounter did offer well over a hundred lines from smaller furniture manufacturers.

The MacDonalds zeroed in on Lexington furniture, an expensive, high-quality line. They wanted a cherry dining room set, china hutch, buffet, and six chairs (two with arms) for their formal dining room. For their master bedroom, they wanted a king-size bed, dresser, two nightstands, and an entertainment center.

Before Amy placed the order, she and Chas dropped by a Denver furniture store that carried Lexington furniture. They knew they couldn't rely on color pictures in a glossy catalog, so they wanted to judge the quality of the furniture in person. They also wanted to double check Edgar B's prices against retail. As it turned out, the store had the bedroom set and entertainment center on sale.

"Is this your best price?" asked Chas, in an opening gambit.

"Let me check with the manager," said the salesman, and the game was on. He soon returned and said they could take one thousand dollars off the sale price. That still did not beat Edgar B's!

The MacDonalds replied that they were going to order the furniture from Edgar B at such-and-such a price, but if the furniture store could match it, they would stay local.

"Let me talk to the manager," said the salesman.

When he returned, the best they could do was three hundred more than Edgar B, and the MacDonalds still would have to pay the 6 percent sales tax! They thanked the salesman for his time and placed the order with Edgar B. How much did they pay? The bedroom set cost $2,670, and the dining room set cost $3,306. Shipping charges were $905, which came to a grand total of $6,881. Since it was a mail-order purchase, there was no sales tax.

If the MacDonalds had paid retail at a Denver furniture store, the bedroom set would have cost $4,450 and the dining room set would have cost $5,750. Total: $10,200 with no shipping charges, but Colorado sales tax (7 percent) would have added $714 for a grand total of $10,914.

So the MacDonalds saved $4,033, or 37 percent over retail, and around 10 percent less than the Denver furniture dealer.

I know, I know. Who can afford seven thousand dollars for new furniture these days? Nicole and I certainly can't. But I tell the MacDonalds' story to illustrate a point: if you are a new-furniture buyer, you can save some heavy coin by using mail-order companies. Besides Edgar B, you can shop from Furnitureland (919-841-4328), Rose Furniture Co. (919-886-6050), Nite Furniture Co. (704-437-1491), and Hickory Furniture Mart (800-462-6278).

Some discounters, including Furnitureland, do not advertise their mail-order business so as to not offend furniture retailers such as Macy's and Ethan Allen, which account for 97 percent of the furniture sold in the U.S. (In other words, Furnitureland risks losing certain furniture lines if the department stores squawk.) Other discounters don't have catalogs, which means you have to visit a retail outlet and jot down model numbers and fabric colors. To thwart mail-order shoppers, some retailers alter model numbers, while others refuse to match the mail-order prices.

You can't buy new furniture on the installment plan with the 800-number companies, but then again, you should *never* buy furniture on credit anyway. Many discounters want a certified check up front since they don't accept credit cards. The MacDonalds said Edgar B does accept credit cards—another windfall of airline miles! But once you order, you're committed . . . no changing your mind. Some discounters will allow disgruntled customers, however, to exchange merchandise for credit.

In the end, the MacDonalds were extremely satisfied with their Lexington furniture. They had been told by the local salesman that Edgar B just dumps the furniture inside the front door and lets you assemble it, but that was not the case. "Edgar B shipped the furniture through an independent trucker, and he and his partner came in, unpacked it, and set it where we wanted it," said Amy. "Then they took away all our boxes."

Were there any nicks? "I found a couple of very minor scratches," replied Amy, "but that comes with the territory. They had paint pens, which they used to touch up the light oak or dark oak. When they were done, they handed the paint pens to me. They also told me I had ten days after delivery to make any damage claims. If we had noticed any problems upon delivery, we could have refused the shipment, and Edgar B would have shipped out a new piece."

If you're going to spring for new furniture, here are some tips if you decide to order through an 800-number discounter:

- **Decide if you can afford it.** It's like shopping for a car: once you test-drive the new model, the used one just isn't good enough. New furniture is outrageously expensive, so you better be sure what you want to do before whipping out the credit card. A decided advantage to mail-order furniture is that you can order exactly what you want.

- **Be prepared to wait.** It will take three to six months for your order to arrive. The discounters fill orders from retail outlets before individual orders. The MacDonalds had to wait six months.

- **Know what you want and order everything at once.** Shipping costs will be lower if the furniture is shipped together. There's no return on these big-ticket items.

If you decide mail-order isn't for you, here's how to shop for new furniture locally:

- **Furniture is frequently a negotiable item, just like a car.** The informed buyer knows that the markup on furniture is 100 to 200 percent. Asking "Is this your best price?" will send a message that you want to negotiate.

- **Give the furniture store a chance to match the mail-order price.** Some salespeople may show you the door, but others would rather make three hundred dollars on you than nothing at all.

• **Don't let the local retailers scare you.** Some salespeople will say the out-of-state discounters won't be able to service the new furniture. What can go wrong with furniture? Sure, a few screws need tightening or some assembly is required, but most furniture is taken out of the crate and placed in its rightful place. Your concern should be whether the item arrives scratched or damaged, but that's true no matter who sells you the furniture.

FURNITURE ON A BUDGET

The previous advice is for people who are financially able to purchase new furniture, but if you're like our family, you probably will never buy expensive new furniture. Like the MacDonalds, we moved from Southern California to Colorado a couple of years ago. The difference in real estate values meant we could afford a much larger home in Colorado Springs. Suddenly, we needed more furnishings.

Nicole investigated every used furniture store in the area, but nothing seemed suitable. We did find a good deal on a bunk-bed kit, which we assembled ourselves and painted white. We also scanned the classified ads, looking for used furniture from private parties. For a month or so, we didn't find anything we liked, but we remained patient since we knew there were no second chances. After several weeks with an empty living room, Nicole spotted a newspaper ad for new sofa sets at a private home.

We went for a look-see. The woman lifted the garage door, to reveal the entire garage stacked to the ceiling with new sofas, love seats, and sofa chairs still in their protective wrapping. "Did these just fall off a truck?" I joked. But I couldn't help but wonder how "hot" these sofas were.

"Oh, no," she assured me. "The sofas belong to a condominium developer. He bought a trainload of furniture, but then never built the condos. I'm selling them for him."

Her explanation sounded good enough. She had about fifty sofas standing on end, and the furniture was definitely new and undamaged. We bought a sofa, love seat, and chair for $675—a savings of $400 over retail outlets.

We finally found a nice master bedroom set in the classifieds—all hand-built by a local furniture craftsman. We paid $500 for a beautiful dresser, nightstands, and bed. I figured that was probably one-third of the original cost.

I highly recommend buying used furniture through the local newspaper ads or "thrifty shopper." You have to be willing to work at it, though. Be patient. It's a hassle to make phone calls and ask about the furniture, get directions, and look it over. In addition, the competition is stiff for name-brand items. Anytime Ethan Allen furniture is advertised, it's usually sold in a matter of hours.

Garage sales are good places to find cheap furniture, but sellers usually sell any nice stuff through the classifieds, since they know they can get more money that way. Estate sales are worthwhile because you can often find high-quality furniture and antiques. But again, the competition is stiff since well-advertised estate sales draw many lookers.

Lou Gage says she never buys furniture new. "There's too much expense involved," she told me, but she has entered furniture stores with the express purpose of buying "scratch-and-dent" merchandise. "Furniture stores usually have a room in the back with damaged merchandise," said Lou. "If it's a solid cherry wood table, ask yourself: Can this be repaired or stained without having to strip the whole top of the table? If so, you might be able to purchase a genuine oak table for $100. If it's scratched, take the finish surface or the varnish off and replace it with another stain or polyurethane varnish. With a little elbow grease, you can save a lot of money."

Lou says if you do buy new furniture, you should look for lesser-known lines that match the quality of the top names like

Thomasville and Bassett. "I wouldn't spend that kind of money for Thomasville, even though it is excellent quality furniture," said Lou. "If you have your heart set on a nice piece, go into a store and ask, 'What do you sell that is equivalent to Thomasville?' They may have something considerably cheaper."

If you're in the market for garden furniture, the time to buy is end-of-the-season. Target, for instance, will make sizable markdowns on garden furniture in the fall. "They are desperate for all that space," explained Lou. "I once paid $4 each for reclining lawn chairs, marked down from $25. Target wanted them out of there because they needed the space for Christmas wrapping and artificial trees. Most stores don't have the capacity to store large items for any length of time."

IN SEARCH OF SCRATCH-AND-DENTS

Lou says her favorite place to shop for furniture and large appliances are the Sears and Montgomery Ward scratch-and-dent outlets in major metropolitan areas. The stores might be called "Ward's Warehouse Outlet" or "Sears Scratch-and-Dent." If you can't find them listed in the Yellow Pages, call Sears or Wards and say, "I'm new to this area. Do you have a scratch-and-dent outlet?" (Since these stores don't deliver, you'll need to borrow a friend's truck—and always return it with a full tank of gas and some homemade cookies!)

Scratch-and-dent outlets offer incredible deals on damaged merchandise. In most cases the damage is cosmetic, and you can't even see the dented sides unless you pull the refrigerator or dishwasher out from the wall.

Lou puts this knowledge to work anytime she's shopping for a big-ticket item. When her oldest daughter moved out of the house, Lou decided she would give her a nice sofa as a housewarming present. She took her daughter to the local Montgomery Ward, where they saw a beautiful sofa for nine hundred dollars—not a three-piece sofa set, but one large sofa with wooden handles and brass!

Lou knew this was way beyond her budget, so she prayed that she would find a sofa for a lesser amount. The figure that came to mind was one hundred dollars. "I know that was asking a lot of the Lord," she said. She then went to Ward's scratch-and-dent in Denver, where items similar to the nine-hundred-dollar sofa were going for four-fifty to six hundred, roughly half-price. That was a good discount, but still a lot more than one hundred dollars.

When Lou is on the hunt, she always asks to see the store manager. Why? Only a store manager can authorize additional markdowns. "Here are the three styles I'm looking for," said Lou, showing her a catalog. "But I can only pay one hundred dollars. Do you have anything else available?"

The store manager scratched her head. "Well, we do have a sofa in the back that was dropped by a forklift. One of the

---

Run, Don't Walk, Out of These Stores

If you've never stepped into a rent-to-own store, be thankful, because those who've walked out with a television set or VCR usually get ripped off. Rent-to-own centers charge an average of 111 percent, but fail to disclose the rates to consumers, according to the U.S. Public Interest Research Group in Washington, D.C.

A report issued by the consumer watchdog group found rent-to-own stores charge between 35 and 396 percent for rental TVs, refrigerators, and couches. A contract for a rent-to-own TV set may be $15 a week for 68 weeks—or a total of $1,019. This, for a TV that costs $269 in a discount store.

Always do your math. If they say you can buy it for $15 a month, how many months do you have to pay before you own it?

boards running along the back was broken when it hit the ground." Lou asked to see it. It was *exactly* like the one her daughter wanted—the one with long wooden handles and brass.

"How much?"

"I'll let you have it for ninety-nine dollars."

Thank you, Jesus, Lou whispered, as she handed over her credit card. When she got it home, she pulled off the back cover and replaced the broken board herself. In one hour, the sofa was as good as new.

Another time, Lou's thirty-two-year-old refrigerator died, which put her in the market for a new one. She traveled to Montgomery Ward's scratch-and-dent outlet and said she was willing to spend one thousand dollars—and no more—for a new, top-of-the-line refrigerator. She had seen the fancy side-by-sides with ice water and ice cube dispensers in appliance stores for sixteen hundred. Did they have anything in her price range?

"Well, we do have what you're looking for, but it's twelve hundred dollars," said the manager.

Lou frowned. "I'll be honest with you," she said. "I have only one thousand to spend."

The store manager said, "Well, we are having this scratch-a-coupon sale today, in which you can earn an additional 10, 20, or 30 percent off. Will you buy the refrigerator if we can get you at least 20 percent more off?"

Lou got her refrigerator for one thousand dollars. "It did have a long scratch on the side, but who will ever see that?" said Lou. "If you're willing to live with imperfections, you can purchase washers, dryers, stoves, dishwashers, and water heaters for 30 to 65 percent off."

Lou added that the managers will try to accommodate you because they have to move the merchandise. "But you can't be arrogant. Don't say, 'How can you sell this refrigerator for twelve hundred dollars?' The whole game of buying and selling is that you are the buyer, but you have to be humble, especially if you're asking for an additional markdown."

Scratch-and-dent appliances come with regular warranties, and you can even purchase extended warranties. The big downside is no delivery. You'll have to borrow a truck from your friend again, and bake another batch of cookies.

WHEN YOU WANT IT OLD

I've always been fond of antiques, and that's because my mom filled our house with beautiful collectibles. I remember the time when I was twelve years old and my mother came upon an antique chest at a garage sale. The inlaid walnut was exquisite, but one of the legs was badly broken.

"Can you tell me more about this piece?" Mom asked.

"Oh, that old thing? I hear it's been in the family for years."

"Will you take seventy-five dollars for it?"

"Sure!"

When my mom took it to a specialist in antique repairs, he made an on-the-spot offer before the chest was even taken out of the car. "I'll give you one thousand dollars for that dresser," he said. That's when we learned my mother had purchased a Queen Anne dresser that was nearly two hundred years old! And no, she didn't take the offer.

Granted, that was a once-in-a-lifetime purchase, but antiques are worth the effort. To discover these treasures, you need to regularly read the classified ads and keep your eyes out for garage and estate sales. Another way to buy antiques is through auctions. As a former antique dealer, Lou knows this. She still dabbles in antiques, but that's like saying Jack Nicklaus dabbles in golf. In recent years, Lou has flown to New Hampshire and returned home with truckloads of antiques, which she then "wholesales" to dealers in the Southwest.

Antiques, Lou points out, rise in price the further west you go. In other words, antiques cost the most on the West Coast.

"The rule of thumb is never pay what they're asking. I don't care if it's an ad in the paper offering a twenty-five dollar antique corset, or a fancy store on Broadway asking five thousand dollars for an eighteenth-century armoire. Most antique dealers double or triple what they paid to leave themselves some negotiating room. For an item like the armoire, you have to decide how badly you want it and how much you're willing to pay."

If you're in the market for antiques, start by going to the library and researching the market value in your area. Ask the librarian for the section on antique pricing guides. Next, scan the newspaper ads for auctions. If you've never attended one, it's wise to watch from the sidelines your first time out. "I can't stress how important it is *not* to be a buyer at your first auction," said Lou. "Go with a friend who will hold your money—and keep your hand down—so you won't be sucked into the excitement. Otherwise, you could get burned."

When you visit an auction, leave your address with the company so you can get on their mailing list. Then you'll receive notices in the mail advertising the next auction. The handbill will also list some of the upcoming items, such as cherry dressers, antique glassware, guns, and jewelry.

If you're looking for a cherry dresser, first go price-shopping in the antique stores. You may learn that they're running about five hundred dollars in your area. If you can afford half that amount, that should be your limit at the auction. It's easy to go over your limit in the heat of the bidding.

On the auction day, be sure to dress down. Leave the gold jewelry and the high heels at home. Instead, wear blue jeans and arrive one hour early to preview the merchandise, because items are sold "as is." Look for cracked legs, loose fittings, warped drawers, missing pieces, or cigarette burns. This preview is important, since your bid will be based on your observations. Remember: the auctioneer's goal is to get as much money out of each item as possible; your goal is to buy as cheaply as possible.

The best auctions—called rural auctions, barn sales, or country auctions—are held in the outskirts of most communities. City auction houses must cover higher overhead, which is reflected in the bidding. And watch out for a "buyer's premium," which means you may have to pay a 10 percent surcharge on your winning bid.

If you're looking for country collectibles, barn sales are the places to go. Let's say you're a newly married couple in need of a sofa, dining room set, and chairs. When bidding at an auction, begin early and start low. The auctioneer will often start at what he wants for a *closing* bid. For a couch, he may say, "Do I hear a hundred?" Never give him that bid. Instead, start at twenty dollars and see where the bidding goes.

Keep in mind the auction industry is rife with dishonest characters. For instance, a savvy auctioneer will notice you looking at a diamond ring during the preview. Knowing the seller wants two hundred dollars for that item, he'll start the bidding by saying "fifty dollars, in the back," and look directly at you. As if on cue, you raise your hand to bid. A dishonest auctioneer will plant a "shill" in the audience who will bid one hundred dollars for the ring. Then you have a decision to make: should you bid higher? If you do, the shill will top that bid, forcing you to bid more. If the shill ends up with the winning bid, the diamond ring will be set out for sale again at the next auction.

If you're new to the auction business, you won't know which auction house does these kinds of dirty tricks. You might find out by questioning people in the audience. "How long have you been coming here?" "Are prices pretty good?" "Is he an honest auctioneer?" "Do they have minimum bids?"

After a couple of auctions, you'll get the hang of it. You may even catch "auction fever" and drag your spouse to the latest country auction every other weekend!

CHAPTER 11

Planes, Trains, and Automobiles

I have a prediction: Thanks to cut-throat competition, the friendly skies will continue to be friendly for families.

Here's the scoop. The major airlines—United, American, Delta, Northwest, USAir, Continental—are being buffeted by smaller carriers who serve peanuts and punch, fly one type of jet, don't assign seats, and won't transfer your luggage to another airline. In other words, Southwest Airlines and its imitators.

For families in need of four or more tickets, this is great news. All you need to do is keep your eyes and ears peeled for one of the periodic "airfare wars" that airlines inflict upon each other every few months. Then you and your family can fly for a fraction of what the first-class and business-class passengers are paying, and they won't arrive any sooner than you do!

The glamour days of flying have vaporized into thin air. Why? Because non-business travelers don't want to pay for all the "frills." We want to board a jet, fasten our seatbelts, and get to our destination. Low-cost airlines such as Southwest and its clones have filled this niche in the world of travel, forcing major airlines to reduce their costs in order to compete.

Southwest flies into only thirty-six cities and has just 4 percent of the market, but its presence is felt from Seattle to Miami. The average round-trip fare on routes between 250 and 500 miles that Southwest *doesn't* fly is $261. Where it *does* fly, the average fare is $115.

Southwest doesn't undercut; they just run a very efficient operation. They don't have a huge computer reservation system connected to other airlines. They fly one type of plane, the Boeing 737, which keeps maintenance costs low. Southwest jets spend less time on the ground—about twenty minutes as compared to forty-five minutes for the industry average. Pilots and flight attendants are paid by the trip, not by the hour. And Southwest doesn't transfer bags to other airlines.

If you're fortunate enough to live in a city served by these low-cost challengers—others include Reno Air, Kiwi International, Private Jet, Family Airlines, or Valu-jet—you know what I mean. More than ninety cities are begging Southwest to provide service, but they're expanding carefully and slowly. In the meantime, we can expect to see more start-up airlines because of the hundreds of 727s and DC-9s being mothballed in the Arizona desert, available for purchase or lease with easy terms.

SHOULD WE DRIVE OR FLY TO GRANDMA'S?

For our most recent summer vacation, Nicole and I debated whether to fly or drive the twelve hundred miles to my parents' home on the West Coast. Then I saw Morris Air—a Southwest wanna-be—advertising $79 one-way summer fares from Colorado Springs to San Diego. That sealed our decision. We had to buy our tickets two months in advance, and were limited to a 5 A.M. departure (ugh!) out of Colorado

Springs and an 11:30 P.M. return (yawn!). Our four round-trip tickets totaled $650.

How would that compare to driving? I figured the mileage at $720 (2,400 miles at thirty cents a mile), two nights in a motel at $100, and four days of fast food for another $100. The grand total: $920. But then I took into account the fact that our time was worth something, as well. The four-hour flight saved four long days of road time. With only two weeks for vacation, that would expend a significant chunk of our available time—25 percent.

While in San Diego, I talked to Michel Schmied, a long-time friend who went to elementary school in Switzerland with Nicole. Michel works as a project manager for Rohr, an aerospace company. Part of his responsibilities include working with Airbus, the European airplane manufacturing consortium.

Michel gave me his assessment of flying versus driving: "It all depends on distance. We did an analysis of traveling costs, and we found that a car will be cheaper up to two hundred miles. The train is more cost-effective between two and four hundred miles, but we're not well-served by trains in the U.S. From four hundred miles on up, planes are the cheapest mode of transportation. When you're driving, every mile costs you thirty to forty-five cents, depending on the age of your car."

If you've determined that it would be cheaper to fly to see the grandparents or vacation at a resort, here are some ways to save on air travel.

• **Develop a relationship with an on-the-ball travel agent.** Travel agents have access to major airlines' computer reservations systems, which contain more than five million fares in the U.S. domestic route system. Each day, more than one hundred thousand fare changes are made. Can a travel agent track all the fares from your hometown to your destination? Yes. Can a travel agent know about every recent fare cut? No. Nonetheless, we should take advantage of a travel agent's expertise and knowledge.

Often, it's better to develop a relationship with an *independent* agent, one who is paid by commission only rather than a salary by a travel agency. That person will be more motivated to give you exceptional service.

Let your travel agent know if you can be flexible on flight times, dates, and destination cities. If you request four tickets for December 19, with a return of January 2, you're not leaving him or her much room to maneuver. Instead you could say: "What is the lowest possible fare for Christmas vacation, and what do I have to do to get it?" By the way, be sure to tell your travel agent your children's ages. Sometimes on certain routes, the airlines offer deeper discounts to children under twelve.

Also ask your travel agent about applicable coupons and specials. You can find significant savings in "Gold C" books (the discount books many schools sell early in the school year) or in newspapers. These coupons are often overlooked, but the savings of twenty-five and fifty dollars often can be used even during fare wars. And more often than not, the coupons are accepted by competing airlines!

Remember: The air fare is the same price whether you purchase your ticket directly from the airline or through a travel agent. Travel agencies lobbied the airlines hard on this point because they receive a 10 percent commission on the base fare (8 to 10 percent on international fares).

• **Take advantage of air fare wars.** Don't rely solely on travel agents. Instead, keep an eye out for announcements of fare wars; the media often gets the information before the travel agents do. On several occasions, I've called my agent and asked about a new fare advertised in the newspaper—and she wasn't even aware of the new fare.

For summer travel, watch closely for fare wars between January and early June. Generally speaking, airline tickets will go on sale at least once during that time. If a fare war does break out, be prepared to purchase your tickets within twenty-four hours of making a reservation—a requirement of most discounted fares.

While you need to act quickly, you don't need to rush and buy tickets on the first day of a major airline sale. The airline business tends to be a "monkey-see, monkey-do" industry. If one airline launches a big sale, you can count on the other carriers to match the lower fares within a day or two. If you wait a couple of days, you might be able to book with the airline where you're trying to build frequent-flyer miles. On the other hand, don't wait too long, because discount seats are limited!

Taking advantage of specials means *planning ahead*. The best fares often require a fourteen-, twenty-one-, or thirty-day advance purchase. Midweek travel dates are sometimes less expensive, but you usually have to stay over for at least one Saturday night.

The catch: you have to be willing to commit your money for non-refundable tickets three to six months in advance. If you're thinking long-range, approach a travel agent who has a reputation for keeping a close eye on fares. Many of them don't want to be bothered—or don't have the time—to watch out for you. Meanwhile, stay on the lookout for announcements of the latest fare war in the media. Two heads are better than one.

• **Be a shrewd customer when you deal directly with the airlines.** First, be aware of "peak" and "off-peak" flying times. Generally speaking, airlines follow the normal school calendar. If you want to fly when the kids are out of school, it will cost more. If you can fly when the kids are supposed to be in school, it will be cheaper. Fares are highest over Thanksgiving, Christmas, spring break, and summer. For instance, don't expect to fly to Honolulu over Christmas or to Anchorage in July on a deeply discounted ticket.

You can often skirt the holiday premium by purchasing your tickets months in advance during a sale, or by taking the kids out of school a day or two early. You may have to be flexible on the return dates, as well. If that won't work for you, consider flying on the Fourth of July, Thanksgiving morning, Christmas Day, or New Year's Day. These are the lightest-traffic days of the year, which means discounts are available. If you homeschool, your flexibility gives you the freedom not to worry about peak traveling periods at all!

• **Ask for "flight specific" fares.** Some airlines offer severely discounted fares on certain flights between major airports. For instance, an airline may have a 5:30 A.M. departure or a 9:30 P.M. return that they will discount, while all other fares are sold at the regular price.

If You're Splurging

Have you ever taken a cruise? I'm serious. Arch-economizer Lou Gage recommends cruising during the "shoulder" seasons (early fall and late spring), when cabins are discounted. If you want to pursue this option, attend a "cruise show" offered by travel agencies. It's a great way to learn about cruise lines, and sometimes they offer "show specials" only to those attending the presentation. You can also ask your travel agent or AAA office for free cruise videos, which explain all the amenities of cruising.

Although cruises can seem expensive, they're actually a good value for the money. One price includes your meals (sumptuous, and you can eat six times a day), evening's entertainment, shipboard recreation, and transportation to the next port of call—all while you're relaxing and sleeping. In the Caribbean, you wake up at a new island each morning.

Many cruise lines offer family specials. Children sometimes cruise for half-price or even free, especially during off-peak seasons when school is in session. You might con-

---

• **Watch for "gimmick" fares.** Sometimes, the airlines offer "companion" fare discounts—fly with a spouse, child, or friend and get a discount. I've seen the airlines offer $29 fares on Christmas Day (fly out in the morning, return that evening), or special discounts if you dress like Elvis when flying into Memphis.

• **Get a group rate.** Do you have a really large family? Are you organizing a family reunion? Are you and another family going to Disney World together? Airlines give discounts to groups of ten or fifteen.

---

sider "repositioning" cruises—special deals offered when a cruise line is moving a ship to a different part of the world (for instance, from Alaska to the Caribbean in the fall).

Cruise specials, discounts, and free-air add-ons abound. If you can travel on short notice, a knowledgable travel agent can find you 50 percent discounts. If you're willing to take an inside cabin (no porthole) at the bottom of the ship, you'll pay a lot less. How much time do you spend in your cabin anyway?

Another way to pick up last-minute cruise deals is to watch the Travel Channel on cable TV. You'll see one-week cruises advertised for between five hundred and two thousand dollars. This channel also features great bargains on domestic travel, as well as foreign destinations. Look for the "daily special," which airs several times a day.

If you're not able to cruise on the spur of the moment, you can receive an early-booking discount by making reservations six months to a year in advance. The cruise line may even offer a cabin upgrade at no additional cost simply because you paid for the cruise so far ahead. Caution: you'll be shipwrecked if you change your mind. The only way to get out of a cruise reservation is to be hospitalized.

• **Ask for military rates.** If you are an active-duty member of the military, or a dependent with an identification card, in active reserve, or retired from the military, airlines offer special rates without blackout periods.

• **Ask for the "senior" discount.** Some airlines will offer 10 percent off its cheapest fares to seniors age 62 and over, and some airlines will even extend the same discount to non-senior companions. Many airlines also offer senior coupon paks, which can be real money savers. Each coupon allows a one-way trip to any destination within the continental U.S. that the airline flies. And the coupon pak is one low price, whether it's coast-to-coast or Dallas to New Orleans.

• **Check out the vacation department of major airlines.** Believe it or not, it's sometimes cheaper to book the airfare through the airline's vacation department. For example, as I write this book, America West's vacation-package department is offering round-trip tickets from Colorado Springs to the West Coast for $158. But if I booked through America West's reservations department, the quoted price would be $240! Your travel agent should know the phone number for an airline's vacation-package department.

• **Be willing to take "red-eye" flights.** Not only are red-eyes cheaper, but your young children may sleep right on through a coast-to-coast flight. You and your spouse? You're going to be tired, but you do gain another vacation day! America West offers many red-eye flights.

• **Volunteer to be "bumped."** If you're flying during a high-traffic vacation period, odds are high that your flight will be oversold. When you check in, tell the agent you and your family are willing to be "bumped" to make room for late-arriving passengers. The airline will usually put you on the next available flight and compensate you for your trouble with credit vouchers for future flights. You might make fifty dollars an hour (or better) just by waiting around—and keeping the kids happy.

• **After purchasing your tickets, still keep an eye out for fare wars.** If your fare drops, you may qualify for a refund, minus a twenty-five or thirty-five dollar service charge. Try to reticket at a downtown airline office or at the airport; travel agencies may also add a service charge.

• **Consider driving to larger airports for more competitive airfares.** We have that situation in Colorado Springs, since only a few airlines service our hometown. We've driven to Denver International (an extra ninety minutes) several times to save a significant amount of money.

• **If you can be flexible, you can often fly a regularly scheduled charter airline to your destination.** Charters typically service vacation hot spots—Orlando, Cancun, Los Angeles, and San Francisco—but many travelers aren't aware that they fly to many other cities as well.

Keep in mind that while major airlines play by the rules and match each other on fares, charters (and the smaller airlines) have to do things differently to remain competitive. Charters are especially good when flying to Europe. Or, if you have family near Las Vegas, Reno, or Lake Tahoe, take a "gambler's red-eye" and save big bucks.

• **Finally, remember to think through your frequent-flyer program.** Sometimes, the airline with whom you're storing up frequent-flier miles (see chapter eight) may not have the cheapest fare to your destination. If the ticket price comes close, you have a decision to make whether it's worth the extra money to gain all those frequent-flier miles. Generally speaking, your frequent-flier airline needs to be within 10 percent of the cheapest fare to make it worthwhile to buy the more-expensive fare.

Consolidators can offer even greater savings. Look in the travel section of your Sunday newspaper for advertisements from "consolidators." When we lived in Southern California, the *Los Angeles Times* travel section was filled with small ads from consolidators. These wholesale companies buy blocks of seats from an airline at a discount, and then resell them on the open market for whatever the traffic will bear. If they can't sell them, they're stuck.

Some consolidators sell nothing but TWA tickets; others specialize in European destinations. How good are the prices? Very good, although they won't be better than the "fare war" prices that pop up every few months. If you missed the big sale, however, check consolidators out because they don't require advance purchase.

Remember this advice in case a family member dies and you need to attend the funeral. Although many airlines offer "bereavement" fares, a consolidator's price might be cheaper yet. Be careful, though: some consolidators may not be able to get you the ticket in time on short notice, unless you're dealing with a local company.

Three national consolidating companies with a solid reputation are UniTravel (800-325-2222), Jetway (800-421-8771), and Travac (800-872-8800). I've used Travac on flights to Switzerland and received bargain-basement prices.

What's the downside? Some consolidators are literally fly-by-night operations that have disappeared and absconded with people's money. If it sounds too good to be true, it probably is. Some travelers prefer to use travel agents as a go-between in booking with consolidators, because they know more about how legit the wholesale company is. Your travel agent could ask the consolidator for its ARC (Airline Reporting Commission) number. A bonafide consolidator is registered with the ARC, an accountability organization for the airline industry.

SAVING ON THE GROUND

Once you arrive at your destination, it can cost at least one hundred dollars a day for a family of four to stay in a motel and eat in coffee shops. Double that if you stay in a hotel and eat out in nicer restaurants.

We frequently save money by staying with friends and relatives. In the last ten years, I can count on two hands the number of times we've booked a room in motels or hotels. We nearly always travel this way for three reasons:

1. It's usually the *only* way we can afford to travel. Staying out of motels and coffee shops saves hundreds of dollars a week.

2. We *enjoy* visiting family and good friends. More importantly, they like to see us (at least we hope so). The best memories are made this way.

3. The kids have buddies to play with. What can be better than relaxing in a lounge chair at the beach or lakeshore and watching your kids play in the sand with their cousins or friends?

We try to be good guests by helping with kitchen cleanup, lending a hand in the yard, respecting our hosts' privacy, buying groceries, and taking them out for dinner. And we always reciprocate and open our home to friends and family.

If you don't have any relatives or friends in other cities to stay with, search the maps for vacation spots within a five-hundred-mile radius. Any national parks within a day's drive? Any big cities with tourist attractions? After you've narrowed down the possibilities, write the chamber of commerce or tourist bureau for information. Describe what you enjoy doing, the ages of your kids, and how much you have to spend. Request informational brochures on museums, scenic areas, amusement parks, restaurants, and lodging.

Realize that summertime is when the whole world seems to go on vacation. The days are long and hot—perfect for family activities. The travel industry has known this for generations, and priced itself accordingly. Still, I don't want to dissuade families from taking time off during the year's best weather. It wouldn't be summer without a vacation, right?

Traveling *before* June 15 or *after* Labor Day can save money. When our kids were in first grade and kindergarten, we flew to Switzerland to see the grandparents. By returning two weeks after Labor Day, we saved hundreds of dollars on the airfare. Also, if you can avoid "bridging" your vacation around the Fourth of July, you avoid the high-season rates charged by resorts and hotels.

If your family wants to put all their vacation eggs in a Six Flags or Disney World basket, go for it! But remember that one day at Disney World means cutting corners along the way. Suppose you budgeted seven hundred dollars for a ten-day vacation. A family will spend a minimum of $125 a day at Disney World. Remind your children that along the way, you'll be eating a lot of picnic lunches and Taco Bell tostadas. Breakfast will be fruit, muffins, and yogurt.

Greyhound and Trailways offer travel packages during the summer months. If you stay within a designated region, you can often purchase thirty-day passes at a reasonable price. Bus tours, like Paragon or Tauck, are available across the country. If you can schedule your trip in the spring or fall, you pay a package price for hotel, meals, and scenery. For older people who don't like to fly or drive, this can be a wonderful way to travel.

If money is tight, you can either camp or stay in an inexpensive condominium or youth hostel. The cheapest vacation is camping, and many of the greatest family memories happen when you pitch a tent and try to get a fire going. Camping is an accident waiting to happen. State and national parks are usually the cheapest places to camp, but fill up quickly during the summer. Make your reservations early. In California, you have to reserve campsites at Yosemite National Park six to twelve months in advance!

If you're driving long distances, consider staying in KOA campgrounds along the way (a KOA book will have phone numbers). You'll need to make reservations at least two days in advance, especially during summertime. You're guaranteed a hot shower and indoor toilets. Some KOAs even have pools for the kids.

Try to participate in group rates. If you belong to an active and large Sunday school class, you might take an annual outing to the mountains and receive a group rate at a resort or group of cabins.

Christian family camps or "conferences" often appeal to both parents and kids. Usually held in scenic retreat areas, these camps provide meals, plan family activities, and offer varied accommodations according to tastes and budget. The average cost for a family of four ranges from five hundred to one thousand dollars a week. To receive a listing of different Christian camps, write for the *GuidePak* (P.O. Box 62189, Colorado Springs, CO 80962-2189), or call (719) 260-9400. This resource costs $10.95.

You can also save by staying in "gateway" towns just outside the national parks or major tourist attractions. Since the U.S. Forest Service allows only a few concessions inside national park boundaries, you'll pay a premium for sleeping inside the park. If you can find lodging twenty miles away, it may be half the price.

I'm a fan of condo vacations. If you've always thought condos were too expensive, a one- or two-bedroom condominium is comparable in price (or less) to a standard hotel room with two double beds, according to the Condominium Travel Associates. Condos have a lot going for them. They are equipped with kitchens, which means you can eat in and save on restaurant meals. Just eating breakfast and lunch at the condo can save fifty dollars a day for a family of four. You can also enjoy a homier environment.

Have you ever considered youth hostels with family rooms? I hear they offer an inexpensive alternative. Yes, the communal bathroom may be down the hall and the walls paper-thin, but a family of four can stay in a Los Angeles hostel for $32.50 a night—just steps from the beach. Or you can stay in a cabin overlooking Estes Park, Colorado, for $22.50, just a few miles from Rocky Mountain National Park.

To stay at one of the one hundred Hostelling International-American Youth Hostels across the country (or any of six

---

Renting a Car?

Car rental fees have risen dramatically in recent years. Do you know why? The Big Three automakers in Detroit were selling hundreds of thousands of new cars to Hertz and Avis at tremendously cheap "fleet prices." But a funny thing happened. Hertz and Avis would rent the cars for about twenty thousand miles and then sell them for considerably less than you could pay for a new model.

When this depressed the demand for new car sales, the automakers responded by increasing prices for their fleet sales. Since the rental agencies now pay more for cars, they have to charge more for their rentals. If you ask for the smallest car, they won't tell you about the cheaper mid-size sedan, so be sure to ask if they have any specials. Renting the cheapest car often pays off because you'll be upgraded to a larger car whenever the economy model isn't available, especially if you arrive late at night.

Try to rent the car over a weekend and for seven-day periods. Single extra-day rates are disproportionately high. If you need transportation for only five days, still book the cheaper weekly rate. When you turn the car in on the fifth day, simply inform the agent that you no longer need it.

Before ever driving off the lot in your rental, be sure to check the car for any nicks or bumps. You'll want the car agency to note them for the record so you're not accused of damaging the car when you return it.

Another way to save on rentals is to bypass the national agencies and rent from a lower-tier company such as Rent-

thousand hostels in seventy foreign countries), you have to join HI-AYH. Family memberships are thirty-five dollars a year—which easily pays for itself. For more information, contact Hostelling International-American Youth Hostels (733 N.W. 15th St., Suite 840, Washington, D.C. 20005) or call (202) 783-6161.

a-Wreck, Ugly Duckling, Rent-a-Heap, or Rent-a-Relic. These companies rent cars three to ten years old with sixty thousand to one-hundred thousand miles on them. The styles may be dated, but, hey, these cars provide clean transportation. Many of these agencies will come pick you up at the airport, but they often close by 9 P.M. Make sure you have a phone number for after-hour breakdowns. The tough part is finding these companies. If you know someone at your destination, ask your friend to check the Yellow Pages for "rent-a-wreck" companies, or you can call information yourself.

Before you leave on your trip, check to see if your car insurance policy covers collision-damage-waiver insurance. This is a favorite way of car rental agencies to clip you for an extra ten to fifteen dollars a day. Nearly all personal car insurance policies will cover you when you're driving a rental car in the U.S.; check with your agent. If not, you can pay for your car rental with any "gold" credit card, which *automatically* pays for the extra insurance.

One last tip: if you're not renting a car, take an airport bus or shuttle service to your hotel or final destination. Don't take a taxi! Unfortunately, some cab companies prey on tourists and take them for a ride—literally. Besides, taxis are always the most expensive way to travel. If you must take a taxi into a metropolitan area, look around the ground transportation area for other people waiting for a cab. Ask them if they would like to share the ride, thus saving everyone a nice piece of change.

Making those asphalt miles fly by—without losing your shirt or your mind. If your family car is on the verge of dying, consider renting a car for your vacation. A local mom-and-pop rental agency can make you a deal on a week-long rental. You'll also be saving on expensive drop-off charges. Many older cars can be rented for twenty-five dollars a day, and it's not uncommon to see weekly rates of seventy-nine dollars.

The other option is renting a motor home, which gives you all the comforts of home (VCR, microwave, even satellite dishes). It's not cheap, but it's cheaper than renting a room in a mid-price motel (or two, if you have a couple of teenagers). You also save on restaurant meals. Motor homes are totally self-contained, so you can pull off the side of the road or stay in a rest area for the night. My parents rented motor homes when I was in high school, and I remember those as our best family vacations!

If you're driving the family car, seek out hotels and motels offering family or AAA discounts. If you're over fifty, an American Association of Retired People (AARP) membership can gain discounts. I know, it's hard to request a "senior" discount when you have three teenagers waiting in the car, but it's worth asking. The same advice goes for military families.

As for breakfast, more and more lodging establishments are catering to families by setting out cereal, muffins, and danish in the morning. Breakfast "in" easily saves ten dollars. Many hotels and motels do not charge extra for children under eighteen who stay in the same room with you. If you have only two queen-size beds but five family members, perhaps someone can sleep on the floor with a sleeping bag you've brought along. That solution has worked for us.

In the lobby, you may find coupons for local restaurants and discounts for gondola rides, rafting trips, and admission fees. (Tourist bureaus or informational offices are also good places to find coupons.) Ask the locals behind the registration counter to steer you away from tourist traps.

Before leaving your place of lodging, be sure to fill up the ice chest and throw in a few cans of pop or juice. Your kids might stay happy for the first one hundred miles. (Stock up on sodas and juice at a local supermarket, since the motel vending machines usually charge seventy-five cents or a dollar for each drink.)

For me, what makes or breaks traveling by car is whether the kids behave in the back seat. We always bring plenty of books, coloring pens, and story cassettes. (*Focus on the Family* has a radio-drama series called "Adventures in Odyssey," which you can request through the ministry. Most kids between five and fourteen love hearing these escapades about children in the fictional town of Odyssey.)

Families, especially those with young children, have to be "vacation smart." Let's say you have a three-year-old and an eleven-month-old baby. You think how nice it would be to take the family to Disney World. But Orlando is a thousand miles away—two long days of driving. And you have only one week off from work.

Obvious conclusion: this is probably not the year to visit Mickey and friends. The kids are just too young and won't appreciate—or remember—the wonders of Disney World. And they will make the drive miserable, too. Instead, you might consider renting a vacation condo closer to home. When our kids were about that age, we rented a friend's condo in the California desert with a nice pool. We all had tons of fun jumping in and out of the water—and life was simplified. Wait until your kids are in grade school for a big Disney trip.

We've exposed our kids to local museums and cultural history, but we know they're too young to enjoy an expensive trip to Washington, D.C. Someday, I'd love to take Nicole and the kids to visit the new Holocaust Museum, the Smithsonian, and all the presidential monuments. But that's a trip better reserved for their early high school years.

Do all these money-saving tips work? Sure, they do! We've employed them over the years and taken some terrific vacations that we never could have afforded at regular prices. I remember the time ten years ago when Nicole and I flew from Los Angeles to Honolulu for ninety-nine dollars each way. Big Pineapple airlines—which consisted of a single 747—offered this special springtime fare. The jumbo jet had one class of seating: scrunched (they squeezed 504 seats in that plane). A flight attendant walked down the aisle with a tray piled high with sandwiches, tossing them to hungry travelers. That was our "meal service."

Our first child, Andrea, was just five months old, and she sat on our laps across the Pacific. In Hawaii, we rented a Wailea beach condo on Maui from a friend for fifty dollars a night (the going rate back then was $115). We had a pool outside the front door, and the beach just a hundred yards away. We stocked the refrigerator with groceries and ate most of our meals in. Even then, grocery prices were frightfully expensive. If we ever go back to Hawaii, I think I'll pack some basic foodstuffs (peanut butter, mayonnaise, nuts, jam, etc.), but I don't think our family will be traveling to the Islands for a long time. It's just gotten too expensive.

But I'm sure glad we went back then!

CHAPTER 12

What's Up, Doc?

Have you seen the bumper sticker that says, "If you think health care is expensive now, just wait until it's free"?

While America continues its ongoing debate on how to finance health care, I'm going to talk about this subject in general terms. Americans—and their insurance companies—spent an average of $2,868 per capita on health care in 1991, nearly 14 percent of the gross domestic product. Whether we pay the doctors and hospitals out of our pockets or the insurance companies cut the check, health care will always be a significant household expense.

Lowering medical costs begins with the person standing in the mirror: you. Only you can eat healthy and cut back on sugar-filled snacks and greasy fast food. Only you can exercise and get enough rest. Only you can listen to *your* body and see a doctor when something doesn't seem right.

Corporate America is starting to see the benefits of employees who take care of their bodies. Companies that offer employee exercise programs ultimately save seven dollars for every one dollar they invest, according to the Center for Disease Control and Prevention. Unfortunately, at least 60 percent of Americans don't exercise regularly. Doctors tell us that thirty minutes of moderate exercise five times a week—which can be anything from walking to doing vigorous yard work—will dramatically lower the risk of heart disease.

Bob Vernon, a former assistant chief of the Los Angeles Police Department, wrote a book entitled *L.A. Justice.* Now in his early sixties, Bob was describing his early morning jog three times a week. "I call it my 'Keep Bob Vernon Alive' program," he quipped. More of us should adopt the same campaign for ourselves.

Young parents are more likely to be in good shape just from trying to keep up with their children. However, this built-in advantage disappears over time. Jim Thorpe, who in 1950 was named the greatest American athlete and football player for the first half of the twentieth century, was asked to follow a two-year-old around and mimic every step, every fall, every sprint. Thorpe tried—but he gave up in less than an hour!

As you watch your children tear around the house with their unlimited energy reserves, ask yourself what could send an unsuspecting tyke to the emergency room. For instance, glass coffee tables with edges hold an unfair advantage over small kids. So do knives, kitchen utensils, and hot plates. Sharp tools next to the Hot Wheels in the garage are not a good idea, either.

Concerning safety, be sure to practice what you preach. Don't insist on bike helmets for your kids if you don't wear one yourself. In the summer, slap sunscreen on *everybody*—including yourself. The dangers of skin cancer are becoming better known every year. If you develop good habits early on, you'll increase your chances—and your children's—of living longer, healthier lives.

A PREMIUM ON PLANS

Why it is so difficult to save on health care? One reason is that much of the decision-making is taken out of our hands. If you work for a large employer, then you're probably enrolled in the company's health plan. It's that simple. If you're self-insured, it's a different ball game. According to my research and interviews, lower premiums may make it cheaper in the long run to have high deductibles, where you pay the first five hundred, one thousand, or even two thousand dollars per person, before the insurance company starts paying its standard 80 percent.

Mary Hunt of *The Cheapskate Monthly* offered an illustration of the cost difference. She said she raised her family's health insurance deductible three years ago to two thousand dollars for each of the four family members. This lowered their monthly insurance bill from six hundred dollars to less than two hundred. But when Mary's husband, Harold, went in for outpatient gall bladder surgery, the one-day bill totaled $21,000! Even after Mary paid the higher deductible and 20 percent of the remaining (for a total $5,600), the Hunts still came out ahead over three years.

Despite the high cost of health care, the odds of your having to file a claim of more than two thousand dollars are only 2 percent, according to one of my insurance sources. Raising your deductible can be an excellent way to go if you have a young family with a history of good health.

Other ways to hold down health-care costs—at least a little bit. Think back to a time when a virulent flu leveled you for days, or the time you were hospitalized for kidney stones or some other serious ailment. You probably didn't feel like living. But you quickly regained your vigor.

Then consider the courage of those who face chronic pain on a regular basis, or have been paralyzed or injured permanently. All of us can learn a lot from such determination. The fact is: many of us will pay anything to feel better when we're feeling lousy. If we don't have our health, what do we have?

• **Know your health care plan.** It pays to be knowledgeable about your health benefits. I know if we go to the emergency room on Saturday afternoon because Patrick can't keep anything down, it's going to cost me a seventy-five dollar co-payment. But if I take Patrick to a "satellite" clinic, my co-payment is only ten dollars, a tidy savings. My health care plan builds in financial incentives so that we use the emergency room only in an absolute emergency—not for my son's stomach cramps.

Read your health care plan thoroughly. For instance, it may specify that you must have pre-authorization, a second opinion, and a complete physical before elective surgery. Check and double check with your doctor that these required hurdles have been jumped. Also, ask your doctor to team up with other physicians who are part of your network, so that you don't end up having to pay for an uncovered bill.

Once inside the health care system, it's hard to shop. Besides, if you belong to a health care plan, the insurance company often negotiates fees with the doctor. Your attention should be directed to finding the best specialist in your health care plan. Once you've stepped into the doctor's office, realize that you are past the point of quibbling over price.

• **Become part of an HMO.** More than forty million Americans belong to health maintenance organizations. The reason is simple: cost. Those with traditional insurance often pay a deductible (anywhere from one hundred to two thousand dollars), plus 20 percent thereafter until a certain figure has been reached. In addition, prescription drugs and immunizations must be paid out-of-pocket.

Those enrolled in HMOs generally make a small co-payment for an office visit, and there are no charges for lab tests, X-rays, etc. The downside is that you often see a *different* doctor with every visit, and you may have to wait a long time for a specialist to be available for an elective surgery.

• **Opt for out-patient surgery whenever possible.** Anytime you can stay out of a hospital overnight, you are going to save a thousand dollars (or several). Thanks to the advances in medical technology, many surgeries that used to require several days in the hospital can now be performed on an out-patient basis, saving you and your insurance company lots of money.

Is shopping for the cheapest medical care a bright idea? Not as a general rule. What you can do is ask your family doctor to name the three best surgeons for a tonsillectomy or a hernia repair. Then you can call these offices and ask questions. How much do you charge for this elective surgery? How many cases have you done? Were there any complications? Are you board certified?

If you don't have insurance, then it does pay to shop.

• **Check out "well clinics" or immunization clinics.** Many cities and towns provide "well-child clinics," which base their fees on a person's ability to pay. Even the full fee will be less than a normal office visit. For example, a physical exam will normally cost fifteen dollars, as compared to twenty-five to thirty-five dollars for a regular office visit. Each shot will be about three dollars, versus ten to twelve at a doctor's office.

Unfortunately, many of these services are not well-publicized, so check with your local health and human services department, or even city hall if all else fails. In addition, many health clubs and even supermarkets offer flu shots every fall for seven dollars or less.

DEALING WITH DOCTOR

I recommend developing a relationship with a family physician based on mutual trust—even mutual faith. A Christian

A Brave New World?

My family doctor, Jonathan Weston, M.D., commented that solutions to the rising cost of health care are popping up like spring daffodils. Some people are trying to eliminate physician costs altogether with the aid of the computer. However, using a CD-ROM entitled *Answers to Common Medical Problems* might miss a serious diagnosis.

For instance, you may type in the symptoms afflicting your child (perhaps headache and fever). The computer will display an answer: "Your child has a virus. Give him plenty of fluids and see that he gets plenty of rest. You don't need to see a doctor."

"But what if the headache and fever turn into meningitis, and your child dies?" asked Jonathan. "That CD-ROM isn't going to bring your loved one back."

No matter where health care is headed, families will always seek the human touch. We instinctively know that a machine can't determine how we are really feeling. Our Judeo-Christian beliefs remind us that human life and the pursuit of happiness have more value than can ever be measured by dollars and cents.

Jonathan predicts that in the next five years insurance companies will focus more effort on determining how much a doctor spends on a per-patient basis. Doctors who order lots of tests may find fewer patients funneled their way by the insurance companies. Furthermore, doctors are receiving financial incentives to keep costs down and will be trying to spend less money per patient. The key question is: How far can medical costs be cut without compromising patient care?

Yes, it will be a brave new world out there. The best thing we can do to control costs is for employees and their families to practice defensive medicine: taking care of themselves, eating properly, and getting plenty of exercise and rest.

doctor can add an important spiritual dimension to your health care.

In fact, it might be smart to establish relationships with two or three family doctors—just in case you lose one when your company switches insurance companies. Businesses are forced to change health care providers like we change undershirts these days. My family doctor told me, "The days of having the same doctor from cradle to grave are over." (If you do change doctors or move to a new town, be sure to take your medical records along. Ask your doctor for a copy. This could save on some expensive tests later on.)

When possible, limit your office visits. If you're an established patient with a family practice, you can frequently get some answers over the telephone. A nurse can answer most of your routine questions. Example: "My four-week-old baby is constipated. What should I do?" The nurse may ask if the infant is on an iron formula. If not, she may suggest the child be given Karo syrup mixed in a small amount of water.

Don't let your doctors run up huge health-care bills just because an insurance company is paying for it. Meaningless office visits, frivolous tests, and excess consultations may be accepted by the insurance company, but eventually we all pay. Large medical tabs are passed along in the form of higher insurance premiums. Also, some insurance companies have a cap on specific categories. For instance, chiropractic care may be limited to five hundred dollars a year, or counseling may have an annual cap of ten thousand dollars.

If you are truly indigent or have high deductibles, ask your doctor (not an office manager or nurse) if fees for routine lab work could be waived or lowered. Some doctors have an unwritten agreement with a lab that allows tests to be done on a *pro bono* basis for patients with no insurance or a high deductible. A certain code on the paperwork sends a "signal" to the lab to this effect. Mary Hunt, who has high deductibles, said this approach worked when her husband needed surgery.

You can sometimes barter with family doctors if you're

short of funds. Do you have a service or a skill that they or their family may need? Perhaps you could do some painting or clean the carpets. Perhaps your spouse could do some house-cleaning or babysitting.

Ask your doctor for help in containing prescription costs. They usually know which generic drugs are equal in quality to the name brand, and when to prescribe a generic. Your pharmacist can be very helpful along these lines as well. Also, remember to ask for free drug samples. Nearly every time I've asked a doctor or a dentist, they've handed me free samples—which saves on buying the prescription. Large pharmaceutical companies put tons of drugs into doctor's hands to sway them to prescribe their brand.

CHAPTER 13

The Insurance Blues

I hate insurance. But Murphy's Law—*what can go wrong will go wrong*—has stalked me all my life, so I buy insurance for my car, my house, and my life.

I've made some mistakes. Seven years ago, an insurance agent dropped by my office and sweet talked me (and many of my colleagues) into buying a "whole life" insurance product. The premiums could be automatically deducted from my paycheck, said the agent. "You'll never miss it."

For a mere forty-two dollars a month, I received thirty thousand dollars worth of life insurance on myself and twenty thousand on Nicole. Part of my premiums were placed into an interest-bearing, "cash-value" account that I could tap into at a later date, perhaps when the kids entered college.

For six years, I paid into the whole life plan at an annual clip of $504. Then doubts began creeping into the back of my mind. When I investigated my options, I came to this conclusion: whole life was not a good idea for our family. So I pulled the plug.

I paid in $3,024 over six years, but when I decided to cash out, my "surrender value" amounted to $1,800. That means I paid $1,224 or $204 a year for two, dinky life insurance policies. "These amounts would barely cover our funerals," I joked to Nicole. As you'll see later in the chapter, two hundred dollars a year can buy a lot of low-cost, term life insurance—$250,000 worth for a forty-year-old.

I've heard the term-insurance gospel preached from many quarters: "buy low-cost, term life insurance and productively invest the rest." Now I'm a believer. Term insurance, in case you're not familiar with the definition, is a contract between you and the insurance company. If you're thirty years old and take out $200,000 in life insurance, then you'll probably pay an annual premium of $225 to the insurance company.

If you die, your beneficiary (usually your spouse) gets the $200,000. If you live, the insurance company manages to build a fund to pay any other claims, business expenses, and insurance agent's commissions. It's clean, simple, and easy to understand, as compared to the complicated and more expensive whole life, universal life, and variable life insurance programs.

GETTING THE MOST FOR YOUR LIFE INSURANCE DOLLARS

I buy my term life insurance from David Holmes, who sells life, medical, and disability insurance out of his office in Cross Plains, Texas. I came across David when I saw his advertisement in *World*, a Christian newsmagazine with a nationwide circulation. David sends his clients a quarterly journal, which is sprinkled with salty opinions and against-the-grain views. (For a complimentary copy of the *American Life Digest*, call 800-LUV-LIFE.)

An insider's view. To learn more about the life insurance industry, I asked David a series of questions. Here are his answers.

Q. How much life insurance should a husband have?

A. I recommend eight times his annual income. A Christian husband has a moral obligation, I believe, to provide for his family if he unexpectedly dies. First Timothy 5:8 states that the man who has not provided for his family "has denied the faith and is worse than an unbeliever."

A husband can't morally and reasonably expect the church or the government to be there after he dies. I normally assume that young fathers have no significant savings, so eight times his annual income will be the right amount.

Here's another way to figure it: for every one thousand dollars a family needs to live on each month, the widow should have one hundred thousand dollars of life insurance. Using that equation, if your family has monthly expenses of $2500, then you would need $250,000 in life insurance. In this way, your surviving spouse could live off the returns (calculated at 12 percent a year) and not eat into the $250,000 lump sum.

Q. What are ten-year, level-premium policies? Should I consider getting one of those?

A. A ten-year, level-premium policy means an insurance company will sell you a certain amount of life insurance and guarantee that premium for ten years. It costs a little more in the first couple of years, but when paid over ten years, it represents a 20 percent savings. I recommend ten-year, level-term policies until you turn forty. After you're forty, you should change to annual renewable term policies every couple of years and shop the best rate.

Q. Why is that?

A. Because it will be much cheaper. If you're willing to undergo a medical evaluation every couple of years after you're forty, the insurance companies will offer you very good rates. Let's say you have a ten-year, level plan ending at age forty. You have every right to continue paying on that policy without a medical exam. But the insurance company has no idea how healthy you are. Since they're in the dark, they must raise the rates to cover the unknown risk. At age forty, a ten-year, level plan costs $328 a year for $250,000 in coverage. At age fifty, without an exam, it jumps to $753 a year!

Q. So what should I do when my ten-year plan is over?

A. If you'll undergo a medical evaluation at the beginning of every third year and prove that you're healthy, I can probably find you $250,000 of annual renewable term life insurance for $340 when you're fifty years old. That's a lot cheaper than $753.

Q. So the insurance company wants me take a blood test to see if I have AIDS, leukemia, or some other life-threatening disease?

A. That's right. To change insurance companies or policies, one has to be insurable. To be insurable, you have to be healthy. Let's say you're forty-nine years old and you *do* have a deadly disease. You know that when you turn fifty, your ten-year plan will run out. That's when you should stay with the old insurance company, because they *cannot* stop you from renewing.

Q. What do you say to those who say life insurance is such a pain?

A. Quit complaining because you haven't collected on it. It's just like house insurance. Do you want your house to burn down so you can collect?

Q. Should I buy life insurance even after I retire?

A. Many life insurance agents are adamant that people need life insurance forever. I'm just as adamant that you *don't* need it forever. I encourage people to be out of the life insurance game by the time they reach sixty-five or seventy. If you have been diligent about investing for your retirement, you could drop out by age sixty to sixty-five. If you have been putting aside several hundred dollars a year into a productive mutual fund for thirty years, you would have accumulated a $250,000 nest egg for retirement or for your surviving spouse. Why would you need life insurance?

Q. If I don't have much retirement savings, how much is it going to cost me to buy life insurance when I am in my sixties?

A. For a sixty-five-year-old person to buy a $250,000 life insurance plan, we're talking about an annual premium somewhere between $1,500 and $4,000—depending upon the type of policy purchased. Most families I know can't afford that.

Q. How many life insurance policies have you sold over the years?

A. Over twenty-three years, I've sold between twelve and fifteen thousand policies. These days, I sell around eight hundred to one thousand policies a year, which makes me the largest single agent in the United States.

Q. Of the thousands of life insurance policies, how many have people collected?

A. None. They're either living or they've died.

Q. OK... I mean their spouses or beneficiaries.

A. Fourteen. Can you believe it? Only fourteen out of all the thousands I've sold. Of those fourteen, six died at age fifty or younger.

Q. Why only fourteen? That seems like an incredibly small number.

A. I advertise in Christian magazines, and my clients don't drink, don't smoke for the most part, and don't live self-destructive lifestyles. Their behavior makes a big difference in how they die and when they die. The insurance companies love me. That's the whole purpose of life insurance: it's there to collect in the unlikely event of someone dying at an early age. It's cheap when you consider how many policies an insurance company needs to fund a single payoff. If you're a smoker or have kidney problems, the insurance companies really can't afford to talk to you.

Q. What are the chances of a life insurance policy not paying off?

A. The last time a life insurance company did not pay on a death benefit was in the 1920s. Do you know why people aren't told that? Because it doesn't sell newspapers—or newsletters.

RECOMMENDATIONS

Based on personal experience, research, and interviews with life insurance agents such as David Holmes, here are my own recommendations.

- **Buy low-cost term life insurance, if you can afford it, and buy eight times your annual salary.** My beef with the whole life insurance products is that they are expensive. If you want $250,000 a year, be prepared to spend $3,000 to $10,000 a year. Who can afford that? Besides, I've never understood exactly what insurance agents were saying with those whole life plans. Remember the maxim: "Never invest in anything you don't understand."

- **Buy a ten-year level plan.** You save 20 to 25 percent going this route.

- **Shop for the best term insurance quotes.** If you want to check your local agent's quotes against a direct marketeer, call USAA Life (800-531-8000), Veritas (800-552-3553), or InsuranceQuote (800-972-1104). Or you can write The David Holmes Agency (P.O. Box 117, Cross Plains, TX 76443) or call David toll-free at 800-327-8963.

- **Buy from top-rated companies.** Look for insurance companies with at least an A-rating from A.M. Best, the oldest and

---

What Term Life Insurance Can Cost

Here are some realistic yearly premiums for a non-tobacco-using male:

Age	$50,000	$100,000	$200,000	$250,000
25	$87	$110	$170	$193
35	$92	$111	$172	$203
40	$119	$128	$206	$215
45	$160	$210	$336	$363
55	$165	$245	$440	$490
60	$207	$371	$692	$678
65	$346	$643	$1,240	$1,420

Source: The David Holmes Agency

most-respected insurance rating company in the U.S.

• **Live a healthy life.** The best rates go to non-tobacco users in good physical condition. Cigarette smokers pay the most.

Five insurance plans to avoid.

Disability insurance. It's expensive, which means it's not worth it. The last time I checked, disability insurance would cost me $36 a month or $432 a year for minimal coverage. That is too much for my budget. David Holmes doesn't recommend disability insurance, either. "In twenty-three years, I have never seen a person who has been totally disabled and couldn't provide for his family. Social Security already provides some disability income. I only recommend disability insurance for preachers who don't pay into the Social Security system."

If you're a small business owner and sole provider for your family, you might consider purchasing disability insurance that pays for a limited duration—perhaps two years—in case you're injured in an auto accident or disabled in another way. Short-term disability insurance is much more affordable.

Mail-order insurance. Toss those pitches you get in the mail. Life insurance can cost up to ten times as much as it would through an agent or a direct marketeer.

Credit-card life insurance. Did you know you can buy life insurance that will pay off your outstanding credit card debts in the event of your demise? But first of all, you shouldn't have any credit card debt, and if you do, you should be doing everything you can to clean the slate.

This insurance is expensive. If you have a $2,000 balance, it costs you $13 a month. For $156 a year, a thirty-five-year-old male could buy $200,000 worth of term insurance, or one hundred times the coverage!

Mortgage accidental death insurance. This rip-off makes me mad, because many decent folks don't understand that it only pays on *accidental* death. If you die of a heart attack or leukemia—or any other illness—your surviving spouse doesn't collect *any* money. Besides, how does one die accidentally these days? Auto accidents, for the most part, and the odds are astronomically low of that occurring.

Accidental death solicitations promise that these policies cost "just pennies a day," but the pennies add up. If you have a $100,000 mortgage, the monthly premium is $15 a month, or $180 a year. Compare this amount to a $111 annual premium for $100,000 of term life insurance (again, for a thirty-five-year-old male), and that would pay on any type of death!

Double indemnity insurance. By paying a "little extra" (only a few pennies a day, right?) for your life insurance, companies pay double if you die accidentally. For instance, a fifty-thousand-dollar life insurance policy would pay one hundred thousand dollars if you die in a plane crash or fall off your roof. But if you're in a car wreck and linger for ninety days or more before dying, your beneficiary won't receive a double payoff. As mentioned before, the odds are very low that you will die an accidental death.

TRAVELING THE INSURANCE HIGHWAY

Car insurance is another pain in the rear end. While most states require minimum amounts of liability insurance, the decision to buy collision insurance rests with the individual. Costs vary from state to state and city to city; North Dakota, Iowa, and South Dakota are the cheapest states to purchase insurance, while New Jersey, Connecticut, and California are the most expensive. In St. Louis, you'll pay $851 for the same policy that costs $1,456 in Los Angeles. Nationwide, the average two-driver family spends $1,000 a year or $83 a month to insure their cars. With that introduction, here are some tips on buying car insurance.

Shop the rate. Insurance companies show all the loyalty of a door-to-door salesperson, so I regularly shop around. I usually ask friends at work where they bought their insurance, which gives me some good leads. David Holmes recommends calling USAA first, then Allstate, Geico, and State Farm.

Lower the deductibles. David recommends a two-hundred-dollar deductible. I would recommend a five-hundred-dollar deductible, and here's why. If you have a small collision with no injuries, you shouldn't report it to the insurance company. You will get taken to the cleaners for having an accident on your driving record. In general, your premiums will increase for a three-year period, so you should pay for the damage out of your own pocket—even if the repair bill totals as much as two thousand dollars. It's cheaper in the long run.

Remember, insurance companies offer their best rates to drivers without any accidents or moving violations over a three-year period. Some go back as far as five years. Your primary purpose in buying car insurance is to protect yourself in the event of a major accident.

Does that mean you should have a one-thousand-dollar deductible? Not necessarily. The savings in premiums, I've found, are just ten to forty dollars for the larger deductible. Stick with five hundred dollars.

Drop collision. Contrary to popular advice, David believes in keeping collision insurance on his older cars if they're still worth more than three thousand dollars. He explained why: "I had a pickup totaled in an accident; having collision coverage kept me from a significant loss. I also recommend buying the normal bodily injury and property damage coverage of one hundred and three hundred thousand dollars."

Once your car is no longer worth more than three thousand

dollars, I think you're better off dropping the collision and walking away from the car if it's badly damaged in an accident.

Check out rebate programs for car and home insurance. In the last year, I've switched over to American National Property and Casualty because it started a new rebate program. If Nicole and I can go for three years without making a claim on our home and autos, American National will refund 25 percent of the first year's auto and homeowners's premium. For us, that would amount to $425!

American National figures customers enrolled in this program make a greater effort to drive defensively and have an incentive to stay with the company. It costs insurance companies more to write "new" business than it does to service a policyholder who returns year after year.

What makes the deal even better is that American National's rates were the same as those of other insurance companies I called for quotes—cheaper in some cases. Obviously, you wouldn't want to use American National if its quotes were 25 percent more than the competitor's.

Check to see if American National is available in your state. Another company, Sentry Insurance, may offer the rebate program in your area, but they require five years without an accident.

CHAPTER 14

The Investment Game

Rich Simons, vice president of Focus on the Family's International division, used to do some financial counseling before he joined the ministry. On one occasion, an airline pilot sought him out for advice. Having just been promoted to the captain's seat, the pilot was finally making more than enough money to support his family.

"What are the hot investments? Where should I be putting my money?" he asked, expecting Rich to describe a new pharmaceutical stock or a mutual fund specializing in Pacific Rim economies. "We both know those who stand still get left behind," said the pilot.

Rich's answer stunned the airline pilot. "Your house."

"*My house?* I've already got a mortgage."

"Until your house is paid for, don't come to me asking for advice on investments. Get your mortgage paid off, and then we'll talk about where to invest."

That, folks, sums up my armchair-quarterback advice on

retirement and investment. If you've got any money to play with, or if you recently came into an inheritance, put it against your mortgage. What can be safer or surer than paring down your principle?

SHRINKING YOUR HOME MORTGAGE

As you know, I am a magazine editor—not a financial advisor with experience in the stock market or precious metals. So I sought out people I respect for advice on investments and retirement. I explained who my audience is: families squeezed by the rising cost of living and a government hungry for more taxes. Their collective advice: prepaying your mortgage is a sure bet.

For those of you who haven't been able to purchase a home, let me amend their counsel: start saving for a down payment.

I know some financial advisors recommend mutual funds or municipal bonds, but paying down your mortgage makes more sense to me. The American dream—owning a three-bedroom, two-bath home in the 'burbs—is the last, great, middle-class tax break that Washington has yet to wrest from our grips. The mortgage-interest deduction is a sacred cow that our elected officials don't have the political courage to take away. Keep in mind that as Washington looks for "revenue enhancements," there is no way they can tax home equity.

You probably already know that prepaying your house mortgage reaps huge dividends down the line. Marc Eisenson, author of *The Banker's Secret*, has built his whole career around this concept. Generally speaking, making one extra loan payment a year will reduce a thirty-year mortgage to seventeen years. Even putting an extra twenty-five dollars a month against your mortgage will save you big bucks down the road.

So, which is a better *investment*? Putting one hundred dollars a month into a savings account or mutual fund, or applying it against a thirty-year mortgage?

For example, if you had a $100,000, thirty-year mortgage at 7.5 percent, your monthly payment would be $699. If you paid an extra one hundred dollars each month, your loan would be paid off in *twenty* years. That means you would save ten years of $699 monthly payments: a total savings of $83,880. If you took that same annual investment of twelve hundred dollars and put it into a savings account paying a steady 5 percent interest, your account would grow to $41,103 in twenty years. But with ten years remaining on your thirty-year mortgage, you would still owe the bank $83,880. By prepaying your mortage instead, you would come out around $20,000 ahead.

Of course, you could gain more by investing in a mutual fund that gave you at least a 10-percent return. In twenty years, a return of 10 percent would earn $68,730; 15 percent would earn $122,932; and 20 percent would earn $224,026. (One important point to remember: you earn the most interest *late* in the twenty-year term, so your mutual fund has to perform very well in the early years to build up a head of interest-steam. Also, mutual funds are not sure things; it is possible to *lose* money on a fund.)

According to David Holmes, whom you met in the insurance chapter, if someone thirty years old began investing $250 annually into a mutual fund averaging 20 percent a year, that person would have accumulated a $295,000 nest egg by the age of sixty.

That's true, but where can you find a mutual fund paying out 20 percent each year? David recommended the *Wall Street Journal*, which prints the five-year average of hundreds of mutual funds in every Friday edition. "It's a tremendous service that the *Wall Street Journal* provides, and it's available at your street corner. But don't trust me or any financial counselor. Read other magazines, including *Forbes, U.S. News and World Report*, and *Kiplinger's Personal Finance* magazine, which list the recent performance of mutual funds once a year, usually in their January or February editions. Another resource I highly recommend is a book entitled *Yes, You Can* by James

Stowers (800-345-2021), which presents the case for equity savings."

The investment route you take—whether to pay off your mortgage or invest in a mutual fund—is the literal $64,000 question for families, and it's one that should be prayerfully and knowledgeably evaluated.

Most people who sell mutual funds will base their marketing on the basis of thirty-year performance. Consider the fact that the greatest economic growth in the history of our country occurred between 1945 and 1975—a period of time when our nation was not carrying the enormous deficit burden and welfare costs we now face. When evaluating mutual fund investments based upon these historic trends, the significant question to ask is: Are the next thirty years going to be as good as the last thirty?

That's why I believe prepaying your mortgage is the *safest* investment you can make. But keep in mind that your mortgage payment is often 90-percent interest in the early years of the loan, so you will reap the greatest benefit if you can start paying down your loan *early*. The downside of this approach is that your money is not "liquid." You can't cash in during an emergency like you could with a mutual fund. And before you start making prepayments on your mortgage, you should have at least three months of living expenses in the bank so you can get by in case you lose your job.

What happens if you accelerate your house payments and pay off your mortgage in ten, fifteen, or twenty years? Won't you be losing a valuable interest deduction? Don't worry. Let's say that you're in the 30-percent tax bracket. That means for every dollar of savings in taxes due to interest, you have to spend $3.33 in real money. You will *always* be better off *not* having a house payment than having an interest deduction. Besides, wouldn't it be a great feeling knowing that no one can take your house away from you if times get really tough?

SIS, BOOM, BAH

If your child were born today, you could expect to pay $175,000 for four years at a top private university. In order to save up enough money, investment planners say you would need to put away $247 a month over the next eighteen years. So who has $247 a month lying around to invest in college tuition eighteen years down the road? Paying for my children's college education—around six years from now—is a daunting prospect. And when I consider how fast the years are passing, I know that high school graduation is just around the corner.

Nicole and I will do everything we can to help Andrea and Patrick earn a college degree. It's not that I want my children to have big-bucks careers. Rather, I want Patrick to have a well-paying job that can allow his future wife to stay home with their kids. Similarly, I want Andrea to be prepared to earn money during the early years of marriage so she and her future husband can save enough to make a down payment for a house. Then, when the grandkids arrive, she can be a stay-at-home mom, if she so chooses. (All of this is assuming that they choose to get married!)

Suzanne Sindt (our Swiss friend introduced in the credit-card chapter), thinks that the greatest gift a parent can give a child is a four-year college degree. "When we're dead and gone, what good will their inheritance do them? We'd rather spend it now on a college education for our daughter," said Suzanne.

My goal, if at all possible, is to put my kids through college the way *my* parents helped me. Mom and Dad paid for my educational expenses at the University of Oregon without my having to hold down a part-time job. Rather, they let me invest my extra time working on the university newspaper (which led to my writing career) and play on the college tennis team (which led to meeting Dr. Dobson on a tennis court, but that's a long story).

Because of their generosity, I graduated with a degree in

journalism and no debts. Although I started my adult career with only a few hundred dollars in the bank, I was worlds ahead of my contemporaries, most of whom had to knuckle down and start paying off college loans.

If there is any way possible, I encourage you to pay for your child's college education on an "as-you-go" basis. That may mean that your son or daughter will have to work hard during the summer and hold a part-time job during school. It could mean the wife has to re-enter the work force. It may mean having your child attend a local college for a couple of years. But if you can enable your son or daughter to get through college without any remaining debt (or with only a short-term debt that can be quickly repaid), neither of you will feel strapped.

Several friends who are in the middle of this college thing were willing to share some of the lessons they've learned. Their experiences may help you to prepare more wisely for such a huge undertaking.

Don't believe the sticker price. Many private universities charge fifteen thousand dollars and up for one year of tuition, room, and board. Yet these same colleges have "endowments," which means generous alumni contribute to the old alma mater—especially after a winning football season. At any rate, these endowments enable the college financial aid office to offer a small number of incoming students "merit grants," or financial aid that doesn't have to be repaid.

A merit grant may be as much as three thousand dollars, which brings the out-of-pocket expenses down to twelve thousand a year—still a large nut to crack, but not as big as fifteen thousand. Do you have that amount saved up? Who does? If the wife's salary is not going to cover that amount, your alternative is to borrow the money. You have several sources:

• **The college.** Most institutions will loan students a couple of thousand dollars a year, but that amount must be repaid by the

Fifteen-Year or Thirty-Year Loan?

Like millions of American families, we refinanced our home mortgage in 1993 to take advantage of the lowest interest rates in twenty-five years. If you were able to lower your interest rate by at least 2 percent, I hope you refinanced as well.

We debated whether to refinance with a fifteen-year or thirty-year loan, but we settled on the longer term for several reasons. For openers, the difference in interest rates was only a half-percent in our area. We could have opted for a 7.5-percent, thirty-year loan with no origination fee, or a 7-percent, fifteen-year loan with no origination fee.

The fifteen-year loan payment was three hundred dollars more a month, which put it beyond our reach. But Nicole and I can effectively make our thirty-year loan into a fifteen-year loan *anytime* we want. All we have to do is increase our payment by three hundred dollars a month, and our loan automatically becomes amortized over fifteen years. I like the security of knowing that we can always revert to making the regular thirty-year payment if we encounter some unexpected expenses. So keep that in mind the next time you're shopping for a mortgage.

One last tip: Don't fall for the "bimonthly" mortgage plans that you periodically receive in the mail. For four hundred dollars, a company will set up a plan in which you pay half your monthly mortgage every two weeks, thus saving you thousands of dollars in interest. Since every year has fifty-two weeks, that means you would be making twenty-six payments a year. In other words, you'd be prepaying one month's interest a year. Of course, that would pay down your mortgage! Remember, you can pre-pay your mortgage anytime you want (as long as you don't have a prepayment penalty clause) without the services of a bi-monthly plan.

time they graduate. The university will also offer a "work-study" program in which a student is paid for working in the dorm cafeteria or the college bookstore.

• **The federal government.** Parents can apply for a variety of loans from the federal government. Most students can receive between two thousand and five thousand dollars annually. The biggest loan provider by far is the U.S. Department of Education, which administers seven different financial aid programs. Loan decisions are based on four major factors:

• parents' income
• parents' assets, such as savings accounts and investments
• student's income
• student's assets

An eighteen-year-old isn't likely to have much in the way of income or assets, so the determination will rest largely on your financial resources. In most cases, these federal student loans must be repaid within ten years of graduation. Unfortunately, parents who have sacrificed expensive vacations and the purchase of a bigger home in order to save for those college expenses may end up being penalized for planning ahead. If your financial income and assets are above a certain amount, your child may not qualify for a federal loan.

For a complete description of federal loan programs, write the Federal Student Aid Information Center, P.O. Box 84, Washington, D.C. 20044, or call toll-free (800) 433-3243. Be sure to ask for a complimentary copy of *The Student Guide*.

• **Your company.** Many large companies, as well as labor unions, have college loan programs for children of employees. It never hurts to ask.

• **Philanthropic foundations.** Community organizations and civic groups such as the American Legion, YMCA, 4-H Clubs, Kiwanis, Jaycees, Boy Scouts, as well as fraternities and sororities, offer grants and loans.

• **The military.** If you or your spouse is a veteran, educational loans may be available. Check with your local Veterans' Affairs office.

• **Investing in your home mortgage or your company's matching retirement plan can be ways to finance your child's college education.** Although some investment counselors don't recommend it, parents can refinance their home or take out a home-equity loan to help get their kids through college. As for retirement plans, you're not allowed to tap into them without a major tax penalty until you reach age fifty-nine and a half. But some retirement plans allow you to "borrow" your pre-tax dollars before then, if the "loan" is repaid within a certain time (usually five years). Be sure to check out all the ramifications before taking this route.

• **Discuss with your child who will pay for what.** Anyone who is college-bound should know exactly what he or she is expected to contribute, and you should outline what sacrifices you are willing to make to cover the high cost of college tuition. You may want to reassure these young adults that you'll stick by them. If the Lord provides a decent job after graduation, then it won't be a great hardship for them to repay student loans. If they don't land a good job, then you'll reconsider what you can do to help.

• **If your child has a talent, push it.** If your child is an excellent student, athlete, musician, actor, or actress, I would have him or her study or practice as much as possible. You might tell your talented teen to look at the extra time spent studying or practicing as a part-time job. Would they rather be practicing their backhand than flipping hamburgers at McDonald's? More and more athletic scholarships are available for young women as well as men, thanks to Title X laws.

• **Have your child take any advanced placement tests and college-credit classes offered in high school.** Almost as an afterthought, I took several advanced placement tests in high school and passed them all. Coupled with a community college political science course I took during my senior year, I entered the University of Oregon with forty-two credits—nearly a year's worth. Although I had to hustle my final year, I graduated from college in just three years, saving my parents 25 percent of my education costs!

More and more schools are offering three-year degree programs to students even without advanced placement credits. Drury University in Springfield, Missouri, and Albertus Magnus University in New Haven, Connecticut, are among those institutions that make it possible to graduate in three years. Check your local bookstores or libraries for a copy of the *College Board Index of Majors and Graduate Degrees* to learn more about this option.

• **Take a video tour of colleges.** Visiting college campuses can be expensive, especially if they are out of state. Collegiate Choice (201-871-0098) produces video tours of over three hundred colleges. These videos average fifty minutes and cost fifteen dollars each.

• **Send your child to a local junior college or university.** Tuition at a community college is *much* cheaper than a state university. In either case, in-state tuition costs far less than out-of-state tuition at state universities. Having your son or daughter remain home saves a lot on room and board. This may not be the ideal situation, of course, since part of the college experience involves cutting the so-called "apron strings" from Mom and Dad. If this is important to your child, perhaps a compromise can be struck by agreeing to finance the last year or two at an out-of-town university.

Parents often debate the pros and cons of deciding in favor of a local college. If son or daughter remains home, remember that he or she will probably need a car, which can cost several thousand dollars a year. At an out-of-town university, most students who live on-campus can get by with just a bike. (I never had a car during college, so there.)

• **Check out EE bonds.** Government EE bonds are currently paying around 4 percent, but if you use them to pay college tuition, they are tax free. They are not a wise investment compared to mutual funds, however.

• **Despite the high cost, consider Christian colleges.** Can I make a pitch for a Christian education here? Yes, private colleges cost more than state universities, but weigh the benefits—perhaps eternal—of having your son or daughter taught by Christian mentors and role models during this crucial time of transition.

Dr. Dobson feels strongly about the importance of a Christian education. In one of his monthly newsletters, he wrote, "The single greatest influence during the college years does not come from the faculty. It is derived from other students! Thus, being classmates with men and women who profess a faith in Jesus Christ is vital to the bonding that should occur during those four years."

You can find some deals on Christian education out there, too. Grove City College in Pennsylvania, for instance, is an excellent institution of higher learning, and 1994 students were paying a little less than $8,000 a year for room, board, and tuition!

THOSE GOLDEN YEARS

Most of us are looking forward to retirement. You better start planning for it, especially if you've hit forty. Nearly 40 percent of U.S. households have no retirement savings at all, and those who do don't have much set aside. Nearly eight out of ten Americans—some seventy-six million households—will have less than half the income they need for their retirement years, according to a study by Arthur D. Little.

I include myself in the latter category. I just turned forty, and guess what? I'm starting to think more seriously about retirement. Until the last year, that's all I was doing: thinking. Then I talked to an uncle in the insurance business about retirement. He offered this advice: "Start doing something, even if it's setting aside twenty-five dollars a paycheck." So that's what I'm doing—putting twenty-five dollars out of each paycheck into a tax-sheltered annuity.

Retirement plans come in different guises—such as IRAs, 401(k)s, or 403(b)s—which allow workers to set aside tax-free money into stocks, mutual funds, and bonds. If your company matches your retirement fund contribution, then you've just made a 100 percent return. Let's see an insurance agent try to match that!

I'm participating in Focus on the Family's retirement plan, but I must "self-manage" it. In other words, I'm responsible for choosing where I put my tax-sheltered annuity dollars. I've listened to several investment counselors pitch their advice, but I've always felt uneasy leaving the decision to a commission-based financial advisor. Why? Simple. I don't trust other people with my money. I feel more comfortable talking to family members, co-workers, and reading newspapers and financial magazines for advice, especially *Kiplinger's Personal Finance* magazine, which offers a "reality check" of how well each mutual fund protected investors' capital when the stock or bond market declined.

Investing in stocks and mutual funds carries varying degrees of risk. An informed buyer—just like an informed car buyer—can educate himself about the investment market. I would encourage you to seek out "no-load" (no sales charge) funds and self-manage your own retirement plan.

I would also be careful about investing in expensive newsletters touting investment advice. I remember the time John Stossel of ABC's "20/20" newsmagazine threw darts against a board printed with all the Standard & Poor's 500 blue-chip stocks. Wherever Stossel's dozen darts landed, he purchased that stock (it was ABC's money, of course). Then he tracked how his stocks performed against those recommended by Wall Street advisors in their "private" newsletters. Stossel's dart-throwing method beat out nearly every financial advisor's advice!

If you want to know how the various investment newsletters' predictions have fared, the *Hulbert Financial Digest* (published out of Alexandria, Virginia) tracks their performance.

A WEEKEND AT BERNIE'S

Bernie Minton, president of Physician Credentialing Services and a financial and management consultant to several medical companies in Southern California, has furnished me with tremendous insights—and funny stories—in my three previous books. For instance, in *Daddy's Home,* he shared his secrets of inexpensively romancing his wife, Elaine, as the "Master of the Cheap Date." In this latest interview, forty-seven-year-old Bernie offered his views on retirement.

Q. What should families be doing about investments and retirement?

A. I have little confidence that I will ever see the money I have put into the social security system. With the economy so uncertain and companies cutting back on retirement plans, I think our parents' generation will be the last one to have had broad-based retirement plans.

Q. Gee, you're a lot of help.

A. Fortunately, we serve a mighty God. I try to put into practice Matthew 6:33-34, which says you should "...give him first place in your life and live as he wants you to. So don't be anxious about tomorrow. God will take care of your tomorrow, too. Live one day at a time."

From the time when Elaine and I got married, even when

we didn't have much, we always tithed to the Lord and lived on what was left over. We wanted her to be at home and raise our children. This meant that many times I carried an extra part-time job, and Elaine did her best to stretch our funds. But I am convinced that it was not just our hard work and budgeting, but our faithfulness in tithing that made our budget balance. Not only did God bring money into the front door, but, more importantly, he arranged opportunities to keep that money from flowing out the back door.

For example, we did not have to buy our kids new clothes until they were eight and ten years old. A neighbor with a son just a little older than ours sold us her son's top-quality, outgrown clothing for a fraction of the cost. Our two boys dressed in styles and brands that I could have never afforded. I keep this example in Matthew 6 in mind when I look at retirement.

Q. So, how has that affected your view of retirement?

A. Although I'm able to earn more now, I still live conservatively. I have saved a little, but my biggest investment is in the Lord's work. I used to think retirement meant kicking back in a rocking chair and puttering around the house. But that view has changed. I don't think there will come a time in my life when I will quit work and live entirely off of what I have saved.

My goal is to get my expenses down. I hope to do this by paying off my home mortgage and getting my two boys through college. When these financial obligations are behind me, I want to cut back on the hours I spend earning a living and spend more and more hours involved in ministry.

My father, who is eighty-one, is still a practicing attorney. He works only five hours a day, but he loves it. It keeps him young. My father-in-law is seventy-eight, and although he has retired from the corporate world, he stays busy building dollhouses for his grandchildren, painting the church, and doing carpentry projects around my house that I just don't have the time to get to.

I tell my boys that a better retirement security than the amount of money you have in the bank is the skills you acquire to support yourself. I believe that if they can develop the talents God has given them, they will be able to provide a service that someone needs. We know a retired man in our community who likes to tinker. He comes to our house to fix our washer and dryer when they break down. He doesn't charge much. He's friendly, skilled, and prompt, and lots of people use his services. He has a real ministry. He meets our needs, and the Lord is meeting his.

Of course, this assumes that you still have your health. I believe that if I am wise in serving the Lord and meeting my obligations while I'm able, then he will take care of me when I'm not able. It is also my impression that wisdom is not building up a huge retirement account. I am not saying that couples *shouldn't* save for the future, because I am doing that. It's just that my motivation for retirement has changed. I'm not saving to provide for myself a life of ease. Rather, as the man who "built bigger and better barns" in the gospel of Matthew, my absolutely secure retirement investment is what I invest of my money and my time into the Lord's work. And that is an investment I will enjoy for eternity.

That's why I don't ever plan to "retire." I plan to *refire*. I want to use my job skills to be a self-supporting missionary. Paul made tents. My "tents" are different, but I want my focus to be the same as his.

Q. How does your wife feel about this?

A. With money beyond our tithe, I tend to be more of a giver, while Elaine tends to be more of a saver. However, my wife trusts me to provide. She tells me that the thing that gives her the most security is seeing me consistently in fellowship with the Lord and seeking his direction.

CHAPTER 15

Advice
for Rent

Ten years ago, frugal-minded families were pretty much on their own. But ever since Amy Dacyczyn's *The Tightwad Gazette* caught the media's attention with some bizarre money-saving tips (my favorite is the Halloween paper-mache masks made out of dryer lint), the floodgates were opened.

These days, a half-dozen frugal advisers are scrambling for attention on the media map. You can see Jim and Amy Dacyczyn (sounds like "decision") featured as "America's Most Frugal Couple" in *Marriage Partnership* magazine, a Christianity Today publication. Then you have Mary Hunt, editor of *Cheapskate Monthly*, appearing on "Good Morning America" and joining Dr. Dobson in the studio for a "Focus on the Family" broadcast.

And what about Ron and Melodie Moore of *Skinflint News* fame hamming it up on the cover of *Kiplinger's Personal Finance* magazine? The editors asked the Moores to dress to the nines on a budget, so Ron found a thirty-five-dollar tuxedo at a consignment store, and Melodie arrived at the photo-shoot in a twenty-one-dollar strapless gown from a vintage dress shop. Inside the magazine, Ron is pictured polishing his shoes with a banana peel. He's not kidding. A banana peel delivers a great shine, he claims.

Tightwad. Cheapskate. Skinflint. Penny-Pincher. Living Cheap. All these publications and more are trying to capture a niche in the crowded—and growing—"frugality newsletter" market. One casualty, *The Frugal Living Gazette*, only attract-ed a hundred subscribers and folded within months of its debut in 1993.

THE FRUGALITY NEWSLETTERS

In researching this book, I subscribed to every newsletter I could find. I'm going to rate them on the following baseball scale:

- **Major League:** a top player, can touch all the bases; defi-nitely worth subscribing to.
- **Triple A:** very good prospect, but doesn't quite have the major-league look.
- **Double A:** either an up-and-coming player trying to break into the major leagues, or a player that may never make it out of the minors.

These are my own personal opinions, of course. Before you take my word on the quality and breadth of these newsletters, you can receive free, sample copies by sending a long, self-addressed, stamped envelope (fifty-two-cents postage, please).

The frugality newsletters I consider major-league material include *The Tightwad Gazette, Cheapskate Monthly, Skinflint News,* and *No-Debt Living*.

The Tightwad Gazette (RR 1 Box 3570, Leeds, ME 04263)

Amy Dacyczyn calls herself the "Frugal Zealot," but she doesn't come across as hard-core. I find her monthly publication erudite, thoughtful, and helpful. I like Amy's style, although I thought some of her newsletters could have used more take-away value. Still, *The Tightwad Gazette* is a strong, well-edited newsletter with fifty thousand subscribers, the largest circulation in its genre.

Format: monthly, eight-page newsletter

Subscription: $12 for twelve issues

Memorable tip: Cheese usually sells in supermarkets for three dollars a pound, but you can buy grated cheddar cheese (among many other items) at the market's deli salad bar for $1.99 a pound.

Cheapskate Monthly (P.O. Box 2135, Paramount, CA 90723)

Mary Hunt racked up one hundred thousand dollars of debt during the go-go eighties before cutting up her credit cards and getting herself and her family back on track. Mary is a Christian mom who uses biblical principles throughout her newsletters, although her audience is primarily secular. She has been featured in *USA Today* and *CashSaver* magazine, and has appeared on national network TV programs. *Cheapskate Monthly* is top-notch graphically, and its strength is advice from readers.

Format: monthly, eight-page newsletter

Subscription: $13 for twelve issues

Memorable tip: Stretch fruit juice by adding club soda.

Skinflint News (1460 Noell Blvd., Palm Harbor, FL 34683)

Ron and Melodie Moore produce an excellent newsletter with a "common-man" feel. The graphics are better-than-average, and the "skinflint" tips from readers are a strong point.

Format: monthly, eight-page newsletter

Subscription: $10 for twelve issues

Memorable tip: If you're shopping for an appliance, the

Moores recommend checking out LVT Appliances (Box 444, Commack, NY, 11727; phone 516-234-8884). LVT carries over four thousand products, including vacuum cleaners, TVs, camcorders, telephones, and word processors. If you know exactly what you want, call for a quote.

No-Debt Living (P.O. Box 282, Veradale, WA 99037; 800-562-3328

Robert E. Frank is doing things right. He bills *No-Debt Living* as a "Financial, Home Management, and Investment Newsletter with a Christian Perspective." Although some issues were weighted heavily on investment and financial advice, Bob also covers consumer areas such as supermarket shopping and couponing. He has recruited some top-name talent to contribute to the publication, including Gerri Detweiler of Bankcard Holders of America, and Christian financial advisors Ron Blue and Austin Pryor.

Format: monthly, eight-page newsletter

Subscription: charter subscribers pay $29.70 for eleven issues

Memorable tip: Take inventory of everything you own in case disaster befalls your home. Use a camcorder (borrow a friend's, if need be) and videotape all your belongings.

Triple A players include *The Penny Pincher* and *The Banker's Secret*.

The Penny Pincher (P.O. Box 809, Kings Park, NY 11754)

When Jackie Iglehart's husband lost his job, the family was forced to decrease their spending by twenty thousand dollars a year. Her own experience with frugal living prompted her to start *The Penny Pincher* in 1992. Although the graphics are not appealing and the newsletter has a bit of a hodge-podge look, the advice is first-rate.

Format: monthly, eight-page newsletter

Subscription: $12 for twelve issues

Memorable tip: Jackie pushes Philips All Earth Light SL Lamps, which use only eighteen watts of electricity, compared to the sixty- or seventy-five-watt incandescents most of us use. This can save tens of dollars each month on utility bills. Write her for more information.

The Banker's Secret (Box 78, Elizaville, NY 12523)

I rate this newsletter "Triple A" because it is a one-note publication: pay down that mortgage. Twenty-five years ago, Marc Eisenson learned the "banker's secret" of prepaying his home mortgage loan by adding small amounts to his monthly payment. Actually, Marc must have been tacking on some pretty hefty sums because he says he paid off his mortgage when he was twenty-seven years old. (You would have to double your monthly payment in order to pay off a thirty-year loan in seven years.)

Marc also sells computer software that will help you calculate how much you owe on your mortgage, and how many years of prepayments it would take to pay off your mortgage. Another program calculates the real cost of credit cards for those who don't pay off their balances. These programs are good, but they are expensive: $64.95 if you purchase both.

Format: quarterly, eight-page newsletter

Subscription: $19.95 for twelve issues; ask for the two-for-one special

Memorable tip: Have an "ace-in-the-hole" business on the side using a skill or hobby you enjoy.

I would give these last three newsletters a Double A rating: *Living Cheap News, Money Monthly,* and *Frugal Times.*

Living Cheap News (P.O. Box 700058, San Jose, CA 95170)

The voice of Larry Roth comes through clearly in this single-spaced newsletter, but his advice seems a bit scattershot. In one issue, he devoted 25 percent of the newsletter to describing the cost of dining out in Budapest (he had just returned from a trip to Eastern Europe). Who cares? Not only that, he's not a warehouse club fan, and I am!

Format: monthly, four-page newsletter

Subscription: $12 for ten issues

Money Monthly (425 Pike St. #403, Seattle, WA 98101; (800) 547-4848

This newsletter is actually two rolled into one. The middle four pages contains a "kid-teen" section written in larger type. These articles aimed at the younger crowd address topics such as how to use traveler's checks and collect valuable pennies.

I recommend their "Money Monthly Curriculum," a program that helps parents teach their children about budgeting and saving money (cost is $19.95). I was impressed with the curriculum and pleased to see that this secular organization included as part of its program "learning to donate to charitable organizations."

Format: monthly, eight-page newsletter
Subscription: $35 for twelve issues

Frugal Times (12534 Valley View St., #234, Garden Grove, CA 92645)

Like Mary Hunt, Tracey McBride was forced to make some drastic lifestyle changes when her husband lost his job in the Southern California aerospace industry. Tracey slashed household expenses to the bone, and began reading every book she could find on economizing. This Christian wife and mom became so enthusiastic with her new-found knowledge that she began publishing the *Frugal Times* newsletter, a promising rookie in this field. I hope she succeeds. When I interviewed Tracey for my cooking chapter, she had some good ideas.

Format: bi-monthly, six-page newsletter
Subscription: $10 for eight issues
Memorable tip: Photocopy a "leftovers" tag (printed in the *Frugal Times*) and place it on the refrigerator. This way, leftover food is less likely to get lost in the family shuffle and grow old and moldy.

Recommendations. First, subscribe to *Consumer Reports*, which entitles you to the free *Annual Buying Guide*. Next, check out several frugal newsletters. *The Tightwad Gazette*, *Cheapskate Monthly*, and *Skinflint News* are homemaker-oriented, while *No-Debt Living* has a broader scope. You'll know which one works for you. Your local library may even carry few of these newsletters, and certainly the consumer magazines. Although you can't check these resources out, you can photocopy what you need.

THE BOOK SCENE

When I visited my local library to check out some financial advice books, I couldn't even count all the titles. They numbered in the hundreds. Most had boring titles like *Investment Strategies for the '90s* and *How to Get Ahead and Get Out of Debt*. Not that those topics aren't important, but a lot of these books didn't strike me as reader-friendly.

I chose not to read many other "money" books prior to writing *Saving Money Any Way You Can*. I didn't want to subconsciously copy another author's approach. As I finished this manuscript, I opened a few more books. Let me point you toward a couple that I especially recommend.

First of all, I praise the work of Christian financial advisors Larry Burkett and Ron Blue, the two big names in this category. Burkett and Blue, who have written books for *Focus on the Family*, are both experienced, forthright people. If I had to generalize, I would say that Larry's advice is clear, simple, and scripturally based, while Ron, a CPA, writes in a more detailed fashion with a specific, analytical approach. Of course, Blue's work is scripturally based, as well.

Austin Pryor, a Christian investment counselor, is a rising star. His recent book, *Sound Mind Investing*, covered the waterfront on the topic—everything from stocks, bonds, mutual funds, and annuities. What made the book extremely reader-friendly were the eye-popping graphics; I'd never seen so many sidebars, pop-outs, graphs, and "pull quotes" in one book. The graphics kept me going in the second half, which bogged down somewhat. Still, if you're going to self-manage your retirement (something I recommend), then this book is for you.

Pryor broke down financial strategies into four levels: 1) getting debt free; 2) saving for future needs; 3) investing in stocks; and 4) diversifying for safety. Most of us may never get past level 2, but at least we'll have a plan in hand for the future.

In addition, Pryor produces an investment newsletter for Christian families seeking more information about no-load mutual funds. Also called *Sound Mind Investing* (P.O. Box 22128, Louisville, KY 40252), this sixteen-page newsletter costs fifty-nine dollars for twelve issues. Before spending that much money, write for a free sample issue.

Jonathan Pond is another author worth reading, although he doesn't target his books toward the Christian market. You may have seen him as the resident financial planning expert on the *Today Show*. In *1001 Ways to Cut Your Expenses*, Pond delivers quick-hitting tips—many under fifty words—on a variety of topics.

Some of these tips are ridiculous, as Pond quickly admits, such as his recommendation to buy a push mower. But much of his advice is right on. For example, tip number 817 says that when your waiter or waitress rattles off the daily specials, be sure to ask the price before ordering. I hate it when the waiter takes three minutes to describe the *emince de veau*, leaving you with the feeling that it would be unseemly to ask what the meal would cost.

Lastly, I enjoyed *Dollars and Sense* by Wilson J. Humber, a Christian and a certified financial planner. I thought he delivered some excellent nuts-and-bolts advice on purchasing a home, buying insurance, and saving for retirement, all coupled with deep spiritual insight.

THE MAGAZINE RACK

My personal pick for best consumer magazine is *Consumer Reports* (P.O. Box 53029, Boulder, CO 80322; twenty-two dollars for twelve issues). I've followed this publication for a long time, and not only has it improved in recent years, but the editors have an uncanny ability to hit my "hot-button" interests. If I'm thinking about a new vacuum cleaner, whammo, *Consumer Reports* publishes their new ratings on Kirbys and Electroluxs. Every subscriber also receives *Consumer Reports'* Annual Buying Guide, chock full of ratings on everything from toasters to Trans Ams.

Consumer Digest (P.O. Box 3074, Harlan, IA 51593; $15.95 for six issues) is a strong magazine, but more investment oriented. I am impressed with *Kiplinger's Personal Finance* magazine (Editor's Park, MD 20782; eighteen dollars for twelve issues), and its annual mutual fund issue.

Consumer's Research (P.O. Box 5025, Brentwood, TN 37024; twenty-four dollars for twelve issues) is printed on cheap newspaper stock and has very few photos or illustrations, which makes it harder to read. The magazine bills itself as an "analyzer of products, services, and consumer issues." A typical story is "FDA Questions Safety of Dietary Supplements." You can pass on this magazine.

CashSaver magazine (Box 16988, North Hollywood, CA 91615; $9.95 for six issues) debuted in 1994, and I was impressed with the initial issues. This is a consumer-oriented publication with helpful tips on extended warranties, how to save in restaurants, and kitchen recipes. However, the publisher is Larry Flynt of *Hustler* magazine fame (or should I say *infamy*), which means I can't recommend it.

INTO THE COMPUTER AGE

Remember back in the introduction where I mentioned the financial software named Quicken? The makers of Quicken (800-986-4100) sent me a program to try out, but my computer didn't have enough memory to store it. I spent an evening "test-driving" the software on a friend's Apple Macintosh. Quicken impressed me with how easy it was to input cash purchases, credit card expenses, and checks into the computer.

The screen actually looked like a checkbook register. Let's say you write in a check for $84.56 to Safeway for groceries. The computer will automatically correct your balance. If you want to know how much you've spent on groceries, you hit a button and the answer will appear on the screen. You can even "split" an individual check in terms of different categories. For instance, you may have bought a fourteen-dollar prescription at Safeway and want to assign that amount to the "prescription" category rather than to groceries.

"Quicken has given me an easy way to track my expenses," my friend told me. "I let my receipts and checkstubs stack up for a few days, then I input them. It takes only a few minutes. I've learned what is costing us more to drive—our Nissan or our Taurus, and I also found out how much Christmas *really* costs our family."

Quicken has cleaned up a lot of awards from computer magazines. Quicken, which is frequently advertised on TV, retails for $29.95. But you will need at least a 386 computer with a hard drive or a new Apple to run the program. Believe me, once you start using it, you'll never go back to checkbooks again.

Quicken is not the only computer software on the market. Microsoft Money 3.0 ($34.95) is the personal finance software for the Microsoft Windows operating system. It can do everything from track your expenses to retirement planning. Also, you may want to consider buying a tax software program, such as MacIntax, and do your own taxes painlessly.

Larry Burkett's organization, Christian Financial Concepts (800-722-1976), offers personal finance software with a twist. After purchasing a new $194 suit, the computer program will ask where to designate the purchase. If you type in "clothing," the computer will inform you that you budgeted only $125 for clothing. Since your new suit is beyond the budgeted amount, the program will ask you how you're going to pay for it. In other words, this software holds you accountable by making sure you maintain a balanced budget.

Those who aren't computer literate or don't have a home PC should consider Code-a-Check (6101 N. Yellowstone, Cheyenne, WY 82009; 307-632-0665). Code-a-Check is a money-management system in which you write down all of your purchases—whether by check, money order, cash, or credit card—into a single register. You write in the purchase, note the date, and then check a column—cash, card, or check.

With each spending designation, you must write down a corresponding code number. For instance, grocery store purchases are 216, gasoline is 233, restaurants are 210, and so on. You also write down your salary and any money earned from part-time jobs. At the end of each month, you send the register to Code-a-Check, and a week later you receive a comprehensive "Personal Income and Expense Report."

Nicole and I participated in the Code-a-Check program for three months, and found it was not for us. It was a hassle to look up the code numbers for each purchase, and some purchases weren't easy to designate to a certain category. The other strike against Code-a-Check is the twenty-five-dollar monthly fee, nearly as much as the cost of Quicken or Microsoft Money 3.0. I suggest you do it yourself and save three hundred dollars a year.

Do you want to know the biggest thing I learned from trying out these various programs? Each one has you input your payroll withholding, which was a sobering reminder of *how much* money we are paying in taxes. If we had to send the federal government monthly checks for income tax and Social Security, there would be a tax revolt overnight!

CHAPTER **16**

The Checkout Line

Whenever we feel the itch to spend money frivolously, a plausible reason seems to follow like a caboose chasing an engine. The list could be endless, but most of these will have a familiar ring:

- "I deserve it because I've been working hard."
- "I haven't bought something for myself in ages."
- "I don't have anything to wear."
- "This will save money in the long run."
- "We haven't gone out in a *long* time."
- "You only live once."
- "We ate breakfast in the hotel room today, so we can afford to splurge."

The next time you whisper any of these rationalizations, catch yourself and think it through. Are there better ways of rewarding yourself? Do you really *need* that new jacket? If money is tight, would a cheaper outing be just as much fun, maybe even more?

WHAT ELSE HAVE YOU GOT TO TELL ME?

Saving money any way you can demands constant vigilance and creativity. Many topics didn't seem to fit elsewhere in the book, so I've lumped the remaining money-saving ideas into this section. The subheadings will serve as a simple index to help you find points of special interest.

Moving

When Focus on the Family moved its headquarters from Southern California to Colorado Springs, I relocated with the ministry. (A good idea, since I wanted to keep my job.) Each employee was given a lump sum to cover moving expenses. If we wanted to rent a U-Haul and drive all our wordly possessions twelve hundred miles, we could pocket the leftover money. Or, we could pay a moving company to box everything up and deliver it to Colorado, which would blow our whole moving allowance.

We chose a middle course. North American Van Lines (800-348-2111) offers a "We Drive" program in which an eighteen-wheeler showed up on our doorstep on moving day. It was our responsiblity to carry the furniture and boxed belongings to the truck, where the driver loaded everything into the van. Then he drove the van to our new home, where we met the truck and unloaded our belongings.

Instead of paying $4,200 for a standard move, our cost was $1,980—not that much more than a U-Haul truck (around $1,200, we figured). To spare my back, I hired three high school kids at six dollars an hour to do all the lifting, so the cost of finding my own help was $150. I saved a cool $2,000 by going this route.

Not only that, I didn't have to drive an unwieldly twenty-four-foot van across the California and Arizona deserts! Focus employees who rented U-Haul and Ryder trucks had horror stories to tell, among them the 2 A.M. breakdown in the middle of nowhere, air conditioning that didn't work, and interminable, twenty-five-miles-per-hour, uphill stretches.

I figure our alternative was money well spent. If you opt for the full treatment, however, you can save up to 50 percent by moving on a weekday.

One last moving tip: U-Haul and other packing stores charge an *outrageous* price for boxes. If you know you're going to be moving in the near future, start collecting suitable boxes from local grocery stores, sporting goods outlets, etc., several weeks earlier. If you don't have storage room, break the boxes down and stack up the cardboard in some out-of-the-way corner.

If you live near a military installation, ask if you can drive onto the base and look for a moving van. If you see one, ask the driver if the family is moving in or moving out. If they're moving in, knock on the door, introduce yourself, and ask if you can take some of their boxes and packaging material away. They will usually be thrilled to have someone dispose of their boxes!

Entertainment

Finding cheap family entertainment is a never-ending quest. Now that most families own a VCR, a ready alternative is close at hand. Purchasing videos doesn't seem like a good idea to me. They generally cost fifteen to twenty dollars, and after you've seen them a couple of times, you know every line by heart. Due to the lack of family entertainment on the tube, it does make sense to buy worthwhile videos for the kids. The Disney classics or the top-notch "McGee & Me!" and "Adventures in Odyssey" videos from Focus on the Family are excellent. (How's that for a plug?)

You can also save a bundle by taping worthwhile programs off of the tube yourself. I have taped dozens of *Leave It to*

Beaver episodes on one tape. Whenever the kids get the TV urge, I just pop in the latest antics of Wally and the Beaver. If you subscribe to cable TV, the Disney Channel offers a free preview weekend a couple of times a year. You can often tape hours of shows for later viewing!

Easter season features several Christian classics, such as *Ben Hur, Jesus of Nazareth, The Ten Commandments,* and *The Robe.* These would be terrific additions to your tape library.

As for video rentals, the average family spends $10 a month, according to *TV Guide.* Supermarkets generally have the cheapest rates. Two video rentals cost a mere $1.50 at my local supermarket (after they filter off the "new release" shelf), but selection is skimpy, especially for discerning Christian parents. Blockbuster has a great selection of worthwhile family videos (films from the forties and fifties) at three dollars a pop.

If you want to see a first-run movie at a local cinema, discounts still abound. Many theaters have matinee prices for the weeknight shows before six. And if you can wait two or three months, you can often see those same films at the bargain movie houses. Really, how many new movies are worth the cost of a full-price ticket these days?

To make sure you don't waste your money, I recommend subscribing to *MovieGuide* (P.O. Box 190010, Atlanta, GA 31119; 800-899-6684; forty dollars for twenty-six issues) or *Preview* (1309 Seminole Dr., Richardson, TX 75080; 214-231-9910; thirty dollars for twenty-six issues). These two publications review the latest Hollywood releases from a Christian perspective, and can steer you away from the losers.

Computers

How often have you heard that the computer system you buy today is outdated by tomorrow? A scary thought, since most home computers carry a hefty price tag anywhere between one and two thousand dollars. The computer market is changing faster than you can say "Intel microprocessing chip." My advice mirrors everything I've read on the subject:

wait as long as you can before buying or upgrading. Then take a close look at the last generation that nobody wants. These days, the hot stuff is the IBM-compatible Pentium; on the Mac side, it's the Apple Power Macs.

If you're a knowledgeable buyer, you can often purchase used equipment for a song and a couple of hundred dollars. The American Computer Exchange (800-786-0717) matches buyers and sellers. Don't buy anything less than an IBM compatible 386; anything older and you won't be able to run many of today's software programs.

Telephone companies

Which long-distance phone company is cheaper: AT&T, MCI, US Sprint, or Metromedia? I wrote Consumer Action (116 New Montgomery St., Suite 223, San Francisco, CA 94105), a non-profit consumer-advocacy organization. They surveyed the four long-distance companies and summarized the results in a newsletter. For a free copy, send a self-addressed stamped envelope to the above address.

It's hard to tell which long-distance company is cheaper. You must study each discount calling plan (outlined in the surveys), then choose the one that fits your individual calling patterns. If you spend more than seven dollars a month in long-distance calls, you can save by signing up for one of the long-distance plans.

Another comparison of long-distance plans was done by TRAC Tele-Tips (send $2 and a self-addressed stamped envelope to TRAC, P.O. Box 12038, Washington, D.C. 20005). *Kiplinger's Personal Finance* magazine published a snapshot of the TRAC survey, which compared monthly bills for light callers and heavy long-distance users. Generally speaking, MCI and US Sprint were about the same, and both were about 5 percent cheaper than AT&T.

We use MCI's PrimeTime plan, which costs $8.45 for sixty minutes of long-distance calls on evenings and weekends, with each additional minute at ten cents. In addition, we signed up for MCI's "Friends and Family Plan" (a 20-percent discount for calls to members of our "calling circle"). We also use an "Around the World" plan so Nicole can keep in touch with her parents and family members in Switzerland; for international calls, we pay three dollars a month plus fifty-nine cents a minute (about half the going rate).

Have you noticed how many car dealers, department stores, and supermarkets are offering free cellular phones with a minimum purchase? What a joke! This ruse starts you on the road of paying monthly "access charges" and long-distance fees, which are considerably more than a home telephone.

Most of us know how teens can tie up a phone for hours. If you don't want to bring a second telephone line into the house, you can ask the phone company to set you up with a special ring program. Our next-door neighbors have a system in which one ring means it's for the teen in the house, two rings is for Mom, and three rings is for Dad.

Refrigerators

You're going to start paying more for a new refrigerator in 1995. That's when federal standards mandate that refrigerators be made without chlorofluorocarbons, which studies have indicated damage the earth's ozone layer. You'll also see manufacturers scrambling to produce more energy-efficient refrigerators, because 20 percent of all household electricity is burned up by this one appliance.

Eyewear

An "optometrist" does extensive eye exams, including testing for glaucoma and peripheral vision. An "optician" can perform ordinary eye exams, but they are not medical doctors. You usually bring him or her a prescription for glasses from an ophthalmologist (eye surgeon) or an optometrist.

Several national chains offer significant savings in eyewear, including Lenscrafters, Peak Vision, VisionMart, Wal-Mart, and Sam's warehouse club. They usually offer basic exams and sell basic frames and lenses (you pay extra for add-ons such as ultra-violet, tinting, and anti-scratch coating). Some are full-care clinics or have an optician on duty in addition to an optometrist. They sometimes offer special deals like a free exam if you purchase a second pair of eyeglasses at the same time.

The winner? Sam's, of course. They don't have an optometrist on site, which means you must get a prescription elsewhere. A Sam's optician will fit your glasses. Basic plastic lenses are $47.00, which *includes* add-ons and warranty. Basic plastic frames are $39.00 to $79.00; metal frames are $29.00 to $99.00. I've purchased three pairs of presciption glasses at warehouse clubs, and the Japanese carbon frame and plastic lenses with all the coatings cost $100.00. I saved $25.00 to $100.00 by going the warehouse club route, and so could you.

Pawn shops

Stop laughing. I'm serious. You can actually walk into a pawn shop these days and not feel like you have to go home and take a shower. Some pawn shops are going upscale these days in order to broaden their customer base. In other words, they want families like you and me to feel comfortable stepping inside the doors.

Colorado Springs, with three military installations, may just lead the country in pawn shops per capita. Several of them are as spiffy as any mall jewelry store. Not long ago, Nicole and I walked into a freshly painted pawn shop. We couldn't help but notice the bright lights, plush carpeting, attractive display cases, and neatly groomed employees. This was a far cry from dingy, storefront pawn shops manned by a scruffy, bearded dude dressed from head to toe in black leather.

Once inside, we were drawn to the handsome jewelry display case, where Nicole saw a beautiful 14K gold ring with a small emerald. She remembered it from the only other time she had been in this same pawn shop—one year earlier! The price back then was around $100. Now it was marked down to

$78. Nicole and I discussed purchasing the ring, and when she convinced me this would be a Christmas present, I nodded my approval.

"Is this your best price?" Nicole asked the fellow behind the counter.

"I can knock another 15 percent off, but that's as low as we can go." We got the ring for $65.

Every town has pawn shops, where people bring in items for a cash "loan." They generally have thirty days to reclaim their item by repaying their loan—plus hefty interest, of course. More often than not, however, they never return, so the item is displayed for sale. Good buys include jewelry, car stereos, computers, camcorders, TVs, VCRs, CD players, tape players, stereo systems, guitars, drums, and photography equipment.

One last tip. If you see a sign that says "Don't Even Ask," that means the management is not in the mood to negotiate.

Carpets

Sooner or later, you'll have to replace the worn carpet in your home. You should call carpet wholesale dealers and ask if they have any seconds or slightly damaged rolls. My hairdresser, Darlene Charlesworth, recently recarpeted her home. She said if you call a carpet store and ask for seconds, the reponse will be no. "That's because they want to sell you *new* carpet. You want to seek out wholesalers because they are the ones who receive the returns on damaged carpet."

Darlene found a carpet wholesaler at her church who sold slightly damaged rolls for two to four dollars a square yard—compared to fifteen and twenty dollars a yard in the regular carpet stores. "But I had to purchase the whole roll, which was enough to recarpet my fifteen-hundred-square-foot home," she said. "I paid eight hundred dollars for the carpet and two hundred dollars for a carpet layer to drop by on his day off." She saved *thousands* by taking this route.

Formal photos

Even going to Sears for a family portrait adds up. Some school districts offer family portraits at a significant discount when the student's photos are taken. Lately, we've stopped buying these "school pak" photos, and ordered a single eight by ten instead. It seems as though we never used all those wallet photos.

Downhill skiing

I know many of you don't live near the Colorado Rockies, Utah's Wasatch Range, or California's Sierra Nevada. But if you do ski, you know how fun—and expensive—this family sport can be. (We come from a skiing family; Nicole used to ski to school when she lived in the Alps.) To save here, you need to pack a lunch and hunt down discount tickets, which are usually offered between Thanksgiving and Christmas, in January, and after the Easter holidays.

For the last three seasons, we've gone to Crested Butte in Colorado every December because they offer free lift tickets. What's the catch? There is none. Crested Butte has discovered the ski area makes more money between Thanksgiving and Christmas by allowing people to enjoy the slopes for free. The ski area benefits by receiving "voluntary" kickbacks from hoteliers and restaurants.

Batteries

One thing I've recently done is purchase a nickel-cadium rechargeable battery system. I had to, since my children share a Game Boy, which they mostly use on auto trips. A recent study says if my children use regular alkaline batteries for three years, it will cost $657.00 to purchase 876 throw-away batteries. (That's a lot of Game Boy!) The cost of rechargeables came to $26, or a savings of $631.00. I hope no one will play that much Game Boy, but you get the message.

When you're in debt

In case your family is swimming in debt, Larry Burkett has trained counselors in many cities across the country who can offer financial counseling. Write Christian Financial Concepts, Attn: Counseling Department, 601 Broad St., S.E.,

Gainesville, GA 30501. Be sure to include a self-addressed stamped envelope.

A low-cost alternative that can still be very helpful is participating in small groups organized by Crown Ministries, an interdominational ministry that trains couples to apply the financial principles from the Bible to their everyday lives. These classes meet once a week for twelve weeks, and cost fifty-five dollars per couple. Crown Ministries does not endorse or sell financial products or services. Write: Crown Ministries, 530 Crown Oak Centre Dr., Longwood, FL 32750, or call (800) 331-6011.

If you are out of debt and looking for solid Christian money management advice, contact Ron Blue's organization at 1100 Johnson Ferry Rd. N.E. Suite 600, Atlanta, GA 30342, or call (404) 255-0147.

Practice frugality at work as well as at home

Organizations as well as individuals have to cut corners to stay ahead. A month or two after arriving at Focus on the Family in 1986, I sent a memo to Dr. Dobson on ministry letterhead. When I received his response, he jotted a P.S. stating that money could be saved by printing memos on non-letterhead paper. Ever since then, I've used blank photocopy paper.

AND FINALLY

Have you ever lived next door to trashy neighbors? You know, a family who parks their broken-down cars on the street, lets the lawn grow into a jungle of knee-high weeds, and lives in such a filthy house that you ban your kids from stepping inside the front door?

Then one Saturday morning, you notice the father mowing the grass. That's the first time you've seen him working in the yard all summer. But he doesn't stop there. He rakes up the remaining clumps of grass and spreads seed and fertilizer across the blotchy expanse. Meanwhile, his two teenage sons join forces to prep the house for repainting. Inside, Mom uses a rented carpet-cleaning machine to get rid of a ton of dirt.

Over the next six weeks, the house undergoes a dramatic transformation. The junky cars are towed away, the driveway is resurfaced, and the house receives a fresh coat of paint from top to bottom. Just when you're ready to allow your kids to play over there, they plant a "For Sale" sign in the lush, green lawn.

You shake your head in disbelief. *With a little effort,* you think, *my neighbors could have gotten their house in tip-top shape all along.*

The same thought applies to our finances. Couples who work steadily at their finances—trimming a bit here, planning for the future there—won't have to scramble when the car dies or one of the kids needs braces. I hope you will use *Saving Money Any Way You Can* to reach this goal.

Let me close with this thought: The reason I try to save money on basic expenses such as clothes, food, and cars is so that our family will be able to support the Lord's work and do fun things together. I want us to continue sponsoring our Compassion International child, Thongchai Neamhorn of Thailand. I want us to participate in the church's building drive and contribute to the "Love Fund."

On the family front, I want Nicole, Andrea, Patrick, and I to visit relatives and family members, camp at the beach, and ride our bikes to the frozen yogurt shop for a Sunday afternoon treat. I want us to enjoy a pizza, attend a Michael Card concert, and go miniature golfing together. In other words, I want to create family memories—joy-filled times my loved ones will never be able to put a price tag on.

Got Any Tips?

I'd love to hear what you thought of *Saving Money Any Way You Can* or about any of *your* money-saving ideas. If you would like to drop me a line, write:

Mike Yorkey
P.O. Box 50592
Colorado Springs, CO 80949

Appendix One

Survey Results

Here are the results of my survey, which was returned by 125 families:

1. Which statement best sums up your experience?
   I worry about finances *all* the time: 5 percent
   I worry about finances *most* of the time: 12 percent
   I worry about finances *some* of the time: 64 percent
   I hardly worry about finances at all : 19 percent

2. Who handles the finances in your family?
   Husband: 29 percent
   Wife: 26 percent
   Both: 45 percent

3. Which statement best sums up your family's financial picture?
   We're able to put some money into savings each month:
   31 percent
   We're doing OK, but it's a struggle to stay ahead:
   46 percent
   We live paycheck to paycheck: 21 percent
   We're living on credit; our expenses exceed our income:
   2 percent

4. Since we've been married ...
Our finances have been improving steadily: 36 percent
We've maintained an even keel: 46 percent
We've been taking on water every year: 10 percent
We're in debt—*too much* debt: 7 percent
Our financial boat could sink at any moment: 1 percent

5. Generally speaking, how do you cut expenses? (More than one answer could be checked.)
Spend less on groceries: 56 percent
Cut out frills, such as health clubs: 72 percent
Skip vacations: 48 percent
Drive older cars: 63 percent
Buy used clothes: 32 percent
Eat out less at restaurants: 76 percent

6. If you work more than forty hours a week, how are you trying to augment your income?
Moonlighting and picking up extra jobs: 22 percent
Working overtime at my regular job: 13 percent
Spouse works outside the home part-time: 17 percent
Spouse works outside the home full-time: 14 percent
Kids work and contribute to the family income: 6 percent
No response: 28 percent

8. What percentage of your annual income do you contribute to your local church or charity?
None: 2 percent
Between one and two: 3 percent
Between two and four: 8 percent
Between five and six: 12 percent
Between seven and eight: 9 percent
Between nine and ten: 36 percent
More than ten: 30 percent

9. Are you currently saving for retirement?
Yes: 72 percent
No: 25 percent
Not sure: 3 percent

Note: The survey also contained six essay-type questions that asked families how they saved money in certain areas. I have tried to include their answers whenever possible.

Appendix Two

Comparison Grocery Shopping Survey

As I mentioned in chapter four, Lou Gage and I shopped at Sam's warehouse club for my third comparison shopping trip (February 1994). For the sake of fairness, I made a concerted effort to purchase comparable products in terms of *name* brands versus *house* brands, as you will see in the table below. Even so, Sam's showed a savings of 15 percent over Cub Foods and 24 percent over Safeway.

The following table details my findings on this third trip. *Size* indicates the size of the purchased product. Because groceries and household products are sold in various sizes and weights, *unit price* provides a common denominator for the size or amount most families would buy. *Price* indicates the actual price paid for each item. *"Comp"* means "comparable price," the cost of the item calculated according to the common denominator. I used this last column of comparable prices to calculate the "tale of the tape." (Boldface type indicates the particular brand or size I chose to include in the final register total.)

Item	Size	Unit Price	Price	Comp
Milk				
Sam's	1 gallon	1.99	1.99	1.99
Cub Foods	1 gallon	2.80	2.80	2.80
Safeway	2 gallons	1.99	3.98	1.99

Item	Size	Unit Price	Price	Comp

Comment: Safeway has a multi-buy program, which means you have to buy two gallons to get the discount. Otherwise, the cost of a Safeway gallon was $2.90.

Eggs

Item	Size	Unit Price	Price	Comp
Sam's	18 Large AA	dozen/.68	1.03	1.03
Cub's	18 Large AA	dozen/.71	1.09	1.09
Safeway	18 Large AA	dozen/1.09	1.09	1.09

Jack cheese

Item	Size	Unit Price	Price	Comp
Sam's	2 lbs.	1 lb./ 1.71	3.43	1.71
Cub's	1 lb.	1 lb./2.29	2.29	2.29
Safeway	2 lbs.	1 lb./1.99	3.99	1.99

Comment: I looked for the cheapest cheese I could find.

Mild cheddar cheese

Item	Size	Unit Price	Price	Comp
Sam's	2 lbs.	1 lb./1.72	3.45	1.72
Cub's	1 lb.	1 lb./1.99	1.99	1.99
Safeway	2 lbs.	1 lb./2.34	4.69	2.34

Cream cheese

Item	Size	Unit Price	Price	Comp
Sam's				
Philadelphia	6/8-oz. boxes	8-oz. box/.86	.86	.86
Cub's				
Philadelphia	8 oz. box	8-oz. box/.99	.99	.99
Cub's house	8 oz. box	8-oz. box/.83	.83	.83
Safeway Phila.	8 oz. box	8-oz. box/.99	.99	.99
Safeway				
Lucerne	8 oz. box	8-oz. box/.95	.95	.95

Butter

Item	Size	Unit Price	Price	Comp
Sam's Mid-Farm	3 lbs.	1 lb./.99	2.99	.99
Cub's Land O' Lakes	1 lb.	1 lb./1.88	1.88	1.88

Item	Size	Unit Price	Price	Comp
Cub's house	1 lb.	1 lb./1.49	1.49	1.49
Safeway				
Land O' Lakes	1 lb.	1 lb./2.49	2.49	2.49
Safeway house	1 lb.	1 lb./1.50	1.50	1.50

Comment: Safeway was running a sale on butter.

Shedd's Country Crock margarine

Sam's	5 lbs.	3 lbs. /1.65	2.74	1.65
Cub's	3 lbs.	3 lbs./2.28	2.28	2.28
Safeway	3 lbs.	3 lbs./2.49	2.49	2.49

Minute Maid orange juice (ready-to-drink)

Sam's				
Minute Maid	96 oz.	96 oz./2.89	2.89	2.89
Cub's				
Minute Maid	96 oz.	96 oz./3.26	3.26	3.26
Safeway				
Minute Maid	96 oz.	96 oz./3.49	3.49	3.49

Store-brand orange juice (ready-to-drink)

Sam's	128 oz.	128 oz./1.98	1.98	1.98
Cub's	64 oz.	128 oz./3.38	1.69	3.38
Safeway	128 oz.	128 oz./3.75	3.75	3.75

Orange juice (frozen concentrate)

Sam's house	6/16-oz. cans	16-oz. can /.91	5.49	.91
Cub's				
Minute Maid	16-oz. can	16-oz. can/1.79	1.79	1.79
Cub's house	12-oz. can	16 oz. can/1.26	.95	1.26
Safeway				
Minute Maid	16-oz. can	16-oz. can/1.49	1.49	1.49
Safeway house	12-oz. can	16-oz. can/1.30	.98	1.30

Item	Size	Unit Price	Price	Comp

Comment: No matter which brand or how you buy it, Sam's is the winner on OJ.

Coke Classic

Sam's	24 cans	4 6-packs/ 6.27	6.27	6.27
Cub's	24 cans	4 6-packs/5.99	5.99	5.99
Safeway	12 cans	4 6-packs/6.78	3.39	6.78

Store-brand cola

Sam's	24 cans	4 6-packs/3.99	3.99	3.99
Cub's	24 cans	4 6-packs/3.96	3.96	3.96
Safeway	6 cans	4 6-packs/3.96	.99	3.96

Diet Pepsi

Sam's	24 cans	4 6-packs/6.23	6.23	6.23
Cub's	24 cans	4 6-packs/5.98	5.98	5.98
Safeway	12 cans	4 6-packs/6.58	3.29	6.58

Store-brand diet cola

Sam's	24 cans	4 6-packs/3.99	3.99	3.99
Cub's	24 cans	4 6-packs/3.96	3.96	3.96
Safeway	6 cans	4 6-packs/3.96	.99	3.96

Comment: Supermarkets often use soda as a loss leader because it's a heavily purchased item.

Applesauce

Sam's	3/48 oz.	50 oz./1.97	5.69	1.97
Cub's Skyland	50 oz.	50 oz./2.18	2.18	2.18
Cub's house	50 oz.	50 oz./1.44	1.44	1.44
Safeway Skyland	50 oz.	50 oz./2.49	2.49	2.49
Safeway house	50 oz.	50 oz./1.99	1.99	1.99

Comment: Cub's house brand holds the advantage here.

Item	Size	Unit Price	Price	Comp

Lay's Potato chips

Sam's	20 oz.	20 oz./2.43	2.43	2.43
Cub's	14.5 oz.	20 oz./2.26	1.49	2.26
Safeway	20 oz.	20 oz. /3.69	3.69	3.69

Comment: Good deal at Cub's.

Doritos

Sam's	24 oz.	14 oz./2.06	3.54	2.06
Cub's	14 oz.	14 oz./2.69	2.69	2.69
Safeway	24 oz.	14 oz./2.56	4.39	2.56

Granola bars

Sam's Quakers	24 bars	10 bars/2.24	5.39	2.24
Cub's Quaker	10 bars	10 bars/2.33	2.33	2.33
Cub's house	8 bars	10 bars/1.56	1.25	1.56
Safeway Quaker	10 bars	10 bars/3.05	3.05	3.05

Oreo cookies

Sam's	42 oz.	20 oz./2.37	4.98	2.37
Cub's	20 oz.	20 oz./2.94	2.94	2.94
Cub's house	9.2 oz.	20 oz./2.80	2.80	2.80
Safeway	42 oz.	20 oz./2.47	5.19	2.47
Safeway house	24 oz.	20 oz./1.65	1.99	1.65

Comment: I didn't count the house brands because they were lower in quality compared to the name-brand Oreos.

Chocolate drink mix

Sam's				
Nestlé Quik	56 oz.	56 oz./4.38	4.38	4.38
Cub's				
Nestlé Quik	56 oz.	56 oz./5.87	5.87	5.87

Item	Size	Unit Price	Price	Comp
Cub's house Safeway	32 oz.	56 oz./4.76	2.75	4.76
Nestle's Quik	32 oz.	56 oz./5.23	2.99	5.23

Decaffeinated coffee

Sam's Folgers	39 oz.	26 oz./5.30	5.30	5.30
Sam's house	48 oz.	26 oz./3.01	3.01	3.01
Cub's Folgers	26 oz.	26 oz./6.93	6.93	6.93
Cub's house	26 oz.	26 oz./3.88	3.88	3.88
Safeway Folgers	26 oz.	26 oz./7.16	7.16	7.16

Comment: Safeway burned here because they didn't offer a house brand.

Tea

Sam's Lipton	216 ct.	100/2.58	5.59	2.58
Cub's Lipton	100 ct.	100/2.99	2.99	2.99
Cub's house	100 ct.	100/2.79	2.79	2.79
Safeway Lipton	100 ct.	100/3.45	3.45	3.45
Safeway house	100 ct.	100/2.49	2.49	2.49

Salted cocktail peanuts

Sam's Planters	2/12 oz.	12 oz./2.43	4.86	2.43
Cub's Planters	12 oz.	12 oz./2.44	2.44	2.44
Cub's house	12 oz.	12 oz./1.98	1.98	1.98
Safeway Planters	24 oz.	12 oz./2.14	2.14	2.14

Bread (Grant's Farm 7-Grain Wheat)

Sam's	2/32-oz. lves	20 oz./.99	3.17	.99
Cub's	20-oz. loaf	20 oz./1.63	1.63	1.63
Safeway	20-oz. loaf	20 oz./1.79	1.79	1.79

House-brand bread

Sam's	2/32-oz. loaves	16 oz./.47	.47	.47
Cub's	16-oz. loaf	16 oz./.33	.33	.33

Item	Size	Unit Price	Price	Comp
Safeway	24-oz. loaf	16 oz./.52	.79	.52

Comment: Cub's house brand wasn't very good; Sam's and Safeway's were OK.

House-brand hot dog buns

Sam's	16 buns	8 buns/.88	1.76	.88
Cub's	8 buns	8 buns/.49	.49	.49
Safeway	8 buns	8 buns/.59	.59	.59

House-brand hamburger buns

Sam's	16 buns	8 buns/.89	1.78	.89
Cub's	8 buns	8 buns/.49	.49	.49
Safeway	8 buns	8 buns/.59	.59	.59

Vegetable oil

Sam's Wesson	1 gal.	1 gal./5.28	5.28	5.28
Cub's Wesson	1.25 gal.	1 gal./6.11	7.64	6.11
Cub's house	1 gal.	1 gal./ 5.39	5.39	5.39
Safeway Crisco	1 gal.	1 gal./5.79	5.79	5.79
Safeway house	1 gal.	1 gal./4.99	4.99	4.99

Comment: The supermarkets were very competitive here.

Flour

Sam's house	25 lbs.	10 lbs./1.82	4.56	1.82
Cub's Gold Medal	10 lbs.	10 lbs./2.75	2.75	2.75
Cub's house	5 lbs.	10 lbs./1.68	.79	1.68
Safeway				
Gold Medal	10 lbs.	10 lbs./2.89	2.89	2.89
Safeway house	10 lbs.	10 lbs./2.29	2.29	2.29

Comment: Unless you bake a lot, the 25-pound bag runs the risk of spoilage. In that case, this is an item better purchased in smaller quantities at the supermarket.

Item	Size	Unit Price	Price	Comp

Sugar

Item	Size	Unit Price	Price	Comp
Sam's C & H	10/2 lbs.	10 lbs./2.44	9.79	4.89
Cub's C & H	5 lbs.	10 lbs./3.98	1.99	3.98
Cub's house	5 lbs.	10 lbs./3.36	1.68	3.36
Safeway C & H	10 lbs.	10 lbs./3.99	3.99	3.99
Safeway house	10 lbs.	10 lbs./3.59	3.59	3.59

Chocolate chips

Item	Size	Unit Price	Price	Comp
Sam's Nestlé	52 oz.	24 oz./3.22	6.99	3.22
Sam's house	10 lbs.	24 oz./1.81	12.09	1.81
Cub's Nestlé	24 oz.	24 oz./2.99	2.99	2.99
Cub's house	24 oz.	24 oz./2.99	2.99	2.99
Safeway Nestlé	24 oz.	24 oz./5.29	5.29	5.29
Safeway house	12 oz.	24 oz./3.98	1.99	3.98

Comment: Sam's house brand is quite good. My Swiss wife, who grew up on chocolate, gives it her seal of approval.

Oats

Item	Size	Unit Price	Price	Comp
Sam's house	2-42 oz	42 oz./2.48	4.96	2.48
Cub's Quaker	42 oz.	42 oz./3.19	3.19	3.19
Cub's house	42 oz.	42 oz./2.65	2.65	2.65
Safeway Quaker	42 oz.	42 oz./3.58	3.58	3.58
Safeway house	42 oz.	42 oz./2.65	2.65	2.65

Pancake syrup

Item	Size	Unit Price	Price	Comp
Sam's Log Cabin	36 oz.	24 oz./2.25	3.39	2.25
Sam's house	128 oz.	24 oz./.53	.53	.53
Cub's Log Cabin	24 oz.	24 oz./2.59	2.59	2.59
Cub's house	24 oz.	24 oz./1.98	1.98	1.98
Safeway Log Cabin	24 oz.	24 oz./3.49	3.49	3.49
Safeway house	24 oz.	24 oz./2.29	2.29	2.29

Comment: One gallon of Sam's pancake syrup? No way!

Item	Size	Unit Price	Price	Comp
Iceberg lettuce				
Sam's	3 lbs.	1 lb./.58	1.79	.58
Cub's	1 lb.	1 lb./.49	.49	.49
Safeway	1 lb.	1 lb./ .79	.79	.79
Tomatoes				
Sam's	5 lbs.	1 lb./1.23	1.23	1.23
Cub's	1 lb.	1 lb./1.49	1.49	1.49
Safeway	1 lb.	1 lb./ .99	.99	.99
Onions				
Sam's	10 lbs.	10 lbs./7.42	7.42	.74
Cub's	10 lbs.	10 lbs./4.49	4.49	.44
Safeway	1 lb.	1 lb./.69.	69.	69
Carrots				
Sam's	5 lbs.	5 lbs./1.32	1.32	1.32
Cub's	5 lbs.	5 lbs./1.88	1.88	1.88
Safeway	5 lbs.	5 lbs./1.49	1.49	1.49

Item	Size	Unit Price	Price	Comp
Russet potatoes				
Sam's	20 lbs.	15 lbs./2.73	3.62	2.73
Cub's	15 lbs.	15 lbs./2.99	2.99	2.99
Safeway	10 lbs.	15 lbs./3.43	2.29	3.43
Granny Smith apples				
Sam's	7 lbs.	1 lb./.66	4.64	.66
Cub's	1 lb.	1 lb./.89	.89	.89
Safeway	5 lbs.	1 lb./ .79	.79	.79
Red Delicious apples				
Sam's	10 lbs.	1 lb./.50	5.02	.50
Cub's	10 lbs.	1 lb./.49	4.99	.49

Item	Size	Unit Price	Price	Comp
Safeway	5 lbs.	1 lb./.79	3.98	.79

Navel oranges

Item	Size	Unit Price	Price	Comp
Sam's	10 lbs.	2 lbs./.68	3.42	.34
Cub's	1 lb.	2 lbs./.98	.49	.49
Safeway	10 lbs	2 lbs./.78	3.99	.78

Mixed frozen vegetables

Item	Size	Unit Price	Price	Comp
Sam's				
name brand	5 lbs.	2 lbs./1.28	3.20	1.28
Cub's house	2 lbs.	2 lbs./1.50	1.50	1.50
Safeway house	2 lbs.	2 lbs./1.99	1.99	1.99

Frozen french fries

Item	Size	Unit Price	Price	Comp
Sam's Ore-Ida	8 lbs.	2 lbs./1.08	4.34	1.08
Cub's Ore-Ida	2 lbs.	2 lbs./1.99	1.99	1.99
Cub's house	2 lbs.	2 lbs./1.75	1.75	1.75
Safeway Ore-Ida	2 lbs.	2 lbs./1.79	1.79	1.79
Safeway house	2 lbs.	2 lbs./1.63	1.63	1.63

Ketchup (squeezable bottle)

Item	Size	Unit Price	Price	Comp
Sam's Hunts	2/40 oz.	40 oz./1.41	2.83	1.41
Cub's Heinz	40 oz.	40 oz./2.59	2.59	2.59
Cub's house	40 oz.	40 oz./1.98	1.98	1.98
Safeway Hunts	32 oz.	40 oz./2.81	2.25	2.81
Safeway house	40 oz	40 oz./2.45	2.45	2.45

Mustard (squeezable bottle)

Item	Size	Unit Price	Price	Comp
Sam's French's	2/26 oz.	16 oz./ .84	2.73	.84
Cub's French's	16 oz.	16 oz./2.59	2.59	2.59
Cub's house	16 oz.	16 oz./1.07	1.07	1.07
Safeway French's	16 oz.	16 oz./1.65	1.65	1.65
Safeway house	16 oz.	16 oz./ .99	.99	.99

Item	Size	Unit Price	Price	Comp

Comment: I don't like mustard, so don't ask me to judge the taste between French's and the store brands.

Mayonnaise

Item	Size	Unit Price	Price	Comp
Sam's Best Foods	60 oz.	32 oz./1.89	3.79	1.89
Sam's house	128 oz.	32 oz./ .97	3.89	.97
Cub's Best Foods	32 oz.	32 oz./2.19	2.19	2.19
Cub's house	24 oz.	32 oz./1.17	.88	1.17
Safeway Best Foods	32 oz.	32 oz./2.19	2.19	2.19
Safeway house	32 oz.	32 oz./1.59	1.59	1.59

Comment: No one in their right mind would buy one gallon of Sam's house-brand mayonnaise—unless you were making potato salad for the church picnic.

Ranch salad dressing

Item	Size	Unit Price	Price	Comp
Sam's				
Hidden Valley	36 oz.	36 oz./4.94	4.94	4.94
Sam's house	128 oz.	36 oz./1.39	4.96	1.39
Cub's				
Hidden Valley	24 oz.	36 oz./6.43	4.29	6.43
Safeway				
Hidden Valley	24 oz.	36 oz./6.73	4.49	6.73

Comment: Even though Sam's house brand was nearly 67 percent less, it came in a gallon container, which is unrealistic for most families.

Raisin bran cereal

Item	Size	Unit Price	Price	Comp
Sam's Post	50 oz.	25 oz./2.99	5.99	2.99
Sam's house	51 oz.	25 oz./2.39	4.89	2.39
Cub's Post	25 oz.	25 oz./4.09	4.09	4.09
Cub's house	20 oz.	25 oz./2.71	2.17	2.71
Safeway Post	25 oz.	25 oz./4.17	4.17	4.17
Safeway house	20 oz.	25 oz./3.33	3.33	3.33

Item	Size	Unit Price	Price	Comp

Comment: Even with a dollar-off coupon for the name brand Sam's Post cereal is cheaper. We buy Sam's Extra-Raisin Raisin Bran, which is quite good.

Grape Nuts

Item	Size	Unit Price	Price	Comp
Sam's	64 oz.	32 oz./3.62	7.25	3.62
Cub's	32 oz.	32 oz./4.45	4.45	4.45
Cub's house	24 oz.	32 oz./3.54	3.54	3.54
Safeway	24 oz.	32 oz./5.17	3.45	5.17
Safeway house	24 oz.	32 oz./3.43	2.29	3.43

Comment: Even though Safeway's house brand was cheaper I'd buy the real Grape Nuts.

Corn Flakes

Item	Size	Unit Price	Price	Comp
Sam's Kellogg's	48 oz.	18 oz./1.11	5.37	1.11
Cub's Kellogg's	18 oz.	18 oz./2.39	2.39	2.39
Cub's house	18 oz.	18 oz./1.83	1.83	1.83
Safeway Kellogg's	24 oz.	18 oz./2.16	2.89	2.16
Safeway house	24 oz.	18 oz./1.71	2.29	1.71

Comment: Even with a dollar-off coupon on the name brands, Sam's wins.

Rice Krispies

Item	Size	Unit Price	Price	Comp
Sam's	38 oz.	19 oz./3.31	6.64	3.31
Cub's	19 oz.	19 oz./2.98	2.98	2.98
Cub's house	40 oz.	19 oz./2.15	2.98	2.15
Safeway	19 oz.	19 oz./3.84	3.84	3.84
Safeway house	13 oz.	19 oz./3.342.	293	.34

Cheerios

Item	Size	Unit Price	Price	Comp
Sam's	35 oz.	35 oz./5.99	5.99	5.99
Cub's	35 oz.	35 oz./6.18	6.18	6.18
Cub's house	15 oz.	35 oz./4.38	1.88	4.38

Item	Size	Unit Price	Price	Comp
Safeway	20 oz.	35 oz./7.33	4.19	7.33
Safeway house	14 oz.	35 oz./5.97	2.39	5.97

Peanut butter

Sam's Peter Pan	5 lbs.	4 lbs./5.27	6.59	5.27
Cub's Jif	4 lbs.	4 lbs./6.98	6.98	6.98
Cub's house	4 lbs.	4 lbs./5.98	5.98	5.98
Safeway Jif	4 lbs.	4 lbs./7.37	7.37	7.37
Safeway house	28 oz.	4 lbs./7.88	3.45	7.88

Comment: Advantage Sam's.

Grape jelly

Sam's Knott's	4 lbs.	2 lbs./1.33	2.67	1.33
Cub's Smuckers	2 lbs.	2 lbs./2.19	2.19	2.19
Cub's house	2 lbs.	2 lbs./1.50	1.50	1.50
Safeway Welch's	4 lbs.	2 lbs./1.24	2.49	1.24
Safeway house	2 lbs.	2 lbs./1.69	1.69	1.69

Comment: Funny how Safeway's name-brand peanut butter and jelly are cheaper than the house brand.

80% lean hamburger meat

Sam's	1 lb.	1 lb./1.74	1.74	1.74
Cub's	1 lb.	1 lb./2.08	2.08	2.08
Safeway	1 lb.	1 lb./1.98	1.98	1.98

Ground turkey meat

Sam's	1 lb.	1 lb. /.87	.87	.87
Cub's	1 lb.	1 lb./.88	.88	.88
Safeway	1 lb.	1 lb./.88	.88	.88

Chicken (whole fryers)

Sam's	1 lb.	1 lb./68.	68.	68
Cub's	1 lb.	1 lb./.79	.79	.79

Item	Size	Unit Price	Price	Comp
Safeway	1 lb.	1 lb./.79	.79	.79

Comment: Look for sales here. Supermarkets often use chicken as a big loss leader item.

Hot dogs (beef)

Item	Size	Unit Price	Price	Comp
Sam's Bar-S	5 lbs.	1 lb./ .95	4.79	.95
Cub's Bar-S	1 lb.	1 lb./1.43	1.43	1.43
Cub's house Safeway	1 lb.	1 lb./ .79	.79	.79
Smoke-O-Rama	1 lb.	1 lb./1.19	1.19	1.19

Comment: Knowing how hot dogs/made, I'd go with Sam's, even though I'd have to freeze some.

Bacon

Item	Size	Unit Price	Price	Comp
Sam's Bar-S Cub's	3/1 lb.	1 lb./1.49	4.49	1.49
Chuck Wagon	1 lb.	1 lb./ 1.25	1.25	1.25
Cub's house	1 lb.	1 lb./ .99	.99	.99
Safeway Bar-S	1 lb.	1 lb./2.09	2.09	2.09
Safeway house	1 lb.	1 lb./ 1.59	1.59	1.59

Comment: You get what you pay for when it comes to bacon.

Chunk light tuna fish

Item	Size	Unit Price	Price	Comp
Sam's	8/6 1/4-oz.cans	3 cans/1.97	5.27	1.97
Cub's	6 1/4-oz. can	3 cans/2.37	.79	2.37
Safeway	6 1/4-oz. can	3 cans/2.07	.69	2.07

Ramen noodles (beef flavor)

Item	Size	Unit Price	Price	Comp
Sam's	24/3 oz.	7/ .93	3.19	.93
Cub's	7/3 oz.	7/1.00	1.00	1.00
Cub's house	8/3 oz.	7/ .87	1.00	.87
Safeway	5/3 oz.	7/1.40	1.00	1.40
Safeway house	3 oz.	7/2.03	.292	.03

Item	Size	Unit Price	Price	Comp

Boxed macaroni and cheese

Sam's Leonardo	12/7.25 oz.	6 boxes/1.63	3.26	1.63
Cub's Kraft	7.25 oz.	6 boxes/3.54	.593	.54
Cub's house	7.25 oz.	6 boxes/1.50	.25	1.50
Safeway Kraft	7.25 oz.	6 boxes/3.54	.59	3.54
Safeway house	7.25 oz.	6 boxes/1.98	.33	1.98

Comment: People have told me the cheap stuff doesn't taste nearly as good as the Kraft. Good item to buy at supermarket.

Spaghetti

Sam's	2/5 lbs.	3 lbs./1.25	4.19	1.25
Cub's	3 lbs.	3 lbs./3.29	3.29	3.29
Safeway	3 lbs.	3 lbs./2.25	2.25	2.25

Spaghetti sauce

Sam's Ragu	2/48-oz. jars	28 oz. jar/1.16	3.99	1.16
Cub's Ragu	28 oz.	28 oz. jar/2.09	2.09	2.09
Cub's house	30 oz.	28 oz. jar/1.67	1.79	1.67
Safeway Ragu	48 oz.	28 oz. jar/1.77	3.05	1.77
Safeway house	26 oz.	28 oz. jar /1.71	1.59	1.71

Comment: Sam's name brand is the winner.

Tomato sauce

Sam's Hunt	s6/15 oz. cans	3 cans/1.26	2.53	1.26
Cub's Hunts	15 oz. can	3 cans/1.65	.55	1.65
Cub's house	15 oz. can	3 cans/1.32	.44	1.32
Safeway Hunts	29 oz. can	3 cans/1.70	1.10	1.70
Safeway house	28 oz. can	3 cans/1.59	.99	1.59

Parmesan cheese

Sam's Kraft	1 lb.	1 lb./4.49	4.49	4.49
Cub's Kraft	8 oz.	1 lb./5.90	2.95	5.90

Item	Size	Unit Price	Price	Comp
Safeway Kraft	8 oz.	1 lb./6.14	3.07	6.14
Safeway house	1 lb.	1 lb./4.99	4.99	4.99

Comment: Sam's is the winner.

Chicken noodle soup

Sam's Campbell	6 cans	3 cans/1.49	2.99	1.49
Cub's Campbell	1 can	3 cans/1.50	.50	1.50
Cub's house	1 can	3 cans/1.77	.59	1.77
Safeway Campbell	1 can	3 cans/1.50	.50	1.50

Comment: Safeway happened to be having an "endcap" sale on chicken noodle soup.

Cut green beans

Sam's				
Del Monte	6/16 oz. cans	2 cans/1.04	3.13	1.04
Cub's				
Del Monte	16 oz. can	2 cans/1.30	.65	1.30
Cub's house	15.5 oz. can	2 cans/1.40	.69	1.40
Safeway				
Del Monte	16 oz. can	2 cans/1.00	.50	1.00
Safeway house	16 oz. can	2 cans/1.00	.50	1.00

Comment: Big sale on green beans when I shopped Safeway.

Converted rice

Sam's house	9 lbs.	5 lbs./2.77	4.99	2.77
Cub's Uncle Ben's	5 lbs.	5 lbs./4.53	4.53	4.53
Cub's house	5 lbs.	5 lbs./2.63	2.63	2.63
Safeway Uncle Ben's	5 lbs.	5 lbs./4.57	4.57	4.57
Safeway house	5 lbs.	5 lbs./1.98	1.98	1.98

Comment: Again, nice sale at Safeway.

Item	Size	Unit Price	Price	Comp

Toilet paper

Sam's

Northern	30 rolls (420)	8 rolls/2.86	10.76	2.86
Sam's medium	24 rolls (500)	8 rolls/3.21	9.64	3.21
Sam's house	45 rolls (300)	8 rolls/1.74	9.79	1.74
Cub's Northern	4 rolls	8 rolls/1.78	.89	1.78
Cub's house	4 rolls	8 rolls/1.32	.66	1.32
Safeway Northern	9 rolls	8 rolls/4.16	4.69	4.16
Safeway house	9 rolls	8 rolls/1.94	2.19	1.94

Comment: Pick your choice.

Facial tissues

Sam's Puffs	8 boxes (175)	2 boxes/1.74	6.97	1.74
Cub's Puffs	1 box (175)	2 boxes/1.76	.88	1.76
Cub's house	1 box (175)	2 boxes/1.78	.89	1.78
Safeway Kleenex	1 box (175)	2 boxes/1.98	.99	1.98
Safeway house	1 box (175)	2 boxes/1.70	.85	1.70

Comment: Dead heat.

Paper towels

Sam's Brawny	12 rolls	6 rolls/4.73	9.47	4.73
Cub's Brawny	1 roll	6 rolls/4.98	.83	4.98
Cub's house	1 roll	6 rolls/2.34	.39	2.34
Safeway Brawny	3 rolls	6 rolls/5.78	2.89	5.78
Safeway house	3 rolls	6 rolls/4.58	2.29	4.58

Comment: Although the Cub's house brand won, quality was very low; these paper towels looked like processed bark.

Paper napkins

Sam's Northern	2/500 ct.	500 ct./2.59	5.18	2.59
Cub's Northern	250 ct.	500 ct./2.88	1.44	2.88

Item	Size	Unit Price	Price	Comp
Cub's house	250 ct.	500 ct./3.10	1.55	3.10
Safeway Northern	250 ct.	500 ct./4.18	2.09	4.18
Safeway house	250 ct.	500 ct./3.38	1.69	3.38

Dishwasher detergent

Sam's Cascade	120 oz.	85 oz./3.42	4.84	3.42
Sam's Electrasol	240 oz.	85 oz./2.47	6.99	2.47
Cub's Cascade	85 oz.	85 oz./4.39	4.39	4.39
Cub's Electrasol	85 oz.	85 oz./3.25	3.25	3.25
Safeway Cascade	85 oz.	85 oz./4.69	4.69	4.69
Safeway house	50 oz.	85 oz./3.04	1.79	3.04

Comment: Price advantage to Sam's Electrasol, but you have to buy a lot.

Powdered laundry detergent

Sam's Tide	280 oz.	280 oz./17.64	17.64	17.64
Sam's house	800 oz.	280 oz./ 4.14	11.83	4.14
Cub's Tide	280 oz.	280 oz./18.05	18.05	18.05
Cub's house	96 oz.	280 oz./14.96	4.96	14.96
Safeway Tide	136 oz.	280 oz./23.03	11.19	23.03
Safeway house	70 oz	.280 oz./15.96	3.99	15.96

Comment: Sam's knocked out the competition cold.

Bleach

Sam's Clorox	2/1.5 gal.	1 gal./ 1.15	3.47	1.15
Cub's Clorox	64 oz.	1 gal./1.78	.88	1.78
Safeway Clorox	1 gal.	1 gal./ .79	.79	.79
Safeway house	1 gal.	1 gal./ .99	.99	.99

Comment: Safeway's loss leader!

Liquid laundry detergent

Sam's Wisk	1 gal.	64 oz./4.98	9.99	4.98
Cub's Wisk	64 oz.	64 oz./8.39	8.39	8.39

Item	Size	Unit Price	Price	Comp
Cub's house	64 oz.	64 oz./3.33	3.33	3.33
Safeway Wisk	96 oz.	64 oz./4.26	6.39	4.26

Aluminum foil

Item	Size	Unit Price	Price	Comp
Sam's Reynolds	2 250 ft.	250 ft./4.99	9.99	4.99
Cub's Reynolds	1 200 ft.	250 ft./6.98	5.59	6.98
Cub's house1	75 ft.	250 ft./6.23	1.87	6.23
Safeway Reynolds	1 200 ft.	250 ft./7.48	5.99	7.48
Safeway house	1 200 ft.	250 ft./6.05	4.84	6.05

Comment: Sam's name brand is the winner.

Zest bath soap

Item	Size	Unit Price	Price	Comp
Sam's		12/5 oz. bars	8 bars/3.99	5.99
3.99				
Cub's		8/5 oz. bars	8 bars/4.99	4.99
4.99				
Safeway	8/5 oz. bars	8 bars/4.69	4.69	4.69

Toothpaste

Item	Size	Unit Price	Price	Comp
Sam's Crest	6/8.2 oz	3/8.2 tubes/3.49	6.99	3.49
Cub's Crest	6.4 oz.	3/8.2 tubes/6.54	2.18	6.54
Cub's house	3/6.4 oz.	3/8.2 tubes/5.11	3.99	5.11
Safeway Crest	8.2 oz.	3/8.2 tubes/7.62	2.54	7.62

Comment: Sam's name brand wins.

Roll-on deodorant

Item	Size	Unit Price	Price	Comp
Sam's Ban	2/3.5 oz.	2.5 oz./2.23	6.26	2.23
Cub's Ban	2.5 oz.	2.5 oz./2.79	2.79	2.79
Cub's house	2/2.5 oz	2.5 oz./1.45	2.89	1.45
Safeway Ban	3.5 oz.	2.5 oz./2.70	3.79	2.70

Diapers (boy's medium)

Item	Size	Unit Price	Price	Comp
Sam's Pampers	72 ct.	72 ct./11.43	11.43	11.43
Cub's Pampers	36 ct.	72 ct./15.34	7.67	15.34

Item	Size	Unit Price	Price	Comp
Cub's house	36 ct.	72 ct./12.98	6.49	12.98
Safeway Pampers	40 ct.	72 ct./17.38	8.69	17.38
Safeway house	27 ct.	72 ct./15.97	5.99	15.97

Comment: Pampers are excellent diapers and they don't leak!

Ibuprofen

Sam's Advil	250 ct	250 ct./11.76	11.76	11.76
Sam's house	500 ct.	250 ct./ 4.98	9.97	4.98
Cub's Advil	65 ct.	250 ct./18.01	11.89	18.01
Cub's house	500 ct.	250 ct./ 3.69	7.39	3.69
Safeway Advil	250 ct	250 ct./14.79	14.79	14.79
Safeway house	500 ct.	250 ct./ 4.99	9.99	4.99

Comment: Great buy on Cub's generic.

Tampons

Sam's Tampax	72 ct.	32 ct./3.80	8.57	3.80
Cub's Tampax	32 ct.	32 ct./4.79	4.79	4.79
Cub's house	32 ct.	32 ct./3.99	3.99	3.99
Safeway Tampax	48 ct.	32 ct./4.32	6.49	4.32

Comment: Don't ask *me* what the house brand is like!

Dog food

Sam's

Purina Chow	50 lbs.	40 lbs./11.90	14.99	11.90
Sam's house	40 lbs.	40 lbs./ 6.99	6.99	6.99

Cub's

Purina Chow	10 lbs.	40 lbs./24.36	6.09	24.36
Cub's house	20 lbs.	40 lbs./11.76	5.88	11.76
Safeway Purina	20 lbs.	40 lbs./11.08	5.54	11.08
Safeway house	20 lbs.	40 lbs./ 6.98	3.49	6.98

Item	Size	Unit Price	Price	Comp
Cat food				
Sam's Purina	20 lbs.	10 lbs./ 4.49	8.99	4.49
Sam's house	20 lbs.	10 lbs./ 3.29	6.59	3.29
Cub's Purina	56 oz.	10 lbs./10.65	3.73	10.65
Cub's house	10 lbs.	10 lbs./ 4.03	4.03	4.03
Safeway Purina	7 lbs.	10 lbs./ 8.55	5.99	8.55
Safeway house	7 lbs.	10 lbs./ 5.70	3.99	5.70
Cat litter (house brand)				
Sam's	50 lbs.	25 lbs./2.79	5.58	2.79
Cub's	25 lbs.	25 lbs./2.64	2.64	2.64
Safeway	25 lbs.	25 lbs./3.69	3.69	3.69

Comment: I figure cat's don't need anything better than house-brand when it comes to litter.

Comet cleanser				
Sam's	4/25 oz	.21 oz./.622	.96	.62
Cub's	21 oz	.21 oz./ .79	.79	.79
Safeway	21 oz	.21 oz./ .86	.86	.86
Pledge				
Sam's	2/18-oz. cans	18 oz./2.98	5.99	2.98
Cub's	12.5-oz. can	18 oz./3.83	2.66	3.83
Safeway	12.5-oz. can	18 oz./5.88	4.09	5.88
Kitchen garbage bags (13 gallon)				
Sam's	210 ct.	100/ 4.26	8.96	4.26
Cub's house	20 ct.	100/14.90	2.98	4.90
Safeway	80 ct.	100/ 6.22	4.98	6.22

GRAND TOTALS:

Sam's $229.47

Cub Foods $266.89

Safeway $285.82

Item	Size	Unit Price	Price	Comp

The tale of the tape showed Sam's as the winner with a savings of 15 percent over Cub Foods and 24 percent over Safeway.

RECOMMENDATIONS

Remember back in chapter two where I advised you to "cherry-pick" the best deals at warehouse clubs and supermarkets? The following listing of comparative prices on common products will help you know more about how to do that. "No difference" means the supermarket's *store brand* and the warehouse club's *name brand* were close in price with a negligible difference in quality.

Milk: Warehouse club was often 80 cents a gallon cheaper, or 40 percent less. Some supermarkets are fighting back by offering the same price as the warehouse club if you buy *two* gallons.

Eggs: No difference.

Cheese: Buy at the warehouse club; one-third cheaper.

American sliced cheese: Warehouse club was 50 percent cheaper, but you had to buy 120 slices.

Cream cheese: No difference.

Butter: Warehouse club was 50 percent cheaper.

Margarine: Shedd's Country Crock, an excellent brand, was 42 percent cheaper at the warehouse.

Yogurt: Warehouse clubs usually sell Dannon yogurt for 40 to 45 cents each, in a box of twelve assorted flavors, compared to 67 cents at the supermarkets. But you aren't allowed to choose flavors, and warehouse clubs offer only one brand. Buy the supermarkets' store brand (which is cheaper) or the more expensive name brands when they go on sale.

Ice cream: Warehouse clubs sell an excellent brand name but

Item	Size	Unit Price	Price	Comp

in one-gallon containers, too big for many freezers. Watch for supermarket sales on half-gallon size.

Name-brand orange juice: The warehouse club was only 15 percent cheaper, and name-brand OJ is often a supermarket loss leader. Look for deals.

Store-brand orange juice: Buy at a warehouse club; 25 percent cheaper.

Coke, Pepsi, 7Up: No difference, except during holidays, when supermarkets heavily discount name-brand pop.

Store-brand soda pop: No difference.

Applesauce: Supermarkets are competitive here; look for sales.

Potato chips: Warehouse club bags are huge, which means the chips may get stale. Buy smaller bags at supermarkets.

Tortilla chips: Ditto.

Cookies: Limited selection at warehouse clubs and not much price difference. Buy at supermarkets, unless you bake your own (good idea).

Nestlé Quik: Buy at warehouse clubs.

Coffee: Warehouse clubs sell name and store brands, and both were 20 percent cheaper than supermarkets' name and store brands, respectively.

Tea: Warehouse clubs sold Lipton for the same price as supermarkets' store brand.

Salted cocktail peanuts: Supermarkets' house brands were cheaper than warehouse clubs' Planters.

Name-brand bread: Warehouse club was 70 percent cheaper.

Store-brand bread: Supermarkets were generally a few cents cheaper, which shows their determination to be price-competitive on this staple.

Hamburger and hot dog buns: Large price variations here. You can find the *best* deal at day-old bread stores.

Vegetable oil: No difference.

Item	Size	Unit Price	Price	Comp

Flour: Warehouse clubs sell in such quantity that you risk spoilage from weevils. The supermarkets often discount Gold Medal flour.

Sugar: Buy at supermarkets.

Chocolate chips: Quality makes a difference here, and if you're a Nestlé-Toll-House fan, buy at warehouse clubs or wait for a sale at the supermarkets. Chocolate chips store well in the freezer.

Oats: No difference.

Pancake syrup: Warehouse clubs sell this cheap in a gallon size, but that's too big for many families. No difference.

Iceberg lettuce: Buy at supermarkets. You have to buy three at the warehouse club to get a price break.

Tomatoes: Little difference.

Onions: Little difference; buy what you need at the supermarket.

Carrots: Little difference.

Russet potatoes: Little difference; shop supermarket ads.

Granny Smith apples: Little difference.

Red Delicious apples: Little difference.

Navel oranges: Warehouse club was 50 percent less.

Bananas: Warehouse club was cheaper, but you have to buy in eight-banana packages.

Mixed frozen vegetables: Warehouse club was cheaper by one-third.

Frozen french fries: Warehouse clubs' brand name was 70 percent cheaper, but you had to buy in five- or eight-pound packages.

Ketchup: Definite warehouse-club winner.

Mustard: Another warehouse-club winner.

Mayonnaise: Don't buy in bulk because of possible spoilage. Watch for supermarket sales.

Ranch salad dressing: Buy at warehouse club.

Raisin bran cereal: Buy at warehouse club.

Item	Size	Unit Price	Price	Comp

Grape Nuts: If you don't mind eating the store brand, no price difference. Otherwise, a big warehouse-club winner.

Kellogg's Corn Flakes: Buy at warehouse club.

Rice Krispies: If you don't mind eating the store brand, you can save money at the supermarket.

Cheerios: Ditto.

Peanut butter: Buy at warehouse club.

Grape jelly: Buy at warehouse club.

80% lean hamburger meat: Buy at warehouse club.

Ground turkey meat: No price difference.

Chicken (whole fryers): Little difference. Wait for supermarket loss leader sale.

Hot dogs (beef): Buy at supermarkets.

Bacon: Cheaper brands available at supermarkets, but you get what you pay for when it comes to bacon.

Chunk light tuna fish (water-packed): Buy at warehouse club.

Ramen noodles: Buy at supermarkets, especially during sales.

Boxed macaroni and cheese: Warehouse clubs' name brand is cheaper than supermarkets' store brands—and much tastier.

Spaghetti: Buy at warehouse club.

Ragu Homestyle spaghetti sauce: Big winner at the warehouse club.

Tomato sauce: Little difference.

Parmesan cheese: Buy at warehouse club.

Chicken noodle soup: Buy at warehouse club.

Cut green beans: Buy at warehouse club.

Converted rice: Store brands were equal in price to Uncle Ben's at warehouse club.

Toilet paper: Warehouse clubs usually win, but look for supermarkets' loss leaders.

Item	Size	Unit Price	Price	Comp

Facial tissues: No price difference.

Paper towels: No price difference.

Paper napkins: No price difference.

Dishwasher detergent: Slight price advantage to warehouse club.

Powdered laundry detergent: Huge price break at the warehouse club, especially if you buy the house brand.

Bleach: Cheaper at the supermarkets (hard to believe!).

Liquid laundry detergent: Check store brand for best price.

Aluminum foil: Buy at the warehouse club.

Zest bath soap: Buy at the warehouse club.

Toothpaste: Warehouse club is half the price.

Roll-on deodorant: Warehouse club is cheaper, although supermarket store brands are competitive.

Hair shampoo: I didn't include this item on my comparative shopping list, but you can frequently buy shampoo on sale for one dollar a bottle, especially if it's not a trendy brand. A recent development is the sale of plastic packages of shampoo you can empty into your old bottle. Style, for instance sells refill packages that are better for your budget and the environment. You can also save by buying a gallon-size container of many name-brand shampoos at a local beauty supply outlet—even better for the environment.

Diapers: Warehouse club is cheaper, but check out Wal-Mart.

Ibuprofen: Any house brand is an excellent deal.

Tampons: Slight price advantage to warehouse club.

Dog food: You'll save big bucks buying the warehouse club store brand.

Cat food: Buy warehouse clubs' house brand.

Cat litter: Buy warehouse club brand.

Comet cleanser: No price difference.

Pledge: Buy at warehouse club.

Kitchen and lawn trash bags: Buy at warehouse club.

Appendix Three

Cutting More Corners on Groceries

What are some of the best ways to save on food bills? Each person who responded to the survey added his or her own unique ingredients to this collective recipe for added savings. (I have included my own comments in boldface.)

- "We have a set allowance, and we always shop with a list."
- "We never buy health and beauty aids in the supermarket, even though it's more convenient. We buy them at Wal-Mart." **(The convenience of one-stop shopping does carry a price tag.)**
- "We buy house brands and generics, unless we can get a better price on a name brand with a coupon."
- "We buy the cheapest possible brand of anything we throw away, such as napkins, toilet paper, sandwich bags, and paper towels."
- "Once a year, the big supermarkets have a sale on sugar. You're usually limited to two five-pound bags per purchase, so I go twice a day until I have enough sugar to last me a long time. A five-pound bag costs ninety-nine cents on sale, so I bought one hundred fifty pounds of sugar for less than thirty dollars."
- "Set limits on how much you're willing to pay for certain items. For example, we like to roast a turkey breast, but I buy one only if the price is under one dollar per pound. Also, I try never to pay more than two dollars for a box of cereal."

- "I comparison shop, and I usually avoid my neighborhood state-of-the-art supermarket."
- "I like to shop at no-frills, employee-owned grocery stores, where you bag your own groceries."
- "I shop the loss leaders."
- "We buy generic when quality is not sacrificed."
- "We shop from a co-op warehouse once a month. We buy items and then store them in a freezer."
- "I breastfed my baby instead of buying formula."
- "We buy milk at a specialty store where it's sixty cents cheaper and the twelfth gallon is free. Our family goes through twelve gallons of milk per month."
- "We buy bread at the day-old store and freeze it."
- "I don't buy kitchen trash bags. Instead, I use the plastic bags from the supermarket. When they're full, I tie a knot at the top and toss them into large lawn bags."
- "Watch for the cheapest per-ounce rating in the stores." **(Too many people overlook this convenient way of determining the best buy per brand and size.)**
- "When meat and butter go on sale, we stock up. We have two refrigerators."
- "Don't buy diapers in supermarkets, unless you buy the store brand. Instead, purchase them at discount outlets, such as Wal-Mart and Toys "R" Us."
- "My husband and I say to each other, 'Let's see how far we can stretch this food.' Normally, we spend four hundred dollars a month, and I have a little one in diapers."
- "When I'm canning peaches, I go to the produce department and ask when they're going to pull the bruised peaches off the floor. When I make jam, I don't care about a few brown spots because I can cut them off. The produce manager is happy to give me an incredible discount because the bruised fruit was minutes away from being thrown into the trash anyway."

- "Buy cream cheese in the square packages, and then put it into an empty plastic margarine tub or a small Tupperware container."
- "Always ask for a rain check when items have run out. You can pick up your discount next week!"

Appendix Four

More Ways to Save on Clothes

Here's what folks I surveyed said about saving money on clothing (my own comments are in boldface).

- "We would always go to the big Patagonia once-a-year sale in Santa Barbara. For the first couple of hours, the discount was 33 percent, and then it increased to 50 percent at midday, and 70 percent the last hour. Of course, all the choice items went early, so we would get there when the doors opened, pick out our stuff, and then have one person from our party stay in the store with the merchandise until the lowest discount was offered."

- "Never buy clothes that aren't sale-priced or marked down. If you see a missing button or a sewing flaw, ask for a discount." **(This works. Remember my story about Nicole getting a discount on Andrea's smudged training outfit?)**

- "I wash my clothes by hand since we don't have a washer and dryer. One towel is allowed per person per week." **(And you thought you had life hard?)**

- "I buy all our clothes marked down at Marshalls and Ross Dress for Less. We rarely pay over twenty dollars for anything."

- "We've cut out new shoes for Mom and Dad."

- "We've been fortunate to have many people willing to pass on clothing items to us when their kids outgrow them. Plus, we home-school our children, which eliminates the peer pressure to buy forty-dollar jeans and hundred-dollar sneakers."

- "Yard sales are definitely a good source of used clothing. I've noticed that the clothes at garage sales don't seem to be as worn as they did a few years ago."

- "I buy cloth diapers and wash them myself. We also try to make do with what we have. For instance, we bathe our baby in the sink instead of buying a baby bathtub."

- "I give my kids a certain amount to spend on clothes per year. They shop harder and take better care of their clothes." (**I think it's a great idea for teens to have their own clothing budget. They learn accountability and gain a greater appreciation for what clothes cost.**)

- "A new dress costs $98.50. I will wear it probably ten times, or ten dollars per use. That's too much!" (**A good way to determine value for a particular clothing item is to figure out your cost-per-use. A two-hundred-dollar jacket may be worth the expense if you wear it fifty days a year, but a fifty-dollar coat worn three times a season is not a good buy.**)

- "I love to find bargains at Marshalls because they have unbelievable sales!" (**The Down-and-Out sales are quite good.**)

- "I cut costs on new clothes by avoiding mail-order catalogs with expensive shipping charges." (**Mail-order companies ship only by UPS, which is more expensive—but more sure—than the U.S. Postal Service.**)

- "Only visit the mall when you're going to make a specific purchase." (**I agree. Doing the "mall crawl" is a fast way to spend money.**)

- "If the boys want name-brand clothes, they have to earn the money themselves. They've learned to wear what they can afford."

- "We check out thrift stores before going into the malls."

- "Almost all of our children's clothes are purchased at rummage sales. We only buy new clothing when stores have 50-percent-off clearance sales."

- "Be creative! Soccer shoes are expensive and seldom get worn out before being outgrown. I run a shoe swap for our school's soccer club. Outgrown shoes are turned into me, and people who need shoes give me a call. I almost never buy new soccer shoes for my kids. This means we have more money available for us to use in the kingdom instead of having it put into retail stores." (**Amen.**)

Appendix Five

Credit Card Choices

American Express

Membership Miles program earns miles on Continental, Delta, Southwest, or USAir.

Contact: (800) 545-5038.

What you get: One frequent-flier mile for each dollar charged. **Annual fee:** Green card: $55.00 for the card, plus $25.00 for frequent-flier program (fee waived in first year). Gold ($75.00) and platinum ($300) are more expensive cards.

Merchant partners: none.

Comment: *Can you can leave home without it? I'm not sure. Unless you have to earn miles with Delta or Southwest, use cheaper programs with individual airlines. Delta's mileage requirement is higher than many airlines: 30,000 miles for a free flight.*

Diners Club

Cardholders can earn miles on fourteen different airlines: Air Canada, American, America West, Continental, Delta, MarkAir, Mexicana, Northwest, Southwest, TWA, United, USAir, British Airways, and Alaska.

Contact: (800) 234-6377.

What you get: One frequent-flier mile for each dollar charged. **Annual fee:** $80.00.

Merchant partners: none.

Comment: *Who accepts Diners Club? Certainly not a lot of supermarkets and retail stores.*

American Airlines AAdvantage

Contact: (800) 843-0777.
What you get: One frequent-flier mile for each dollar charged. Limit of 60,000 miles per year.
Annual fee: $50.00.
Time limit: three years.
Merchant partners: MCI, Hilton, Avis.
Number of miles needed for free trip: 25,000 (beginning February 1, 1995).
Comment: *American has a wide domestic and international route.*

United Mileage Plus

Contact: (800) 537-7783.
What you get: One frequent-flier mile for each dollar charged. Limit of 10,000 miles per month or 50,000 per year.
Annual fee: $60.00.
Time limit: three years.
Merchant partners: Hilton, Hyatt, Marriott, Sheraton, Avis, National, Hertz, and Dollar.
Number of miles needed for free trip: 25,000 (beginning January 1, 1995).
Comment: *United's friendly skies extend to Hawaii, where many frequent-fliers travel.*

Continental One Pass

Contact: (800) 446-5336.
What you get: One frequent-flier mile for each dollar charged, plus a 5,000 mile sign-up bonus.
Annual fee: $45.00 for standard, $65.00 for gold.
Time limit: none.
Number of miles needed for free trip: 20,000.
Comment: *Continental has been so buffeted by financial turbulence in recent years, I wonder if they'll still be flying in five years.*

Northwest

Contact: (800) 945-2004.

What you get: One frequent-flier mile for each dollar charged.

Annual fee: $55.00.

Time limit: none.

Merchant partners: MCI, several car rental companies and major hotels.

Number of miles needed for free trip: 25,000.

Comment: *Northwest now flies to the Pacific Rim and Europe. It is also the only airline that allows you to use flight coupons for one-way travel.*

USAir

Contact: (800) 241-6295.

What you get: One frequent-flier mile for each dollar charged.

Annual fee: $35.00 for standard, $55.00 for gold. 2,500 miles for signing up.

Time limit: none.

Merchant partners: none.

Number of miles needed for free trip: 25,000 miles (beginning January 1, 1995).

America West

Contact: (800) 242-5722.

What you get: One frequent-flier mile for each dollar charged.

Annual fee: $35.00.

Time limit: three years after receiving awards certificate.

Merchant partners: car rentals and several hotel chains.

Number of miles needed for free trip: 20,000.

Comment: *Miles can be used for flights on Northwest and Aeromexico.*

Alaska

Contact: (800) 552-7302.

What you get: One frequent-flier mile for each dollar charged.

Annual fee: $25.00 for standard or gold.

Time limit: none.

Number of miles for a free trip: 15,000 miles (increases to 20,000 miles on February 1, 1995).

Comment: *Flying to Anchorage next summer?*

AUTO COMPANIES

If flying is not your thing, Detroit can help you spend your way toward a new car. These credit cards are free, and seven million people have signed on so far. It's a smart move by the auto companies: not only are they assured of a sale, but they also have a built-in audience for any direct-mail campaigns.

Ford

Contact: (800) 374-7777.

What you get: 5 percent of purchases, up to $700 a year. This means you would have to charge $14,000 a year. Rebate of up to $3,500 can be applied toward purchase or lease of any Ford, Mercury, or Lincoln car, van, or light truck.

Annual fee: $20 waived first year, $50 rebate credit issued in following years.

Time limit: five years.

Merchant partners: none.

Comment: *Have you driven a Ford lately? If not, you might want to consider doing so with the help of Ford's credit card.*

General Motors

Contact: (800) 846-2273.

What you get: 5 percent of purchases, up to $500 a year with free card, $1,000 a year with gold card. This means you would have to charge $10,000 a year with free card and $20,000 with gold card.

Annual fee: none for standard card, $39.00 for gold card; $39.00 rebate issued on gold.

Time limit: seven years.

Merchant partners: MCI, Avis, Marriott, Time-Warner, and Mobil Oil.

REBATE PROGRAMS

Credit card spending can also win rebates and cash. If you're on a tight budget and won't be spending that much, I recommend the GE Rewards card, which has no annual fee. At least you can earn rebates on household items. An increasing number of businesses are issuing cards, including those mentioned below.

Sears: The Discover card—which can be used at a wide variety of businesses—promises "cash back up to 1 percent," but the rebate is rather stingy. If you spend $12,000 annually, you can expect only $72.50 in cash. No annual fee.

H&R Block: This nationwide company offers a 1 percent rebate toward income tax preparations. Annual fee is $9.00. Contact (800) 934-0101.

General Electric: The GE Rewards card gives back 2 percent of purchases in the form of coupons that you can take to 27 different retailers (including Macy's, Kmart, and Pier 1) for rebates on any GE products. If you're in the market for a new refrigerator, this might be your ticket to frost-free happiness. Participating retailers also mail out additional discount coupons of their own. No annual fee. Contact: (800) 437-3927.

Shell: Using this credit card earns a rebate of up to $70 a year on Shell gasoline purchases (at a 3 percent rebate). Annual fee of $20.00 is waived when the card is used a minimum of six times. Contact: (800) 373-3427.

Apple Computer: This company offers a rebate that can be used on Macs and other Apple accessories. The rebate is 2.5 percent on purchases up to $3,000 a year, and 5 percent on purchases greater than $3,000 for a maximum rebate of $500 a year and $1,500 over three years. The annual fee is $20.00. Contact: (800) 950-5114.

Keep in mind that new credit cards are being issued all the time. Recent entries into this market include: US West (800-872-2699) offers a maximum rebate of $500 per year on long-distance calls; Start (800-955-7010), is a credit card company that will deposit a rebate in a tax-deferred annuity in $100.00 increments, equal to 1 percent of your charges; and Kroger, a supermarket chain, offers a MasterCard with no annual fee and discounts on certain products.

Appendix Six

More Ways to Save on Cars

What are some extra ways you can save on cars and keep them running longer? Here's what those who responded to the surveys had to say (with my comments in boldface):

- "I'm considering taking the bus to work for forty dollars a month instead of parking downtown for $135.00 a month." **(This fellow lives in Portland, Oregon, and I can understand why he is wrestling with this issue. Most people choose not to leave their car at home unless persuaded by financial incentives or disincentives. In his case, saving a tidy sum in monthly parking fees offers a financial incentive. But what about the extra time it takes to commute? Many of us drive to work so we can spend more time with the family.)**

- "I cook homemade meals for single-guy friends who change my oil." **(Good idea for single-parent mothers.)**

- "Living in a rural area, we spend three hundred dollars per month on gas. We use an honest Christian mechanic. We buy old Suburbans for our teenagers. That way, if we get into an accident, we will win out."

- "Drive old cars and put new engines in them. This saves on car payments and insurance." **(I did this with my GMC pickup. It had 93,000 miles when the engine blew two years ago. I had it rebuilt for two thousand dollars, and have had no trouble since then.)**

- "Check out the warehouse club for buying a car. The Price Club had 'fleet sale' prices, and I saved about two thousand dollars on my Dodge Grand Caravan."

- "I try to have one day per week when I don't use my car at all."

- "I get rid of my cars when they start to become expensive. I replace them with well-maintained cars, 'in-the-family' cars that have been handed down."

- "My husband bought a repair manual and taught himself how to fix our car. Also, I ride in a car pool, so our truck is used only three thousand miles per year." (**Cutting miles saves big bucks.**)

- "I recommend buying a two-year-old car with twenty to thirty thousand miles. Maintain it well and then trade it in at sixty thousand miles while it's still worth something."

- "Try to lower the three biggest car costs: interest, depreciation, and insurance. I do that by looking for a low-mileage, older, and bigger used car for a great value."

- "Our cars are old and paid off. That sure beats high monthly payments, costly insurance, and high registration fees."

- "Don't get the extended warranty." (**When I bought my Subaru years ago, my father overheard two salesmen talking in the next booth. One said, "How much does the extended warranty cost us?" The other replied, "It costs us one hundred fifty dollars, but we sell the extended warranties for five hundred. We sometimes make as much on those warranties as we do on the car."**)

- "A rebuilt Chevy three-fifty engine costs less than the interest for one year on a new car loan." (**Not really. Interest on a ten-thousand-dollar car loan at 8 percent in the first year totals eight hundred dollars, and a new engine costs two thousand dollars or so. But if you keep the car for a few years, the rebuilt engine does pay off.**)

- "One gas station in town has discount hours, and that's when we buy gas." (**Discount hours on gas? I've never seen that in the western U.S. Does your hometown offer that option?**)

- "Don't waste gas or time. I do most of my errands in one day and plan my travel route accordingly."

- "I wash the van myself the old-fashioned way: a bucket of soapy water, hose, and old towels." (**A visit to a car wash costs five to eight dollars these days. Wash it yourself and save. If you don't want to do that, pay one of your children or a neighborhood kid to wash it for half the price.**)

- "I ride a bike to work and insure only one car." (**The savings probably comes to about three thousand dollars a year.**)

- "Don't get into car payments." (**If you do, it's hard to get out.**)

- "I drive my cars until they won't drive any more. We now have two cars with over 150,000 miles on them." (**Bravo! But I hope they're putting the savings aside for an eventual automobile purchase. Cars don't last forever.**)

- "Buy good, clean, low-mileage cars that qualify for an extended warranty, which, in turn, provides for peace of mind. We also did our homework on current book and loan values before starting our search for a newer car. We nearly always sell our older car for top dollar. Again, maintenance is the key."

- "I do preventative maintenance, like changing my oil every three thousand miles." (**More and more car advisors extol the virtues of three-thousand-mile oil changes.**)

- "Take an adult-ed class to learn minor repair."

- "We purposely bought our home near a shopping center, library, and bus routes. I ride my mountain bike to work or take the bus."

- "Buy wisely. You can lust after cars, too." (**Yes, the smell of new upholstery can be intoxicating.**)

- "We buy second-hand cars. We save a little each month so that when we need a car, we have enough to pay cash. We pray and wait for a sturdy, quality car under two years old with less than twenty thousand miles. God answers our prayers." (Prayer works time after time.)

- "This is one area of difficulty, because I am helpless when it comes to cars. I'm at the mercy of the mechanics and have to pay whatever is asked." (A single mom wrote this. Ask around and find a good Christian mechanic.)

- "We've bought one good traveling car and one beat-up pick-up, called 'Ol' Blue.'" (My Uncle Bopper—see chapter three—named his cars "Balthazar" and "Greenie." They had a lot of character.)

- "Don't buy a car until you can pay cash. Pay off the car you have, then keep sending that payment to a bank account until you save enough for a used car. We *never* buy new."

- "Never trade in your car to a dealer. You can get a lot more selling it yourself." (A Christian auto dealer gave me this advice.)

- "Try not to get speeding tickets!" (Insurance goes way up after a traffic violation. Nicole got caught going too fast on a surface street when we lived in Southern California. She went to "traffic school" and kept the ticket from appearing on our record. If your state has the same program, it's worth the eight hours of mind-numbing boredom.)

- "My husband drives the small car for commuting to work and doing errands. We use our van when all or most of us go somewhere, saving on gasoline and repair costs. The van is older (1987), and we bought it used."

- "We lease the car that gets beaten to death on a long work commute." (Watch out! You'll probably be charged fifteen cents a mile when you drive more than fifteen thousand miles a year on a lease.)

- "Look for God's hand in financial matters. Did a car repair that was estimated at five hundred dollars turn out to be only two hundred? Thank God for the three hundred dollars you didn't have to spend. Maybe ask him if there's something he wants you to do with it!"

Appendix Seven

Extra Cooking Tips

What are some other ways you can save in the kitchen? Here's what the surveys said (my comments are in boldface):

- "We're learning new methods of cooking in order to avoid buying processed foods. We make our own taco seasoning, salsa, bread, and cakes from scratch." **(Good idea! I recently bought some sloppy joe mix in a glass jar for $1.29. When I got home and showed Nicole, she said she could duplicate the same sauce for a fraction of the cost by using spices and tomato sauce.)**

- "We are semi-vegetarians, so meat bills are low. We rarely use prepared food and don't drink much alcohol." **(That's a good way to save: dodge those Silver Bullets.)**

- "We always have two or three convenient meals in the refrigerator and freezer. This helps us withstand the temptations of eating out."

- "This summer, I mixed juice in pitchers and then had plastic cups with magic markers for names. This saved on dishwashing and provided more juice for less money."

- "We have our kids take their lunches to school." **(For the life of me, I can't understand why some parents don't pack school lunches for their kids. And buying individual servings of pudding or applesauce is a waste of money, as well. We buy a large jar of applesauce and serve it in small Tupperware containers.)**

- "My wife makes double recipes of lasagna, chili, and spaghetti sauce. Then she freezes the leftovers for future meals."

- "We rarely eat out, but when we do, we find something at a discount."

- "When I get hungry, I want a Burger King Whopper! Then I remind myself of the thirty grams of fat. 'A moment on my lips and a lifetime on my hips.' So I go home and eat a turkey sandwich. I save $2.50 and one pound!"

- "I cook stew or chili once a week, usually on Fridays, and we eat it all weekend. These dishes assure that something is available for my son and his bottomless-pit friends."

- "Buy healthy food. You'll have fewer doctor bills and higher insurance deductibles."

- "By using a lot of whole grains, we stretch meals. We spend very little on junk foods, like chips, soft drinks, and processed foods."

- "My husband goes hunting several times a year, so we live on venison most of the year. Plus, we have a pretty big garden." (Self-sufficiency is great.)

- "I like to bake, so I don't purchase ready-made desserts at the market."

- "In winter, we always have a kettle of homemade soup, which makes for great on-the-go meals."

- "Eat vegetarian." (Actually, I was a vegetarian for two years during my twenties. It was healthy and light on the food budget. I went back to eating meat when my fiancee, Nicole, issued an ultimatum: her or the vegetarianism.)

- "Avoid the pre-cut vegetables, like baby carrots, cubed celery, carrot sticks, and prepared salad. The couple of times we've bought these items, they've gone stale and we had to throw them out."

- "Buy at a farmer's market." (Good idea. Buying direct from the farm is cheaper, healthier, and tastier!)

- "We buy in bulk, raise our own sheep and pigs, have a vegetable garden and orchard, and make most of our meals from scratch."

- "We eat meat only two or three times a week. We concentrate on beans, which are cheap, convenient, and low-fat, plus grains and vegetables."

- "We have a 'breakfast dinner' once a week." (Nicole will do that, too, cooking up scrambled eggs and toast.)

- "We make friends with people who have a garden." (Do you barter anything in exchange for some zucchini or corn?)

- "We cook in advance for thirty days. We also eat beans and rice once or twice a week. We lived twelve years in Central America, so this is not a hardship for us." (From a "once-a-month" cooking fan.)

- "We like to go fishing and eat what we catch."

Appendix Eight

Survey Input on Insurance

The people who responded to the surveys had a lot to say about ways to save on insurance. (I've added my comments in boldface.)

AUTO INSURANCE

- "Don't make claims." **(I talk more about this in detail in chapter thirteen.)**
- "Pay your premiums annually or semi-annually. It's cheaper that way." **(In other words, pay your insurance premium in one lump sum and avoid monthly interest charges.)**
- "We use USAA, which restricts policyholders to individuals who have some type of relationship with military officers. They are better-risk clients, which equals lower-cost insurance with higher-quality coverage."
- "We took a thousand-dollar deductible on the house and cars. Once our cars were valued at less than ten thousand dollars, we dropped the collision protection. We took the risk and saved money." **(Until the cars were worth less than $10,000? I dunno.)**
- "I look at my coverage every six months, and I usually 'hop' at renewal time." **(Loyalty is a two-way street, and there isn't much of it on either side these days.)**
- "We have one car, so we don't have to insure and maintain a second one." **(If you can make do with one car, you can**

save hundreds of dollars a month this way.)

- "For teenagers, get driver's training and good-student discounts. That can lower insurance by 10 to 25 percent." **(Auto insurance may be too expensive by the time my kids turn sixteen, which means they may have to wait until they're eighteen to drive. When Nicole grew up in Switzerland, the minimum driving age was eighteen.)**

- "When our teenage boys reached sixteen, we offered them an option. If they chose to wait to get their driver's license, we would give them the money that we would have had to pay in insurance. Our first son waited until he was eighteen. Our second son is nearly eighteen, and he still hasn't asked for his license. They both drive with us on permits and are excellent drivers now." **(See, my idea can work!)**

- "Shop around! Use one carrier for all types of insurance, such as auto and home. Maintain a good driving record, install smoke detectors in the home, plus other items that allow a discount." **(Such as fire extinguishers and carbon dioxide detectors.)**

HEALTH AND LIFE INSURANCE

- "If you come up with any way to save on medical insurance, let me know. Our health insurance alone costs two hundred dollars a month. Add that to insurance for two cars... aaargh! **(A job with good health benefits is worth its weight in gold.)**

- "Medical insurance is a toughie. Some of the cheaper ones cost a lot in time and hassle: filling out numerous forms, ironing out problems through numerous phone calls, etc."

- "Never buy whole or universal life. Buy term insurance for maximum protection and invest the difference in a steady mutual fund." **(Now, that's more like it.)**

- "Buy only term life insurance for the years when you're supporting children."

- "We are putting money into a life insurance policy for college." (I didn't hear too many of these.)
- "We use insurance for a catastrophe, not to get rich."
- "Buy a ten- or fifteen-year, level-term insurance policy for the breadwinner of the family." (That's what I did.)
- "Take out good life insurance with a low, fixed premium when you're young. If you wait until you're older and making more income, those premiums will become much higher and perhaps harder to maintain. The loan value appreciates rapidly and can serve you well in emergency situations." (This is from a fan of traditional life insurance. I'm still not convinced it's the best way to go.)
- "I found a good broker who represents numerous companies. I let him do research on life insurance policies." (Good idea. Brokers can shop dozens of companies for the best rates.)
- "We call around for the best quotes on our home and cars. On life, we both have had health problems, which made us uninsurable for a time. Now we are at-risk clients."

Appendix Nine

Keeping a Lid on Housing Costs

How can you save more on housing and upkeep? Here's what the surveys said (with my comments in boldface):

- "Learn to do things yourself." **(And that takes time.)**
- "We're buying a townhome until we can afford a house."
- "When times were better, we doubled up our mortgage payments and paid off our mortgage in twelve years. But the downside of that is we don't have a tax deduction." **(Don't worry about it. It will always be cheaper not to have a mortgage than to have the interest deduction.)**
- "We're renting a less-appealing apartment than we'd like, but we're saving for a home." **(Landlords will tell you that good renters are hard to come by, which means solid families are always in demand. Often, you can rent for under market value. Nicole and I were excellent tenants because we mowed the lawn, fixed up the garden, and kept the property in tip-top shape.)**
- "I dropped my security alarm service." **(Security systems are expensive—twenty-five dollars a month and up, plus installation fees of a thousand dollars or so. And if burglars really want to gain entry, they can cut your phone wires. When I lived in Southern California, I worried about break-ins, but we could never afford a security system. We prayed that the Lord would place a hedge of protection around our home. Another time, I saw a home that posted a sign for "Shedd-Blood" protection**

agency. I assumed it was a real security company until I read the small print describing how Christ was protecting their home. Clever idea.)

- "We bought a home with my parents, who are elderly and in need of physical assistance. They help with the payments and we care for all their practical needs."

- "Right now, I'm putting a lot into our fixer-upper house, and the equity is my ace in the hole."

- "We occasionally are tempted to build an addition to the house, but usually handle this by cleaning closets and making a run to the Salvation Army instead." (When interest rates are low, many owners are tempted to move up. I advise using any extra money to pay off the mortgage more quickly.)

- "When you purchase a new home, put as many of the upgrades into the loan to save out-of-pocket costs." (Not a good idea. Your five-thousand-dollar hardwood floors could end up costing you nine thousand. Lou Gage said her daughter purchased a three-hundred-fifty-dollar refrigerator and a five-hundred-dollar fence, and added them to the mortgage. It ended up costing her thirty-two hundred with the added interest.)

- "We've lived in the same house for twenty-four years." (I'm sure it's paid off!)

- "Everyone wears house shoes, which saves on carpets." (The Yorkey family wears house shoes or slippers, too, and it really does save on the wear and tear of carpets.)

- "We don't use cable TV." (We do, and I can't imagine life without it. I rarely watch the network channels—except for sports events.)

- "We paid off our mortgage. That made a huge difference, especially going from making hefty monthly payments to no payments at all." (Am I jealous? Nah....)

- "The house we built cost more than we planned on, so after two years of scrimping on everything to hang onto it, we decided to sell. We bought a more affordable house with a smaller mortgage, and that has given us more disposable income."

- "We don't hire people to do things in the yard, and my husband makes an attempt to do all the repairs himself before calling a specialist." (Nicole has complained about washing the windows, but it costs eighty dollars to have someone else clean them. When she does "do windows," I remind her that she just earned eighty dollars. Then she tries to collect!)
- "We heat our house with a wood-burning stove. We have trees on our property, so the wood is free."
- "We keep our thermostat down to 55 degrees at night and wear layered clothing. We bought a set-back thermostat, and that saved a lot on gas and electricity."
- "We cut out our lawn fertilization program, and now I do it myself... but not as well."
- "Mow your own lawn. Lawn mowers these days are so good, so easy to start and use, that you can do an average-sized lawn in less than an hour. Buy a weed-eater, too." (I've been a lawn maniac ever since I mowed lawns in high school to earn pocket money. I often mow our lawn after work on weeknights. That way I don't lose precious time on Saturday!)
- "I once needed $1,550 dollars worth of roof repairs. I paid someone $650 cash and traded a chain saw and log splitter for the rest."
- "We do home repairs or big jobs only when we have enough cash saved. We wait to do a big project."
- "We do-it-yourself around the house, but my husband hates plumbing." (I remember the time Nicole wanted to retile a bathroom floor. We had never removed a toilet in our lives, but we did it! It was a great feeling of accomplishment—but messy!)
- "We adopted a simpler decorating style and purchased a house in a 'borderline' neighborhood, which is filled with wonderful people!" (It's always a good idea to buy the cheapest house in a nice neighborhood rather than the

most expensive home in a not-so-nice neighborhood.)
- "When it's raining, I turn the automatic sprinklers off. It's pretty easy to push a button and have them go on when the warm weather returns." (You're lucky. Most systems aren't that easy.)
- "I wash dishes by hand. That saves lots of water." (We lived in Southern California during the drought years, and the Department of Water and Power told us dishwashers actually use less water than hand-washing.)
- "Barter with your landlord to save rent." (During our renting years, I always offered to mow the lawn to save money. Or offer to paint, but be sure the landlord pays for the material.)

Appendix Ten

Bonus Saving Tips

Finally, here are some quick-hitting tips from the surveys that didn't fit elsewhere (with my comments in boldface):

- "Order gifts from catalogs. It saves on going shopping and buying impulsively." **(I disagree. I've never found catalog shopping to be a good deal, plus you pay all those shipping and handling charges.)**
- "We try to plan ahead for gifts, and purchase 'generic' baby gifts during 'baby week' or 'baby month' sales."
- "We're making do after building our house two years ago. Presently, we need a new mattress and landscaping. We have an overall landscaping plan, and we're trying to do it a little at a time." **(Good idea... pay as you go.)**
- "I price-check several sources before making a major purchase, and then I try to locate a used source. That's great for furniture and seasonal equipment." **(Ask your friends about any used appliance stores in your area. Sometimes a Christian business directory will list them.)**
- "We entertain ourselves with board games, puzzles, reading, and just talking around the table."
- "I buy most everything used, and I watch for 'good junk' by the side of the road." **(Good junk by the side of the road! What could that be?)**
- "In my spare time, I buy, repair, and sell lawn mowers and other machinery." **(It's great to have an "ace-in-the-hole" sideline that can be parlayed into a home business.)**

- "I discovered from experience that a working woman incurs a lot of costs—gas, clothes, dry cleaning, take-out lunches. All those expenses really cut into the benefits of working. Stay-at-home moms can reduce costs because they have the time to research sales and bargains." (**Dry cleaning can be done in dry-cleaning machines at some laundromats. The savings is between 60 and 75 percent. But of course it takes extra time—usually a precious commodity for working moms.**)

- "For pleasure-seeking pursuits, we read and stay at our cheaply rented cabin in Michigan for one week a year. We rarely go anywhere. We invite friends for dinner and then watch a video."

- "We're teaching our kids the value of money so they're not always wanting more 'things.'"

- "We take the saved money from grocery coupons, put it in a savings jar, and watch it grow!" (**When I was young, my parents painted an old coffee can and wrote "Vacation Fund" on it. And that's what we used to pay for our holidays.**)

- "We rarely eat out (we have six kids), so we order pizza for the family once a month. If there's a movie we want to see, we wait until it comes out on video. We don't buy new clothing unless it's absolutely necessary and on sale."

- "Stock up on sale cards, gifts, and wrappings. When a special occasion comes, you aren't in a big hurry to buy those extras at regular price."

- "Trim the entertainment budget by ditching expensive entertainment, such as movies, in favor of cheap or free activities, such as library programs, nature center programs, parks, and parades. Our major entertainment expense is eating out once in a while at a cheap restaurant. When money is tight, we just go to Dairy Queen. It's not how much you spend, but the fact that you do it together as a family."

- "We minimize TV watching. Commercials just make us want to buy things we really don't need."

- "I have four small electric candles that burn four-watt bulbs in each of the four windows facing the street. Those rooms aren't used much, since we live in the back of the house. That makes the lights in those rooms cost-effective."

- "We go to Tijuana for car upholstery, car paint, and Christmas gifts. (From a mom who lives in San Diego.)

- "We bought a motor home for family vacations and save on hotels and restaurants. I'm not really sure if this will actually result in overall savings, but it sure is fun." (You can rent one for two weeks and save on upkeep, maintenance, and insurance. It's much more cost-effective than buying.)

- "I try not to fall into the trap of having to acquire things to be happy." (If you're not happy without money, you won't be happy with money.)

- "I write letters and make fewer long-distance phone calls to friends and family." (I thought the art of letter-writing had died.)

- "We don't carry around much cash. That makes me think twice before buying something frivolous."

- "Garage sales! We buy most of our 'wants' from garage sales. I also get my boys' 'treats' from garage sales."

- "I have a contract with the state police, and they call me to pick up a deer after a car collision. Free food! I rebuilt a trailer and have paid for it many times by hauling those dead deer around."

- "Around 11 percent of my husband's pay is set aside for retirement. We never see it. This is mandatory, and we can't do anything to change it up or down." (My father-in-law, Hans Schmied, recently retired on a pension. He said his company had a mandatory 6 percent deduction for retirement. "I could have used that money back then, but I'm sure glad I have a pension now.")

- "We scrutinize our phone, cable, and other bills for sneak add-ons that creep in. Last month, we saved over one hundred dollars by having unrequested charges removed."

- "Barter! We exchange baby-sitting for having our oil changed." (I string tennis rackets out of my home, and I've bartered string jobs for many things, including a stereo and a new lawn with a sprinkler system.)

- "We make jewelry, and I have successfully bartered for items we want or need, from fixing the truck to ordering a book by mail (from small companies only). A piece of jewelry costs me six dollars, but when I'm finished with it, it's worth thirty dollars. Although I put some time into the piece, I've saved twenty-four dollars!"

- "We have a raspberry patch. Friends of ours have blueberries. We let them come and pick raspberries, and they let us pick blueberries."

- "Lumber has gone through the ceiling. I had to build extensive shelving in our barn, and I found a great wood supply at our local dump. A contractor had just remodeled and thrown away enough wood for me to do the job free! I had to pull lots of nails, but with a coat of paint, the shelves look fine." (You can approach local contractors who are building new homes in your area. They usually have scraps you can haul away, but you must ask permission.)

- "I believe in returning items that aren't living up to their guarantee of quality or workmanship. My money is too hard to come by to accept or bear the cost of unsatisfactory merchandise. I only shop at stores with a good return policy!"

- "I put Shoe-Goo on my tennis shoes." (I've done that!)

- "I rinse out my Zip-Loc bags. Cheap, huh?"

- "I love to roll up all my loose change and put it in the bank."

- "I make my gifts. Nothing is cheap in the store, so I save by making them myself."

- "I don't go golfing every week, although I'd love to." (I can't believe it when I hear golfers say fifty dollars isn't much for eighteen holes of golf these days. Give me a break! In Hawaii, golf courses cost over one hundred dollars a round.)

- "Have everyone take showers right after each other. Then you won't waste water waiting for the hot water to arrive."

- "I write a check for savings whenever I pay the bills." (**Why is it that I never have anything left in the checkbook to put into savings?**)

- "Switch to natural gas for major appliances, if you can." (**A couple of years ago, my electric hot water heater died. A gas heater cost four hundred dollars more, but I purchased one anyway. Then I had the plumber put in an extra outlet for a gas dryer, sold my electric dryer, and replaced it with a used gas dryer. My utility bills dropped significantly.**)

- "The local swimming pool is cheap at one dollar a visit."

- "Instead of skipping vacation altogether, we have stayed home when finances were tight and taken inexpensive day-trips."

- "We use creativity to meet a need. Discontinued rolls of wallpaper are cheaper, prettier, and more durable than shelf paper. For Christmas presents to my children's teachers, I decorated cans of potato chips, turning them into 'Kris Pringles.' I also wished them a 'chipper Christmas holiday.'"

- "I like to see how long I can keep a twenty-dollar bill in my wallet." (**This won't work for most people.**)

- "To be honest, both my wife and I work right now, and though we're usually pretty good at sticking to our budget, there's enough fat to cover our little spending splurges. Our first baby is due in March, and I'm sure that the hard facts of sticking to a tight budget will sink in then. Between now and then, we're trying hard to pay off our last non-house debt: the car."

- "I try to keep the pioneer spirit alive and look at the past generation's typical housing, wardrobe, foods, and compare my wants versus my needs. I try to be missionary-minded: what satisfies the poor believer in Russia or India?"

- "Have you heard that 'work expands to fill the time allotted'? Well, needs expand to fill the funds available. I think it was Christian author and speaker Tony Campolo who suggested deciding how much you will live on, and make any excess income designated for giving to the kingdom. One of our friends, with a wife and two kids, decided to live on twelve thousand dollars a year. He went through seminary in Iowa. People gave him anonymous donations, which to his delight exceeded his needs. He passed the excess along. His goal was to keep his 'needs' to the lowest level so he could be free to minister in the streets and neighborhoods on a part-time income. He's currently teaching in Mexico!"

- "Our finances have often been tight in the eight years we've been married. We taught English as missionaries overseas for a year. This depleted our savings. Upon our return to the States (about five years ago), we were unemployed for quite some time. I explain this to say that it is my nature to worry about finances most of the time, but these past experiences have desensitized me and built my faith. God has always helped us pull through."

- "We visit museums on Thursday afternoons, when they admit everyone free. I keep my eye out for coupons, discounts, and freebies at parks, museums, zoos, and historical attractions. Our family outings—despite the fact they are low-budget affairs—are nearly always refreshing."

- "I leave my checkbook and purse at home and go window shopping."

- "We have only basic phone service. We limit our long-distance calls to one or none each month." (I can't do that, and I don't think many families can.)

- "Keep your wife happy. That saves on alimony."

- "Marry in-laws who love to spoil grandchildren."

- "Send your kids to Christian schools. It can save on a bail bondsman later on." (I don't think this person was kidding.)

- "If you're buying a big-ticket item, such as a camcorder, call around to different stores. Tell the manager that such-and-such store will sell this model at this price. Can they beat that? Very often, they will."

- "We're a double-income couple with no kids. If kids come along, Mom will stay home. We're not saving for retirement yet because we're saving for children right now."

- "We were encouraged at the start of our marriage (three years ago) to live on one income and save the other. This will ease the transition if and when we have children and I stop working. I didn't like it then, but I'm used to it now, and we've saved a lot so far. The trick is to keep the finances separate from personal feelings."

- "Don't buy any item until you are ready to throw one out. That will slow you down!"

- "I do the theory of finances around the home. My wife does the application."

- "I tithe, so God protects me. To not tithe is to rob God. To rob God is to be foolish."

- "Before Christ was in our lives, pride knocked us out of good bargaining. But now we jump at every 'needed' garage sale or thrift shop bargain."

- "At the beginning of the week, we both get cash for spending, and when it's gone, it's gone."

- "Too few parents discuss finances with their kids."

- "Having savings taken out of paycheck is the way to go. That way, I never miss the money!"

- "We go to restaurants where you don't have to tip, such as buffets and smorgasbords."

- "Do a family outing that's creative instead of costly. We went to an apple orchard last week and picked harvest apples. It was a lot of fun."

- "Stay home! Going out and being in the stores is the easiest way to spend too much, especially if the kids are with me."

- "I've got more ideas, but they'll cost you big time. I want ten dollars an idea." (This comment came from my college buddy, Bob Welch, who enjoys playing hardball with me.)

- "We only get the basic cable." (We do, too. My only splurge is getting Wimbledon on HBO every July. I figure spending ten dollars for my Wimbledon fix is a lot cheaper than traveling to London.)

- "My favorite way to save money is to turn my wife loose. If there's a way to save, she's the one who will think of it."

- "Never buy warranties on appliances or cars. I always take the risk."

- "Always evaluate: Where can we cut back? What are flexible and inflexible expenses?

- "My husband always negotiates prices down on big items, such as furniture, musical instruments, autos, and appliances. He drives the salespeople nuts!"

- "I gave up some personal hobbies that cost money, such as snowmobiling and hunting."

- "Buy a budget book and decide on an allotted amount for all expenditures, and stick to it. It worked for us!"

- "I show up at friend's home around dinnertime." (This tip came from Eddie Haskell of "Leave It to Beaver" fame.)

- I like G.K. Chesterson's quote: 'There are two ways to have enough: One is to acquire more, and the other is to desire less.'"

- "A babysitting co-op in our neighborhood saves on babysitting costs. We exchange poker chips instead of money for hours of child care."

- "I wish I had better ideas for saving money, but I'm not very good at it. My husband is the expert. What do you recommend for a couple where one is a miser and the other is a compulsive shopper?" (Uh... have the compulsive shopper read this book. Another idea is to sit down and make house rules for shopping.)

- "Try not to buy anything for a few months but gas and food."
- "Throw catalogs in the trash without looking at them."
- "I don't like planned budgeting. I just go on a spending diet and cut back in all areas."
- "My wife sits at home with the kids instead of sending them to preschool." (**I'm sure your wife is not sitting when she's home with the kids!**)
- "We're caring for my senile mother-in-law rather than putting her in a nursing home. This keeps her money in the family so that when she dies, what's left is ours. We've cared for her seven years so far. (**I'm sure you're not doing this primarily for the money. Caring for an elderly parent is a real ministry.**)
- "We've found you can't outgive God!" (**Amen.**)